# Reforming the Indian Public Sector Banks

## The Lessons and the Challenges

# Reforming the Indian Public Sector Banks

## The Lessons and the Challenges

T.R. Bhat

GYAN

First Published, 2018

*Published by*

Gyan Publishing House
5, Ansari Road
Daryaganj, New Delhi-110002
Phone: 9811692060
E-mail: books@gyanbooks.com

*Printed at:* G. Print Process, Delhi.

**Cataloging in Publication Data—DK**
Courtesy: D.K. Agencies (P) Ltd.
<docinfo@dkagencies.com>

**Bhat, T. R. (Thekkekare Ramachandra),** 1949- **author.**
Reforming the Indian public sector banks: The Lessons and the Challenges / Thekkekare Ramachandra Bhat.
pages cm
Includes bibliographical references.
ISBN 9788121214209 (HB)

1. Banks and banking—India—History. 2. India—Economic policy—1991- I. Title.

LCC HG3284.B43 2018 | DDC 332.10954 23

# Contents

## SECTION - III
## Further reforms (2004-2014)

## SECTION - V
## The way forward

# Foreword

Like the diversities of the Indian economy, the banking sector also displays wide diversities in the nature and efficiency of banks. It is a conglomeration of banks big and small, young and old, state-owned and private-owned. Drastic changes in their operations have taken place after the nationalisation of 14 banks in 1969. Before that, the State Bank of India and its associate banks were the only banks in the public sector. Since 1969 there have been remarkable changes in the banking sector and more players were added. This process continues still now.

This book traces the dynamics of the reforms of public sector banks since 1991, when the banking reforms were initiated. Weaknesses of public sector banks in 1991, which prompted the Government of India to initiate the reform process are explained in the first section. In the second section, the impact of reforms on the banking sector in the initial years is explained, analyzing their internal weaknesses. The additional reforms initiated during the next decade, 2004 to 2014 are critically evaluated in the next section. The impact of the global financial crisis of 2007-08 on Indian banking sector is briefly discussed in the next section. The factors contributing to the crisis of 2014-16 which necessitated the introduction of fresh reforms are objectively assessed in the fourth section. The last section deals with an evaluation of the feasibility of merger of public sector banks, or their privatization. In addition to this, the probable challenges likely to be faced by the banks in future are briefly predicted.

The whole gamut of reform measures introduced over the years and their impact on the development of the banking sector since the beginning of Independent India are meticulously recorded in this little volume. The author, Sri T R Bhat, being a veteran banker, who had long innings in one of the public sector banks- Corporation Bank - has been successful in making an elaborate documentation of Financial Sector Reforms in India. He has witnessed the transformation of the Bank from the private sector into public sector in 1980. His observations of the banking sector's response to the changing conditions reflect the practical side of the reforms. On the whole the explanation has come out with clarity and objectivity.

This book becomes very useful in appraising the changes which have taken place in the Indian banking sector in the recent years as a result of the initiative taken by the owner of the public sector banks. Sri Bhat's presentation is simple and easily readable.

Mangaluru **Dr N K Thingalaya**

Chairman & Managing Director (Rtd.),
Syndicate Bank

# Preface

Banking industry is intimately connected with the society in several ways. In the pre-independence days good many banks were set up by nationalist leaders so as to promote self reliance and inculcate savings habit among the people of an emerging nation. In India traditionally banks restricted their business to mobilising savings of the community and providing them financial assistance in times of need or to pursue their calling. After nationalisation of major commercial banks in 1969 banks became part of the social milieu. What they achieved during 1969 and 1991 in terms of branch network, business growth, social banking and contribution to productive economic activities was unparalleled in the world.

When the Indian economy opened up in early 1990's, the state owned banks entered a critical phase with a new road map for the sector's business strategy and performance. Banks went for a process of radical changeover from 1991 and, the process continues even beyond 2017. The evolution of Indian banking sector during these 25 years offers an interesting as well as challenging study for the discerning observers and laymen. This work is an attempt to document these changes. As public sector banks still continue to enjoy a lion's share in the banking business I have primarily focused my study on them with incidental references to banking developments in the private sector.

As an insider in the industry, although a cog in the wheel, I had observed from very close quarters as well as experienced the transformation taking place in the public sector banks. It was a great learning experience spread over three decades. Documenting this transformation from an insider's angle would be, according to me, very useful to the society at large. My association with several top bankers, board members, policy makers, union leaders both at the bank and national level and exposure to many decision making bodies and study groups was indeed an enriching experience. This has had a bearing on this work.

The frontiers of my understanding have been greatly widened by the voluminous literature credited to several authorities, analysts, journals and newspapers, reports of committees and also my own articles on the subject in different occasions and places as cited in the footnotes at the end of each chapter. Studying them was itself a learning experience.

A work of this kind serves two purposes. One, it documents the evolution of the institution of public sector banking over five decades after nationalisation although the primary focus is on the reforms era (1991-2017). Such documentation by an insider provides inputs which are authentic and reliable. And second, in the dynamic world of constant change, policy makers could draw appropriate lessons from the documentation so done and on the basis of the lessons bring about policy changes needed.

I am greatly benefited by the advice of Dr N.K. Thingalaya, Economist and former distinguished Chairman & Managing Director of Manipal based Syndicate Bank. Despite his advanced age he painstakingly went through the draft, patted my effort and gave very valuable suggestions. His foreword acts as a curtain raiser on the work. I am beholden to him.

A former colleague of Corporation Bank, S.A.Hiremath from Dharwad, Karnataka went through the draft and gave me encouraging feedback about the contents and the presentation.

My wife, Sumathi Ramachandra, who was herself a banker did a lot of work related to compiling data, corrections in the draft and suggestions for refining certain observations.

Several other former colleagues constantly kept on nudging me to undertake the project.

I am grateful to all of them.

There are bound to be shortcomings in a work of this kind spanning a period so large and covering a subject as complex as banking. I will be grateful for a feedback from the learned readers on such shortcomings.

I am thankful to the publishers M/s Gyan Publications, Delhi who agreed to take up publication of the book. They have done a good job and in record time.

**T R Bhat**

Mangalore
'Mitra'
Kotekani I Cross Road,
Ashokanagar,
Mangalore-575006
Karnataka
Email: bhat_tr@yahoo.co.in

# List of Tables

## CHAPTER - 12



## CHAPTER - 13



## CHAPTER - 15



## CHAPTER - 17



## CHAPTER - 19



## CHAPTER - 21

# Prologue

As part of the wide ranging economic reforms started in the early years of 1990s the financial sector in India was also subjected to radical changeover. The reforms have been sweeping and continuous. During the period of over 25 years between 1991 and 2016, although the political leadership has moved from one end of the ideological spectrum to the other, with minority, coalition and single party led governments at different times, the process of reforms continued unabated. Apparently there was consensus among the divergent political leadership that reforms were necessary. The latest round of changes was unleashed with a change in the regime in 2014. Have these reforms helped the financial sector? Have they complemented the wider changes experienced in the country? As banking industry is in the core of the financial sector has the industry gained substantially from the changes effected in the past 25 years? Have they contributed to the real economy?

These and a host of other questions stare at the observers of the financial sector. The answers will obviously be divergent for diverse reasons. We have been constantly observing such divergences from the beginning of reforms. For that matter when the major scheduled commercial banks were nationalised in July 1969 the opinions were sharply divided so much so that the original act of bank nationalisation was struck down by the Supreme Court necessitating a fresh act in 1970. Notwithstanding such differences the country witnessed fundamental changes in the financial sector after the nationalisation of major banks.

At the exact moment when certain decisions are taken by the policy-makers reactions are bound to come; they could endorse the decisions or, they could be critical of the efficacy of the decisions. It is only after the efflux of time that one can evaluate the performance and make an objective assessment on the basis of hard facts.

Considerable volume of literature is now available about the circumstances which warranted certain reforms in the financial sector, the progress of such reforms, their outcome and the future challenges. Even with a score and five years behind us, there is still no consensus in the country about the impact of the reforms. In a country as diverse as ours such divergence is a fact of life.

A critical review of the whole reform process and its impact would help an informed debate on the whole issue. The lessons learnt and to be learnt could help the policy-makers to steer clear of the pitfalls or the dangers the financial sector could be exposed to in the days ahead.

This volume is an attempt to study the whole gamut of reforms in the banking sector as part of the larger financial sector. Although the current spate of reforms began in 1991, what happened before that year is also relevant for a study of this kind. The reforms emerged as a strategy to tackle the perceived shortcomings and challenges before the banking industry around 25 years ago. Further the assessment becomes fair when the impact of reforms is juxtaposed with the situation that triggered the reforms. The period of reforms has been quite long and the scale of reforms wide ranging. And this necessarily takes us to the future challenges.

To meet this need the study will broadly be in five sections. The first part (chapters 1 to 3) is an attempt to reconstruct the situation leading to the reforms. The second part (chapters 4 to10) will chronicle the gamut of reforms during the first 12 years (1992-2004) and its evaluation. The third part (chapters 11 to 15) will examine the progress between 2004 to 2010 to 2014 followed by an assessment of its impact on the PSBs. As the global financial crisis of 2007-08 did have lessons of significance for India, one chapter on that is included in this part. The fourth part (Chapters 16 to 19) looks at the turmoil in the banking industry starting from 2014 to 2017, the factors that led to it and the measures taken by the regulator and the new government. The concluding part is an attempt to reflect upon the current status, future challenges and the path that could be followed.

Considering the fact that the changes were interconnected and spread over a long period and the problems were recurring some developments and actions get repeated references in different chapters. Similarly over years certain basic problems relating to governance, management and accountability have remained unaddressed necessitating a recurring comment on them. This type of narration makes every chapter to stand on its own and at the same time give a total picture over a time zone.

The process of reforms is on-going. Although for the purpose of this work the indicative period is 25 years between 1991 and 2016, developments that have taken place after that cut-off are also recorded and discussed. For practical reasons the period starting from April 2017 is not included although some references do appear during the course of the discussion of the reform process from 2014.

# SECTION - I

# Towards reforms
# (The pre-1991 years)

## Chapter - 1

# Banking in India in the Early Years of Independence

Until the advent of the East India Company, the Indian financial sector was dominated by indigenous bankers. With the arrival of the Company, modern banking made its appearance with Bank of Hindustan as the first bank to be set up in 1770 in Calcutta (as it was then known) by Alexander and Company, an agency house. A number of banks were set up by individuals and the managing agents of trading companies of British origin. The concept of joint stock banking came into existence in the late Nineteenth Century. A major thrust was received with the setting up during that century of the Presidency banks in the erstwhile Bengal (1806), Bombay (1840) and Madras (1843) presidencies under the royal charter and the control of the East India Company. But due to inherent weaknesses, bank failures were frequent. It is instructive to know the reasons for such failure as pointed out in 1868 by C. Jackson Commission, one of the earliest panels which enquired into bank failures in that century. According to that Commission[1]:

> The reasons were abuse of powers by weak and unprincipled secretaries; the managers were almost all young and inexperienced and the negligence of the

directors who were thoroughly unscrupulous and mischievous. The government directors also neglected their duty.

A more scathing indictment of the amoral practices of the banks came from Charles Northcote Cooke in his treatise '*Rise, Progress and Present Condition of Banking in India*'. He said then:

> ...after the discreditable failure of the Union Bank of Calcutta, the disgraceful fraud of the Benares Bank, the delinquencies of the North-Western Bank of India, and the rascality of the London and Eastern Banking Corporation, the commercial and banking morality of India- Calcutta in special- have been loudly called in question.[2]

One historic development of the early Twentieth Century was the merger in January 1921 of the three Presidency banks based in Calcutta, Madras and Bombay (now Kolkata, Chennai and Mumbai, respectively), to form what was then known as the Imperial Bank of India. There was as yet no central banking authority to control and monitor the working of banks. The financial sector continued to be fragile with recurring bank failures till the middle of Twentieth Century. The lessons from the bank failures of the earlier years were apparently not learnt. The deep-rooted problems were once again brought to the public domain by the Central Banking Enquiry Committee (CBEC) in 1931 in the following words[3]:

(1) The incompetence of the Directors, 'too innocent of banking practice or business prudence' to check the manipulations of designing Directors and Managers.

(2) Unrestricted loans to Directors or concerns in which they were interested.

(3) Dishonest management and bad, speculative and injudicious investments.

(4) Paid up capital and reserves were insufficient, while a large proportion was held in immovable property, and short-term deposits were utilised for long-term loans, leading to poor liquidity.

(5) There was no co operation among banks for joint action in the hour of need, no central banking institution for timely assistance and no organisation for effecting schemes of amalgamation.

The setting up of the Reserve Bank of India (RBI) in 1935 in terms of RBI Act, 1934 as the central banking authority was intended to be a decisive step in reforming the fragile banking industry. The central bank itself was, however, not sufficient to regulate the industry as more banks failed. A comprehensive legislation became imperative and the new government enacted in 1949, the Banking Companies Act (BCA). It became the bulwark aimed at strengthening the banks and enhancing public confidence in them. RBI could monitor the working of banks through inspection and, liquidate those who were afflicted by serious illness. It could also encourage voluntary merger of weak banks with sound ones.

It was ironic, however, that banking industry continued to be plagued by failures triggered by the same reasons which the Jackson Commission in 1868 and the CBEC in 1931 pointed out. Many banks were not amenable to RBI's counsel. By a further amendment to BCA in 1960, the central government on the recommendation of RBI could order compulsory amalgamation of a weak bank with a sound one. As a consequence of the steps initiated by the now empowered RBI, the process of consolidation and mergers of banks helped reduce bank failures. The number of banks fell drastically from 567 in 1951 to 295 in 1961 and to 91 in 1967[4].

In the meantime, the model of economic development that was adopted for the country in the early years of Independence required the banking industry to perform a more active role in mobilising the financial resources from the far corners of the country and in making them available to those who were in need of them. There was also the report of the Rural Banking Enquiry Committee (1950) which suggested the involvement of commercial banks in providing rural credit. A direct offshoot of this was the nationalisation of Imperial Bank of India in 1955 to form State Bank of India (SBI). SBI had a specific task of opening branches in the rural areas and lending to agriculture and small industry both of which received priority in the economic policy- to meet the goals of food security and generation of employment. This was followed by establishment in 1959 of the seven subsidiaries of SBI, by takeover of the banks in the then princely states empowered by an act of Parliament in 1958. The list of subsidiaries is given in the *Annexure* - 1.

In furtherance of the government's strategy of industrialisation more institutions were set up during this time. For financing industry, term lending institutions in the form of Industrial Finance Corporation of India (1948) and Industrial Development Bank of India (1964) in the public sector and Industrial Credit and Investment Corporation of India (1955) in the private sector were set up. In 1955, life insurance business was nationalised to form Life Insurance Corporation of India which was also mandated to lend for infrastructure building. This development helped streamline the financial sector with commercial banks providing financial resources on a short and medium term basis and the term lending institutions providing long-term funds necessary for industrialisation of the country.

The private banks in the mainstream, however, continued to be guided by their own commercial considerations. Their business was urban oriented, clients were primarily industrialists and traders and as the ownership and control vested with large industrial houses, the farmers, the marginalised sections of the society and those entrepreneurs who wanted to be on their own could hardly expect the banks to come to their help. It was reported that in 1967, 64 per cent of the bank advances went to the big industries, and 6.6 per cent to small scale industries and just 2.1 per cent to farming including plantations. The branches of the banks were concentrated in urban areas; in 1969, just 22.2 per cent of the branches were in the rural areas. While the per-branch average population was 65,000 there were many smaller towns (444) without branch of any bank. In short, financial exclusion was a serious shortcoming of the banking industry in the late 1960's.[5] A balanced regional growth, sustained growth of agriculture, encouragement to employment generating small industries and foreign exchange generating export oriented industries were not feasible with the then existing structure of banking.

The prevalent state of affairs of the banking industry was attributed primarily to the interlocking of control and ownership of banks with industrial houses which cornered the lion's share of bank finance. For example, Central Bank of India had H P Mody as Chairman and its main client was the Tata Group of Companies; United Commercial Bank was headed by G.D. Birla and its principal customer was the Birla Group of Companies and Punjab National Bank with S.P. Jain as Chairman was the principal banker to Dalmia-Jain group of companies.[6] The Dutt Committee on Industrial Licensing (1969) had gone on record that '11 banks were under the direct control of large industrial houses'.[7] There was, as a result, not only growth of monopolies but also concentration of economic power in a few hands.

The situation necessitated a radical shift in the policy of the state. The first signal of this policy shift came in the form of social control of banks in 1967-68. The scheme of social control over banks (adopted by the Indian Parliament in late 1968 and implemented in early 1969) had a three-pronged strategy to regulate the banks. First, the business policies of the banks were to be reshaped to meet the needs of the economy through equitable allocation of resources. Second, the boards were to be reconstituted to give representation to different stakeholders like agriculture, chartered accountants, small industries, rural economy etc. And third, if a bank did not fall in line with this policy, government could take over the bank violating the law. To implement this policy a formal body called National Credit Council (NCC) was set up in February 1968 with Finance Minister as Chairman and RBI Governor as the Deputy Chairman and three other permanent members. The NCC was empowered to influence the directional flow of credit to desired sectors of the economy.

Social control had its own limitations. The promoters of the banks continued to wield considerable influence on the banks which could neutralise the impact of NCC's directions.

It was in this background that the central government headed by Prime Minister Mrs Indira Gandhi decided to nationalise major banks. Accordingly in July 1969, 14 major private banks with deposits of Rs 50 crores and above were nationalised through a Presidential Ordinance which was later replaced by Banking Companies (Acquisition & Transfer of Undertakings) Act 1970. With nationalisation, 72 per cent of the deposits and 65 per cent of the advances of the banking industry came under the government control. Having acquired the control over the financial resources, the government's intention was to re- allocate them into the sectors that were in need of them.

With the government as the owner of major banks, branch expansion in unbanked areas could be speeded up; savings could be mobilised from such centres and credit could be reallocated to marginalised sections of the society and risk of bank failures would be minimal. It was a forerunner of inclusive banking which concept came into currency in the first decade of this century. A little over a decade later six more private banks each with deposits of Rs 200 crores were taken over by the government in April 1980. (*Names of banks nationalised in 1969 and 1980 are given in Annexure 2*). With the second batch of nationalisation around 80 per cent of banking business came directly under the control of the central government.

In the meantime, in 1975, Regional Rural Banks were started with a PSB as the sponsor and central and state governments as joint sponsors. Each RRB had its operations in the district/s earmarked for it; it was primarily intended to meet the banking needs of the rural areas with the backing of a PSB and support of the state and central governments. Thus, the nationalised banks (numbering 20), the State Bank and its associates (numbering 8) and the RRBs (numbering 196) constituted the core of Indian banking primarily under the ownership and control of the state. As we shall see in the next chapter state takeover of banks became a watershed in the evolution of banking in Independent India with far reaching implications.

**Annexure - 1**
**List of the subsidiaries of State Bank of India established in 1959**

1. State Bank of Bikaner & Jaipur
2. State Bank of Hyderabad
3. State Bank of Indore*
4. State Bank of Mysore
5. State Bank of Patiala
6. State Bank of Saurashtra*
7. State Bank of Travancore

*Merged with SBI in 2008

## Annexure - 2
## List of private banks nationalised in 1969/80

| *Sl. No.* | *Name of Bank* | *Year of nationalisation* | *Headquarters* |
|---|---|---|---|
| 1. | Allahabad Bank | 1969 | Calcutta |
| 2. | Bank of Baroda | 1969 | Baroda |
| 3. | Bank of India | 1969 | Bombay |
| 4. | Canara Bank | 1969 | Bangalore |
| 5. | Central Bank of India | 1969 | Bombay |
| 6. | Dena Bank | 1969 | Ahmedabad |
| 7. | Indian Bank | 1969 | Madras |
| 8. | Indian Overseas Bank | 1969 | Madras |
| 9. | Bank of Maharashtra | 1969 | Poona |
| 10. | Punjab National Bank | 1969 | Delhi |
| 11. | Syndicate Bank | 1969 | Manipal, Karnataka |
| 12. | United Commercial Bank@ | 1969 | Calcutta |
| 13 | Union Bank of India | 1969 | Bombay |
| 14. | United Bank of India | 1969 | Calcutta |
| 15. | Andhra Bank | 1980 | Hyderabad |
| 16. | Corporation Bank | 1980 | Mangalore |
| 17. | New Bank of India* | 1980 | Delhi |
| 18. | Oriental Bank of Commerce | 1980 | Delhi |
| 19. | Punjab & Sindh Bank | 1980 | Delhi |
| 20. | Vijaya Bank | 1980 | Bangalore |

@Subsequently renamed as UCO Bank. *Merged with Punjab National Bank in 1993.

## References


1. Tandon, Prakash 1989, Penguin: *Banking Century-A Short History of Banking in India and the Pioneer: Punjab National Bank* (pp. 188-9).
2. Quoted by Thingalaya, N K. 1997, *Banking Development in Independent India,* Pigmy Economic Review, July-August 1997, monthly economic journal of Syndicate Bank.
3. Tandon, Prakash, (1989), p. 196.
4. Shukla, S.P. 2006, *Report of the Independent Commission on Banking and Financial Policy* (p. 12) Pub: AIBOC.
5. Shukla, S P, *ibid*, p. 14.
6. Da Costa, E P W, *Reserve Bank of India –Fifty Years,* 1985 Published by RBI; p. 97.
7. Shukla, S P, *ibid*, p. 14.

# Chapter - 2

# Banks after Nationalisation Till 1991

The nationalisation of 14 major private banks in 1969 opened up a new era in the financial sector in India. In the decade following the first nationalisation, Regional Rural Banks came into existence almost entirely owned by the state. A decade later, in 1980, six more private banks were nationalised. During the two decades following the first round of nationalisation, the banking scenario underwent a radical change. The present chapter briefly discusses the developments in the years following State-takeover of banks.

## Objectives of nationalisation

A reference has already been made in the earlier section about the objectives of nationalisation of banks. A more detailed study of the specific goals of that change will be necessary to understand the contribution of the banking sector during the first two decades of nationalisation.

It will be instructive to recall the objectives of nationalisation as enumerated in the preamble to the Banking Companies (Acquisition & Transfer of Undertakings) Act 1970 (BNA). It reads:

> An Act to provide for the acquisition and transfer of the undertakings of certain banking companies, having

> regard to their size, resources, coverage and organisation, *in order to control the heights of the economy and to meet progressively and serve better, the needs of development of the economy in conformity with national policy and objectives* and for matter connected therewith or incidental thereto. (*emphasis added*)

The original Nationalisation Bill of 1969 was more specific:

> The banking system touches the lives of millions and has to be inspired by larger social purposes and has to subserve national priorities and objectives such as rapid growth in agriculture, small industries and exports, raising of employment levels, encouragement of new entrepreneurs and the development of the backward areas. For this purpose, it is necessary for government to take direct responsibility for the extension and diversification of banking services and for the working of the substantial part of the banking system.

Although the decision was inspired by 'larger social purpose', in practical terms it had clear economic rationale of promoting an inclusive banking with conscious strategies related to branch expansion, deposit mobilisation and credit deployment. The concept of 'inclusive banking' popular today was yet to gain currency 45 years ago; but the nationalisation of banks had inclusive banking as a subtext to its goal.

## Performance of nationalised banks

There were initial hiccups as well as criticisms. The original Bank Nationalisation Act of 1969 was struck down by the Supreme Court of India in February 1970 on two grounds. One ground was that there was 'hostile discrimination' against the 14 banks nationalised in as much as their former owners were not allowed to carry on banking business whereas those who were left out could continue their business. The other ground was that the principles and method of determining the compensation to the erstwhile owners of taken over banks were untenable. A new Ordinance plugging the loopholes of the original act was immediately issued followed by a new Act in March 1970 renationalising the 14 banks.[1]

Criticisms came from different quarters- academics, political leaders and business and industrial communities. For example, the eminent economist P.R. Brahmananda at a later occasion recalls his views expressed immediately after the nationalisation in a seminar held in Pune in these words:

> I argued (at the seminar) that the bank nationalisation would not achieve the grand objectives specified. On the other hand, nationalisation would open the gateway, allegedly in social interest to misuse depositors' funds. I took the same position at a seminar organised by the Indian Merchants Chamber in Bombay immediately after bank nationalisation.[2]

The first 25 years of nationalisation saw that the banking sector moved in the direction set forth at the time of take-over in 1969. A series of measures were initiated at the national level to translate the goals into reality.

In 1970, the Lead Bank Scheme was introduced with every PSB being assigned the role of Lead Bank in selected districts of the country. It was the responsibility of the Lead Bank to identify the banking needs of the allotted district and evolve strategies to meet these needs through branch expansion and credit allocation. Along with the RRBs, the PSBs were made the instruments to penetrate into the unbanked areas of the country. The RBI's branch licensing policy was reoriented to give a push to rural branch network. This, coupled with the radical thinking on the part of the policy-makers of the country, was 'instrumental in revolutionising the structure of banking in the rural areas'.[3]

Banks were mandated to allocate 40 per cent of their aggregate credit to what came to be called priority sectors comprising agriculture, small industry, employment generating small enterprises and foreign exchange earning exports. The goals of food security, employment generation, self-reliance and foreign exchange build-up to contain balance of payments difficulties were expected to be realised through such directed lending. This direction from the government amounted to a radical departure from the purely commercial oriented lending of the pre-nationalisation era. The PSBs were also directed to lend to the socially vulnerable groups under special schemes.

As a result of these measures, the banking sector moved in the direction of fulfilling the broad objectives of nationalisation. Several official and non-official studies confirmed this trend. Three broad areas of achievement could be identified. They are:

(a) Rapid branch expansion even in unbanked, remote corners of the country.
(b) Spread of banking habits as evidenced by sharp growth in the deposit accounts.
(c) Availability of bank finance to agriculture, rural areas and schemes generating employment (directed lending).

When the government itself was the owner of the business enterprise it could reorient its business policy to meet the needs of a larger purpose. Therefore, the idea of government ownership and control over resources had its grounding in the economic compulsions of the country.

Did nationalisation of banks actually achieve its goals or as opined by Prof P.R. Brahmananda open the gateway to misuse of scarce resources? Enormous data are available about the tangible contribution made by the government owned banks in the years following state-takeover. Statistics apart, three decades later, in 2002, I.G. Patel who as Finance Secretary in 1969 had actually worked out the modalities of implementing the government's decision to nationalise banks sums up its success in the following words:

> By all accounts, the nationalisation of major banks was a great success initially. ....it greatly increased popular confidence in the banking system and thus increased the mobilisation of private savings through banks. The savings so mobilised were also used now for supporting public borrowing as well as for meeting hitherto neglected genuine credit needs.[4]

Six years later, in 2006, Patel's views were substantiated by a panel, of independent experts drawn from relevant fields, called Independent Commission on Banking and Financial Policy (ICBP) headed by another former Finance Secretary, S.P. Shukla. After a careful evaluation of the performance with facts and figures collated from the Reserve Bank archives, ICBP commends the performance of the Indian financial sector in the following words:

> Even the ardent critics of India's growth strategy would admit that what the country achieved in the area of financial sector development....particularly after bank nationalisation was unparalleled in the financial history of any other nation in the world.[5]

The Commission provides the following facts:

1. The SCBs (scheduled commercial banks) opened a vast network of branches in the rural areas and unbanked and under banked regions of the country in a short span of 20 years. Out of 62,000 branches as on March, 1991, as much as 35,000 (58 per cent) were in the rural areas.
2. With the expansion of branches, there was sustained increase in the share of deposits mobilised and credit disbursed in the rural areas. The share of rural deposits went up from 6.3 per cent in

December 1969, to 15.5 by March 1991 and of credit from 3.3 to 15.0 per cent.

3. Three historically under banked regions and also underdeveloped economically, namely, north-eastern, eastern and central regions received special attention in the branch expansion programme of banks. Apart from opening branches, the public sector banks supported the state governments in these regions by investing in the securities and bonds of their institutions like electricity boards, improvement trusts and other statutory bodies.
4. There was a decisive shift in credit deployment in favour of the farm sector. From an extremely low level in 1969, the share of farm credit went up to 11 per cent in mid-1970s and to a further level of 18 per cent by the end of the next decade.
5. The share of small scale industrial sector in total bank credit shot up from 6.9 per cent in 1968 to 12 in 1973 and further to 13.5 until the beginning of 1990s.
6. The small borrowal accounts (which signify inclusive banking) went up phenomenally during this period. Between 1972 and 1983, 21.2 million additional loan accounts were opened; out of this as much as 19.8 million (93.1 per cent) were accounts with credit limits of Rs 10,000 or less. This cut-off was revised to Rs 25,000 from 1983 on account of inflation. Between 1983 and 1992 another 38.1 million loan accounts were added. Out of this 36.0 million (95 per cent) belonged to the category of small loans.

Speaking about the share of small loans granted by the SCBs the ICBP lauds the achievement in these words:

> This ability of SCBs to service small borrowal accounts-a peak of 62.5 million with credit limits of Rs 25,000 or lessfrom various sectors and regions of the economy

could be said to be one of the outstanding achievements of bank nationalisation. It is this aspect of banking development that aroused the aspirations of the common man and gave him a sense of participation in the development process.

The progress achieved by the nationalised banks in the areas of branch expansion, advances to priority sector, staff strength, establishment expenses, equity and reserves between 1969 and 1991 given in the tables provided at the end of this chapter is further evidence of the achievements of the banks after government takeover.

With these laudable achievements to the credit of the banking industry after nationalisation in 1969, there were shortcomings as well which regularly figured in public debates. These shortcomings, in turn, triggered the demand for reforms in the financial sector. The next chapter examines them at a greater length.

**Table 1: Progress of Banking at a Glance 1969-1991**

| | *Indicators* | *June 1969* | *March 1991* |
|---|---|---|---|
| 1. | **Number of commercial banks** | 89 | 276 |
| | a. *Scheduled commercial banks: Of which* Regional Rural Banks | 73<br>- | 272<br>196 |
| | b. *Non-scheduled commercial banks* | 16 | 4 |
| 2. | **Number of Bank Offices in India out of which:** | 8262 | 60220 |
| | a. *Rural* | 1833 | 35206 |
| | b. *Semi-urban* | 3342 | 11344 |
| | c. *Urban* | 1584 | 8046 |
| | d. *Metropolitan* | 1503 | 5624 |
| 3. | **Population per Office (in thousands)** | 64 | 14 |
| 4. | **Deposits of Scheduled Commercial Banks (in Rs Crore)** Of which: | 4646 | 201198 |
| | a. Demand | 2104 | 38300 |
| | b. Time | 2542 | 162898 |
| 5. | **Credit of Scheduled Commercial Banks in India (in Rs Crore)** | 3599 | 121865 |
| 6. | **Scheduled Commercial Banks' Advances to Priority Sectors (in Rs Crore)** | 504 | 44572 |

| | | | |
|---|---|---|---|
| **7.** | **Share of Priority Sector Advances in total credit of Scheduled Commercial Banks (in per cent)** | 14.0 | 37.7 |
| **8.** | **Investments of Scheduled Commercial Banks in India (in Rs Crore)** | 1361 | 75817 |
| **9.** | **Investment-Deposit Ratio** | 29.3 | 37.7 |

*Source*: RBI Statistics.

### Table 2: Equity and Reserves of Public Sector Banks 1969-1991

(*In Rs Crores*)

| ***Year*** | ***1969*** | | ***1990*** | | ***1991*** | |
|---|---|---|---|---|---|---|
| ***Bank Group*** | ***Equity*** | ***Reserves*** | ***Equity*** | ***Reserves*** | ***Equity*** | ***Reserves*** |
| State Bank group | 10.63 | 18.14 | 264.00 | 1031.75 | 313.00 | 1310.00 |
| Nationalised Banks | 30.05 | 42.10 | 2046.00 | 1206.10 | 2800.00 | 1577.00 |
| Total for the Public Sector Banks | 40.68 | 60.24 | 2310.00 | 2237.85 | 3113.00 | 2887.00 |

*Source:* IBA Bulletins, March 1992 and July 1994.

### Table 3: Staff Strength of PSBS 1969-1991

| ***Bank Group*** | ***1969*** | ***1991*** |
|---|---|---|
| State Bank Group | 1,23,735 | 2,97,859 |
| Nationalised Banks | 1,87,559 | 5,71,133 |
| All Public Sector Banks | 3,11,294 | 8,68,992 |

*Source:* IBA Bulletins March 1992 and July 1994.

### Table 4: Branches of PSBS 1969-91

| ***Bank Group*** | ***1969*** | ***1991*** |
|---|---|---|
| State Bank Group | 2602 | 12,371 |
| Nationalised Banks | 5197 | 29,952 |
| All Public Sector Banks | 7799 | 42,323 |

*Source:* IBA Bulletins 1992, 1994.

**Table 5: Establishment Expenses of PSBs 1987-1991 (as percentage of total expenses)**

| ***Bank Group*** | ***1987*** | ***1991*** |
|---|---|---|
| SBI | 22.16 | 17.12 |
| SBI Associates | 25.46 | 19.20 |
| Nationalised Banks | 20.14 | 17.53 |
| All PSBs | 21.07 | 17.55 |

*Source:* IBA Bulletin March 1999.

**Table 6: Return on Equity of PSBs 1987-1991**

(*In percentage*)

| ***Bank Group*** | ***1987*** | ***1991*** |
|---|---|---|
| SBI | 30.34 | 53.65 |
| SBI Associates | 8.18 | 37.97 |
| Nationalised Banks | 22.69 | 11.60 |
| All PSBs | 22.26 | 15.36 |

*Source:* IBA Bulletin March 1999.

## References


1. Da Costa, E.P.W., *Reserve Bank of India –Fifty Years,* 1985 Published by RBI; p. 98.
2. Brahmananda, P.R.: *Bank nationalisation-Story of ad hocism and arbitrariness: The Hindu,* July 26, 2000.
3. Da Costa, E.P.W.: p. 150.
4. Patel, I.G., 2002: *Glimpses of Indian Economic Policy: An Insider's View,* Oxford University Press, pp. 139-140.
5. Shukla, S.P., 2006, *Report of the Independent Commission on Banking and Financial Policy* (pp. 17-20) Pub: AIBOC, Bangalore.

# Chapter - 3

# Weaknesses of Public Sector Banks in 1991

As explained in an earlier chapter, while externally the public sector banks (PSBs) acquitted themselves admirably in furthering the goals of nationalisation, internally they suffered from several weaknesses. These weaknesses can be identified under the following heads:

1. Political interference
2. Slow technology adaptation
3. Mounting non-performing assets
4. Lack of accountability
5. Poor customer service
6. Poor human resources management
7. Poor performance in terms of productivity and profitability

Each of these shortcomings needs elaboration.

### *Political interference*

By virtue of BNA, the taken over banks became autonomous corporations incorporated under the said Act and wholly owned by the Government of India. The government as the owner had enormous powers to run the undertakings, encompassing areas like appointment of staff, formulating business strategies, credit deployment and declaration of dividends. In principle banks were independent corporations.

The reality, however, was different. As the owner, the government had a legitimate right to give directions to the banks; but this power when exercised beyond a point would be counterproductive particularly when the banks were commercial enterprises. Complaints of interference even in day-to-day matters were frequently heard during the post-nationalisation years. A commercial enterprise would be hamstrung by undue interference by the owner whose duty was to ensure that the banks complied with the policy directions given by the government. The critical areas of political and governmental interference in the public sector banks' (PSB) working could be listed as under:

1. Appointment of top level management personnel
2. Recruitment of manpower
3. Sanction and disbursement of credit.

As owner the government had the power to appoint the Chairman (CEO) and the directors of the banks' boards. However, the selection of CEOs left much to be desired. There was no transparency in the criteria and the process of selection. As usual with most government departments, merit would not by itself be the sole criterion for selection. The term of their appointment was also not standardised. Many had terms ranging from one to two years. Such short tenures would make long range planning impractical.

In the appointment of directors on the boards of the banks, the government had the sole authority; consultation with the RBI was a formality. The BNA under its different sections provided for appointment of directors to represent specific interest groups like, farmers, small scale industries, chartered accountants, depositors and employees. Very often political considerations weighed with the government in selecting candidates for the posts of directors.[1]

As a measure to promote participation by employees as stakeholders in the management of the PSBs and as mandated by the Indian Constitution under Article 43A, the BNA contained a provision to appoint a representative each from the supervisory (officer) staff and non-supervisory staff (the award staff). After adopting that system in the late 1970's, the government gave up the system of selecting representatives of the officer-staff. The concept of performance was introduced as a criterion for selection giving room for favouritism. Ultimately in September 1989 the Supreme Court had to intervene on a petition by bank officers' associations to restore the representative system of appointment.[2]

When the board as the top policy-making body of a corporation does not have competent personnel the corporation suffers. Several PSBs were victims of such attitude of the government from time to time. This ailment continued even during the post-reforms period.

The staff strength in the PSBs was continuously increasing during the two decades after nationalisation. This was necessitated by the rapid expansion of the branch network even in the remotest corners of the country. The PSBs were given additional responsibilities like setting up and running lead bank offices in each district, promoting and managing Regional Rural Banks (RRBs) and lending under special schemes to beneficiaries identified through the Integrated Rural Development Programmes (IRDP).The business had also grown as shown in the supporting tables in the earlier chapter. In the middle of 1980's the government suddenly imposed a cap on the recruitment in PSBs linking it to the existing staff strength. The measure, therefore, was unrealistic. The objective of the government decision was to cut down the operational cost. This cap introduced in the second decade of nationalisation and continued till late 1990's created serious shortage of trained and experienced manpower in the PSBs during the second decade of the present century.

Another major area of interference was essentially political, in the form of the infamous 'loan *melas*' of the mid-1980s. The elected representatives and their party activists would bring pressure on the field level functionaries and the top management of the banks to sanction and disburse loans ostensibly to the small and marginalised sections of the society. Public functions would be organised to hand over 'sanction' letters giving room for serious malpractices. In the presence of the assembled loan aspirants the bank staff including the top executives would be admonished by the representative. The normal business prudence had to be compromised if the loans were to be sanctioned in that manner. Both the Central Vigilance Commission (CVC) and the Central Bureau of Investigation (CBI) had found fault with that practice. There was countrywide debate on this kind of political interference in loan sanctions. Although the amount involved in each sanction was a few thousand rupees, the process affected the functioning of banks and demoralised the staff.[3]

A more serious problem was in the form of pressure on sanctions of large loans to bigger borrowers who were close to power centres and the tendency to write them off when they turned sticky. *(More about this is discussed later)*

## Technology

PSBs were slow in adopting technological innovations for their day-to-day operations. Initially there was resistance from the well-entrenched trade unions for fear of job losses. But with the revolutionary changes taking place in information technology and its application to service industries, banking sector could not lag behind. For the first time in 1983 there was an agreement between the bank unions and the managements which allowed the banks to mechanise certain key transactions signalling a definite shift towards computerisation of operations.

In 1984, the RBI-appointed Rangarajan Committee on mechanisation had submitted its recommendations for computerising the banks' operations on a large scale. Starting with ledger posting machines in the branches and inter-branch reconciliation through computers at the controlling offices the banks graduated to total branch automation (TBA) by the middle of 1990s. Although the unions were taken on board through agreements, the process was slow for two reasons: the investment needed was huge and the PSBs did not have adequate resources for such investment and, the human resources had to be adequately trained to work in an unfamiliar environment. The slackness in adoption of technology put the PSBs under a disadvantage before the new generation of educated and techno-savvy customers and the new banks which started springing up in the early 1990s.

## Mounting non-performing assets

A serious development observed during the two decades following nationalisation was that the loan over-dues were surging and there were recurring attempts to write them off. The new, rigorous norms for classification of loan assets were yet to come into practice and the current nomenclature of Non-Performing Assets (NPA) was also yet to gain currency. The data provided below is an indicator of the magnitude of overdues during that period.

In 1993, out of the outstanding advances of Rs 1,67,340 crores as much as 39,253 crores (23.2 per cent) were NPAs. The method of computing the NPAs current at that time would conceal the actual NPAs. Whether the interest on loans were actually received or not, the interest receivable would be shown as income earned resulting in two consequences namely, that the actual earnings would get inflated and that the loan would be deemed as interest earning.

The genesis of this problem had to be traced to the process of appraisal and sanction of loans, the method of their disbursement, the system of monitoring and the strategy to recover sticky advances.

The PSBs in the initial years after nationalisation lacked the skills required in evaluating the loan proposals. Most of the employees were grass root workers who grew with the banks; the banks lent generally by the rule book, the eligibility to get a loan linked to the test of conventional three 'C's- meaning character, capital and capacity to repay- of the loan applicant. Many did not have the skills to assess the creditworthiness of a borrower. The power to sanction loans was centralised at the controlling offices with very limited delegation of authority. Large loans were invariably to be sanctioned at the highest level-by the CEO or the board of directors. The loan proposals would be prepared in a way to facilitate sanction.

Even in respect of advances to agriculture and small scale industry, the PSB officers did not have adequate knowledge of the activity. A large majority of the urban based employees had no idea of the farming operations or starting and running a new enterprise. They would either shy away from sanctioning or where they entertained the loan proposals, far lower amount than applied for by the borrower would be considered with numerous conditions and multiple documents, possibly to avoid risks and accountability.

Post-sanction supervision and monitoring of advances also needed skill to read the signals in time and initiate corrective actions. Most managers were not trained in that area; monitoring was limited to sending notices of interest, obtaining stock statements from the borrowers and inspecting the stocks hypothecated to the bank without knowledge of the quality of the stocks.

While these were the problems at the operational level, at the top level 'the behest culture' had contributed to bad loans. Using this phrase, S.Venkitaramanan who was

Governor of RBI during the beginning of the reforms era, between 1990 and 1992, wrote as follows (in 1996)[4]

> Rare is the Chief Executive Officer (CEO) who can resist the blandishment of a minister or his panjandrum who asks that a particular loan be expedited. The CEO exists at the sufferance of the government and has at least to consider their requests even when they are unreasonable...Behest will be behind many of the loans that have turned sour in the latest saga of Indian banks. Combine behest with the human tendency of CEOs to be seen as benevolent boss. The mixture can be explosive even in a corruption-free bank.

There was another practice which also came up for public scrutiny. The banks resorted to writing off of bad debts (meaning loans which were deemed irrecoverable). After the loans were so written off, the promoters of the firms or enterprises which received the munificence would be granted fresh loans in a different name. There was no check or scrutiny of such write offs by the PSBs. Very often these benefits were extended to borrowers who had political clout and who were close to the power centres. More often, the beneficiaries were the larger borrowers. For example, during 1988-89, the composition of debts written off by one PSB was as under:

| | ***Loan amount*** | ***Number of accounts*** | ***Amount written off (in Rs lakhs)*** |
|---|---|---|---|
| 1. | Loans of Rs 50,000 or less | 2436 | 62.67 |
| 2. | Loans of above Rs 50,000 | 43 | 494.35 |

Under the present standards the amounts may look too small, but it is to be appreciated that the figures were for 1988-89, nearly three decades ago.

As the regulator the RBI had, in July 1986, given the following prescriptions to control the growth of bad loans and their write off.

(a) Efficient functioning of the credit department

(b) Maintenance of quality loans and advances

(c) Timely identification of irregular accounts/sick units

(d) Time discipline to implement these measures.

These guidelines of the RBI were hardly implemented. When the loan accounts went bad, the banks would routinely write them off or enter into compromises and settlements with borrowers.

The process was shrouded in mystery; the internal audits and the inspection by RBI were unable to point out the lapses in the process of sanction and monitoring of loans and the efforts for recovery.

The impact of this development was on the viability of the banks as observed by this author in a paper presented in 1993[5]:

> By 1986 itself the viability of the banks was a matter of concern for RBI. Debts had already been contaminated by then. Urgent corrective measures were called for. RBI stressed on this in October 1985 when it initiated two-year action plan for all banks. The plan covered strategies to improve credit administration. Then followed the guidelines for write off given in July 1986. In spite of these guidelines, the systems prescribed and the RBI's monitoring the incidence of bad debts has not only not come down, on the other hand it has grown into a proportion threatening the very existence of the banks. New Bank of India became the first casualty. Others in the list are UCO Bank, Syndicate Bank, Indian Overseas Bank, Bank of Baroda, Vijaya Bank, Bank of India, Bank of Maharashtra and Central Bank of India- all of whom had reported huge losses this year; one cannot be sure with the others. Many more have reported large scale erosion of their profits.

According to the data published by IBA during 1991-92, 20 PSBs had written off Rs 660.90 crores, which went up to 1534.41 crores next year and to a further level of Rs 2437.06 crores in 1993-94 (*IBA Bulletin* June 1994). Their equity in 1993 was Rs 4554.50 crores.

In November 1986, Gurudas Dasgupta, as a Member of Parliament, had introduced a bill to set up an independent audit authority on the lines of Comptroller & Auditor General to go into the gamut of debt write-offs. The bill also spelt out a provision to mandatorily disclose bad debts and sticky loans.

In the early 1990s there was a demand by a bank officers' association to subject such write-offs of bad debts to Parliamentary scrutiny through a social audit.[6]

At the policy makers' level there was hardly any serious action to arrest the setback, which failure made the PSBs more fragile in the early 1990s.[7]

## Lack of accountability

A serious lacuna in the working of the PSBs in the immediate two decades following state takeover was the absence of accountability for failures and questionable loan decisions. The government had enormous power to fix accountability on the CEOs and the board for their failure to provide efficient leadership to the banks. There was no yardstick for performance evaluation of the CEOs or for holding them accountable for serious losses due to their decisions. On rare occasions, when driven to a corner, the government would ask the CEO to take leave as it happened in the case of Bank of Baroda in 1985.[8] There was another case in 1992 in Syndicate Bank whose Executive Director who was officiating CEO was asked to go on leave for his alleged involvement in the scandal associated with Fairgrowth Financial Services Ltd.[9] In the same year the Andhra Bank CEO had reportedly ignored the auditors' suggestion to make a provision of Rs 44 crores for bad and doubtful debts in the balance sheet.[10] The lack of decisiveness on the part of the government in handling cases of this kind had greatly impacted the working of the PSBs.

The terms of the CEOs were not governed by set rules. (The CEOs at that time combined the posts of Chairman and Managing Director in nationalised banks. In 2015, the government started splitting the post. In SBI the posts were split much earlier with a full time Chairman as CEO and many Managing Directors). In several PSBs, the CEOs had tenures varying from one year to less than three. Such short tenures would affect the long range planning and monitoring of the plans drawn. And after declaring the adoption of a plan if the CEO demitted the office, his successor would not be held answerable to ensure its implementation. He would have his own vision. Such approaches affected the efficiency of individual banks.

Accountability was limited to the lower level officials in conformity with the government guidelines on vigilance and the conduct and disciplinary regulations.

## Poor customer service

When the PSBs made rapid strides in their business, the existing staff who were exposed to new kind of business and customers, had difficulty in adapting to the transition. The massive recruitment that followed did not solve the problem immediately as they did not have the required customer orientation. The banks did not possess the infrastructure to provide them the necessary skills and influence their attitude. Internal training systems were yet to size up themselves to the challenges.

The result was increasing customer complaints against the poor quality service of PSBs. Responding to these complaints both the Government of India and RBI set up committees to study the problems and recommend corrective measures. The R.K.Talwar Committee (1977) appointed by the government and M.N.Goiporia Committee (1991) appointed by the RBI went into the issues and suggested a host of measures to be undertaken by the banks and to be in turn monitored by the RBI. In implementing many of the suggestions made by these committees some of the banks took employees' unions on board at individual bank level. At the level of IBA too, customer service figured in the bipartite meetings with apex level unions of bank employees.

In 1995, RBI introduced the Banking Ombudsman Scheme to create a platform for the aggrieved bank customers to seek expeditious redress of their complaints on certain identified issues. It was intended to be inexpensive and easily accessible to the public and was organised under the aegis of the RBI itself.

All these measures were indicative of the fact that the quality of customer service in PSBs left much to be desired.

## Poor human resources management (HRM)

As mentioned earlier the manpower in the PSBs grew rapidly after 1969 primarily to meet the new challenges of social banking. The concept of 'human resources' was, however, alien to the PSBs which were earlier operating under a feudal system of master and servant. The departments handling the staff were being called by different names like Staff Department, Establishment Department, Personnel Department, Administration Department or simply Labour Department. It is in the late 1980s that the banks started rechristening the department as Human Resources Department. But the change was in the nomenclature without change in the approach and attitude.

The recruitment process was standardised with the constitution of Banking Services Recruitment Board (BSRB) paving the way for broad based selection of employees at the entry levels of clerks and officers through competitive examinations. But such recruitment was not complemented by adequate conceptual and on the job training. Training itself was a low priority issue for PSBs.

Many PSBs did not have proper placement policies governing the posting of their staff. Officers with specialised foreign exchange training would be posted to rural branches; officers without much of practical branch banking experience would be posted as branch managers and those with little knowledge of credit appraisal would land in loans department of the banks. Many PSBs did not have fully equipped staff training colleges and where they had, the faculty were not adequately oriented towards human resources training.

The service and conduct rules were archaic adopted as they were from the Central Civil Service (Classification & Control) Rules (CCSR). The compensation packages were hammered out through protracted negotiations with the unions, often preceded by industrial unrest. As the government would impose a cap on salary increases and pay structure, the salaries were unrelated to market realities. Disciplinary system was also linked to the CCSR which was ill-suited to commercial enterprises where decision-making required exercise of discretion and judgement by an individual officer. These realities were instrumental in demoralising the huge manpower of the PSBs resulting in less than optimal utilisation of their strengths and capabilities.

It is pertinent to mention that for almost three decades after nationalisation, there was no serious attempt to understand the complexities of human resources management in PSBs. The first attempt came in 2000 when the Ministry of Finance, Government of India appointed a Committee on Human Resources Management in Public Sector Banks (CHRM). It was mandated to examine all aspects of human resources management in PSBs and suggest measures for converting this resource into a viable asset. Another Committee was set up in 2010, under the Chairmanship of Anil K.Khandelwal. But by that time the quality of human resources had already suffered.

A comprehensive study of the issues connected with human resources management was made by the

Independent Commission on Banking & Financial Policy (ICBP). In its report released in 2006 ICBP pointed out the shortcomings of the then existing human resources management policies of the banks and made a number of recommendations.[11]

Obviously when the banks were on the threshold of newer challenges in 1991 the human resources policies of the PSBs needed a drastic change.

## Poor performance in terms of productivity and profitability

While the business of the banks in terms of deposits and advances grew after nationalisation receiving uniform accolades, it is the performance parameters which caused concern. The opinion was divided, though. The productivity, profitability, earnings, return on capital and efficiency ratios were considered to be unsatisfactory. A look at certain key parameters is necessary to understand the then prevailing situation. Some of them are explained below.

## The Non-Performing Assets (NPAs)

The most serious issue was related to the bulging over-due loans most of which were not recoverable. Technically called Non-Performing Assets after 1991-92, the volume of these loans was growing alarmingly. By early 1990 NPAs as percentage of advances of PSBs had crossed 20; by 1993 it had reached a staggering 23.4 per cent surging to 24.8 a year later. In absolute terms, out of Rs 1,69,340 crore of advances of PSBs as much as Rs 39,253 crore had become bad in 1993; in 1994 out of Rs 1,65,621 crores of advances Rs 41,041 crores were NPAs. It related to their equity and reserves the gravity would be starker. In 1993, the equity of the PSBs was Rs 4,685 crores and the reserves were Rs 4,554 crores and that year alone the PSBs (other than SBI group) had written off as much as Rs 1,534 crores of bad debts followed by another Rs 2,437 crores in 1994. PSBs had become financially very weak threatening their viability.

## The efficiency parameters

Different efficiency parameters were also cause of concern to the government.

Interest earned as percentage of working funds in 1991 was 8.46 (8.69 for private banks and 11.46 for foreign banks). The net profits as percentage to working funds for PSBs was 0.18 (0.35 for private banks and 1.45 for foreign banks). The spread as percentage to working funds for that year was 2.95 (5.48 for private banks and 3.57 for foreign banks).

The establishment expenses of the PSBs in 1991 as percentage of total expenses at 17.55 were also considered to be on the high side. (That for the private banks was 23.36, though and for foreign banks in India, 7.32).

The return on assets of the PSBS in 1991 was 0.36 per cent (0.75 for private banks and 3.15 for foreign banks). The return on equity for the PSBs in 1991 was 15.36 per cent (99.51 for private banks).

It will be useful to recall what C. Rangarajan -at that time he was a member of the Planning Commission and later became the Governor of RBI- said in 1992 about the state of affairs in relation to the financial sector.[12]

> While the progress made by the financial system in general and the banking and other financial facilities to a larger cross-section of the people is well-recognised, there is a growing concern over the operational efficiency of the system. There has been a perceptible decline in the productivity and profitability of commercial banks. It is estimated that in 1989-90, gross profits before provisions were no more than 1.10 per cent of working funds. In 1990, the spread between interest earned and paid as a proportion of working funds was 3.2 per cent. The establishment expenses as a proportion of working

funds in the same year was 2.05 per cent. With the decline in the quality of loan assets (the sticky advances account for more than 20 per cent of the credit outstanding) the need for provisioning has become urgent and several banks are not in a position to make adequate provisions for doubtful debts. The financial position of RRBs is far worse with the accumulated losses completely wiping out the capital in most banks. The balance sheet of the financial sector is thus mixed, strong in achieving certain socio-economic goals in general, widening the credit coverage but weak as far viability is concerned.

We need to take these efficiency parameters with a rider. In absolute terms the ratios appeared abysmally low; but the performance of the Indian private sector banks was no better. And with social banking as mandatory requirement for the PSBs, their performance could not be compared to that of foreign banks operating in India.

These shortcomings, both actual and perceived, juxtaposed with the stage set for an overhaul of the country's economic policy provided the rationale for a relook at the banking policies in the beginning of the reforms era.

## References

1. In a Karnataka based PSB, a person who was the primary school teacher of a central minister was appointed director. Another director would frequently drop the name of his patron who was Speaker of the State Legislative Assembly. One more was a former member of the State Committee of the ruling party. This author was a colleague of the latter two on the board. None of them represented any interest; their contributions to the board deliberations were minimal.
2. See Bhat, T R. (1999): *In search of an identity, CBOO through 25 years;* Pub: CBOO, Mangalore, p. 193.
3. See Bhat, T R (1999), pp. 162, 163 and Bhat, T R (1998): *Voice of CBOO- Collection of Editorials in Officers' Voice 1982-1998, Pub CBOO,* pp. 253-259.

4. S.Venkitaramanan, (1996): *Bankers and their dilemma* in *Times of India,* August 25.
5. See Bhat., T.R., (1993): *Bad debts written off and their impact on Banks' Balance Sheets,* a Paper presented at the Triennial Conference of AIBOC in 1993 held in Agra, reproduced in the aforesaid book (1999), pp. 174-182.
6. See Letter no. CO/213/122/90 dated February 8, 1990 written by General Secretary, CBOO to the then Finance Minister, Government of India- document published in Bhat, T.R., (1998) pp. 168-173; also see Bhat, T.R., 1993.
7. The issue becomes again relevant in the context of the problems of loan losses and write-offs faced by the banks during 2015-17.
8. Thakurta, Paranjoy Guha, (1985): Cover Page article in *Update,* August 23-September 5, 1985: *Fraud at Bank of Baroda* pp. 25-29.
9. Report in *Business Standard*: August 18, 1992: *Syndicate Bank Chief Asked to go on leave.*
10. Reports in *Times of India,* June 29 and 30, 1992.
11. Shukla, S.P.(2006): *Report of the Independent Commission on Banking and Financial Policy 2006* pp. 77-88.
12. Rangarajan, C and Jadhav, Narendra *Issues in financial sector reform* published in Bimal Jalan (Edit) 1992: *The Indian Economy-Problems and Prospects* Viking/Penguin India pp. 149-150.

# SECTION - II

# The first 12 years of reforms (1992-2004)

# Chapter - 4

# The Early Years of Reforms

## The trigger

The year 1991 is a watershed year in post-Independence India. Faced with an acute balance of payments crisis, the Government of India had to quickly find an enduring solution. The magnitude of the crisis could be understood from the fact that in May that year the country's foreign exchange reserves had depleted to a level sufficient to meet only the imports of fifteen days with a serious risk of default in fulfilling its repayment obligations towards loans borrowed earlier. The care-taker government headed by Chandra Shekhar had to pledge 67 tonnes of gold to avail a bailout loan of $2.2 billion from international financial institutions. In July 1991, a new government with P.V. Narasimha Rao as Prime Minister and Manmohan Singh, a former Finance Secretary and RBI Governor as Finance Minister took office. A series of policy changes to meet the conditions imposed by the international institutions were initiated immediately. There was a radical shift in the model of economic development till then followed in the country under the Nehru-Mahalanobis strategy of economic development.

One critical sector to be opened up was banking. The conditionalities imposed by the International Monetary Fund and World Bank for providing financial assistance to

India to tide over the balance of payments difficulties required major changes in the financial sector.

## The first Narasimham Committee

In August 1991 the government appointed the Committee on the Financial System (CFS/NC-I) headed by M.Narasimham, a former RBI Governor and Finance Secretary to *"examine all aspects relating to the structure, organisational function and procedures of the financial system"*. The CFS submitted its recommendations in three months that is by November 1991. The next few years saw the government and the RBI implement these recommendations to bring about sweeping changes in the entire financial sector.

The committee aimed at seeking "to consolidate the gains made in the Indian financial sector while improving the quality of the portfolio, providing greater operational flexibility and most importantly greater autonomy in the internal operations of the banks and financial institutions so as to nurture a healthy, competitive and vibrant financial sector...". To achieve this, the CFS underlined the need for deregulation of the financial sector and measures to improve the health and competitive vitality of the banks which would enable "the Indian financial sector to forge closer links with the global financial markets."[1]

## The Basel Accord on capital for banks

Across the globe, the financial system was undergoing rapid transformation through regulatory framework evolved out of experience of failures due to banks' exposures to huge risks. The collapse of West Germany's bank, Bankhaus Herstatt, in June 1974 sent shock waves in developed countries. The Franklin National Bank of New York had followed suit the same year. Compelled by these disruptions the central bank governors of G10 countries set up during the end of 1974 a Committee on Banking

Regulations and Supervisory Practices. It was renamed as Basel Committee on Banking Supervision.

> Its aim was and is to enhance financial stability by improving supervisory knowhow and the quality of banking supervision worldwide. The Committee seeks to achieve its aims by setting minimum standards for the regulation and supervision of banks; by sharing supervisory issues, approaches and techniques to promote common understanding and to improve cross-border cooperation; and by exchanging information on developments in the banking sector and financial markets to help identify current or emerging risks for the global financial system.

The Committee is a forum for formal consultation among the member nations on banking supervisory issues. A member country is represented by the governor of its central banking authority. Although its recommendations have no binding legal force, it sets standards of supervision for implementation by countries.[2] From time to time the Basel Committee has been laying fresh standards for bank supervision.

## A paradigm shift

The recommendations of the NC-I laid the road map for a paradigm shift in the banking policy in the country. New standards of accounting, capital adequacy and disclosures were set; government ownership of public sector banks was reduced; new banks were allowed to be established; interest rates were liberalised and the statutory impounding of the banks' resources through cash reserve and statutory liquidity ratios was eased. Emphasis was laid on improving internal control and monitoring.

These changes had far reaching implications. It is appropriate at this stage to dwell upon them at greater length.

### *New accounting norms*

The loan assets were required to be classified as standard and substandard assets according to the risks associated with each loan. Loans which carry normal risks associated with lending with no problem of recovery were required to be classified as Standard or Performing Assets (PAs). Those loans whose record of recovery indicated more than the normal risk- where the repayment of instalment and/or interest remain overdue beyond a stipulated period of say 90 days- would be classified as Non-Performing Assets (NPAs). NPAs in turn were to be graded into Sub-standard, Doubtful and Loss Assets. This kind of classification of assets with objective norms helped streamline the loan portfolios of the banks.

Income and/or other charges debited to the loan accounts would be recognised as income depending on the class of advances. For performing assets as and when the interest and/or other charges accrue they would be classified as income. In case of NPAs only when the interest due was actually realised it would be treated as income.

Banks were required to make provisioning against the likely losses on loans according to the classification of loans and realisability of securities. For standard assets, the provisioning would range from 0.25 to 0.40 per cent of amount outstanding. Among the NPAs the sub-standard assets would require a provision of 15 per cent, for doubtful assets it would be between 25 to 100 per cent depending on the security and the duration of the loan and for loss assets it would be 100 per cent.

### *Capital adequacy standards*

The concept of capital adequacy for banks as laid down by Basel Committee was made applicable to Indian banks as recommended by NC-I. Intended to strengthen the viability of banks by shoring up their owned funds, the

Capital Adequacy Ratio (CAR) also known as Capital to Risk-Weighted Assets Ratio (CRAR) is the ratio of capital and reserves to total risk weighted assets of each bank. Capital was divided into two tiers. Tier I comprised of core capital and different kinds of reserves. Tier II capital comprised of hybrid capital, subordinated term debt and general provisions. The banks were mandated to achieve a level of nine per cent capital adequacy by 1999.

Most banks were able to comply with this mandate given by the RBI in the backdrop of the specific measures intended to enhance their performance efficiency and infusion of capital through government's contribution and initial public offer of shares in selected banks as part of the plan to progressively privatise government owned banks.

### *Entry of new players*

In pursuance of the emerging World Trade Organisation's architecture of integrated global financial system, the financial sector in India was opened up for new players. In 1993, the RBI issued fresh guidelines on setting up new banks with certain conditions on capital adequacy, setting up the registered office in Tier II cities, priority sector lending and other regulatory guidelines of the RBI. Ten new private sector banks were licensed. Notable among them were Global Trust Bank, ICICI Bank, UTI Bank (later renamed as Axis Bank), IndusInd Bank and HDFC Bank. While ICICI Bank was promoted by the development financial institution of the same name, Axis Bank was started by Unit Trust of India and HDFC Bank was the off-spring of Housing Development Finance Corporation Ltd. Both the GTB and IndusInd Bank were promoted by private individuals. Many more banks also opened their shops.

Simultaneously, more foreign banks were allowed to open their offices in India; banks already operating in the country were permitted to expand their network of branches.

***Reduction of government's shareholding***

On different grounds the government started diluting its ownership from 100 per cent up to 51 per cent. One ground was the new argument that it was not the business of the government to be in business. The second reason was that the government did not have adequate financial resources to infuse capital to meet the continuously rising capital requirements to conform to international standards. There was continuous pressure from the pro-liberalisation lobby that government banks should also be privatised.

Further to this thinking, in 1994, the government amended the Banking Companies (Acquisition & Transfer of Undertakings) Acts, 1970 and 1980 and State Bank of India Act 1956 (Bank Nationalisation Acts) to enable the state-owned banks to raise capital through public issues and/or preferential allotment. The amendments facilitated reduction of government holding from 100 per cent up to a level of 51; the boards could have directors elected by the shareholders and the banks could be listed in the national level stock exchanges.

As a result of this measure, over a period of time the government ownership in public sector banks was progressively diluted through public issue of shares. The public issues of most banks received overwhelming response from the share markets demonstrating that the investing public continued to have immense faith in the soundness of these banks. By raising capital from the market, they were able to augment capital to meet the now mandatory capital adequacy ratio. The government, however, retained its majority holding. The shares of the banks were listed in major stock exchanges. The listed banks also resorted to raising additional capital through bonds and other instruments which strengthened their Tier II capital.

While the government claimed that the dilution of government share holding was not privatisation, the amendment to the Bank Nationalisation Acts was a radical departure from the concept of 'a wholly owned government of India undertaking' which in 1969/1980 gave the government the full control over the commanding heights of the economy to subserve the goals of achieving an egalitarian society.

### *Liberalised branch licensing*

Another major change in the banking policy related to the branch licensing scheme. In the aftermath of nationalisation, as the regulating authority the RBI laid great emphasis on a broad based branch expansion in its licensing policy. The banks were mandated to open branches in unbanked and under-banked rural and semi-urban centres. This mandate was given to ensure that the banking facility would be made available at the remotest corners of the country. The branch licensing policy required the banks to obtain prior permission from the RBI before opening new branches and shifting of existing offices.

Under the new policy, the discretion to open new branches, close the existing ones or shift them was given to the boards of the respective banks. This liberalised licensing regime had mixed results. There was further expansion of bank branches but banks developed cold feet in opening new branches in the rural areas or unbanked centres. As the government and the RBI laid increasing emphasis on profitability of banks, banks could close down those branches which were chronically loss-incurring. As a result, the share of rural branches in the network of branches progressively came down. The emphasis on financial inclusion which gained currency in the early years of this century was a fall-out of this shift in the policy.[3]

### *Reduction in the cash reserve ratio and statutory liquidity ratio*

Another major shift in the regulatory regime of the central bank was to reduce both the cash reserve and statutory liquidity ratios of the banks as part of the reform package.

In the background of a series of bank failures in the first half of the Twentieth Century, the concepts of cash reserve ratio (CRR) and statutory liquidity ratio (SLR) as percentage of demand and time liabilities (DTL) were incorporated in the Reserve Bank of India Act, 1934 and the Banking Regulation Act, 1949. Section 42 (1) of RBI Act provided for the CRR ranging between 3 and 20 per cent and section 24 of BR Act provided for SLR ranging between 20 and 40 per cent. They would provide liquidity to the banks to meet unforeseen heavy demand for cash from the depositors and internal strength as their funds would be invested in cash, in current account with RBI, in gold and in interest yielding, approved government securities. RBI had the power to vary the ratio from time to time.

While both the provisions were originally intended to strengthen the liquidity, the RBI as the monetary authority would use them as instruments to regulate credit expansion. During inflationary situation the ratios together or singly would be hiked which would have the effect of sucking the lendable resources of the banking system; contrarily when credit expansion was needed the ratios would be lowered so that banks could lend their surplus fund. It is relevant to note that on several occasions as much as 50 per cent of DTL were virtually impounded by the regulator through enhanced CRR and SLR. The impounding of the banks' funds would affect the earning capacity of the banks as on CRR balance kept with RBI no interest would be admissible and the investment for SLR purposes would yield low rates of return.

These ratios were also subjected to downward revision progressively by the RBI in furtherance of loosening the regulatory regimen.

### *Freeing interest rates from the control of RBI*

A major area of reforms was in the form of giving autonomy to banks in fixing interest rates on both deposits and advances.

For long, to prevent unhealthy competition and to incentivise savings the RBI was fixing the interest rates the banks could offer on the deposits. Similarly the lending rate was also prescribed by the RBI. The interest rates on advances were generally linked to the bank rate (the rate at which the banks can avail funds from the RBI as banker to the banks). The interest rates were interlinked. If people's savings were to be attracted into the banking channels higher rates were required to be offered to the public on their deposits. This was intended not only to attract domestic savings but wean them away from unscrupulous non-banking saving organisations (known in the common parlance as 'Finance Companies') who would offer high rates of return and would close their shops with impunity causing serious hardships to gullible depositors. In a way banking habits could be developed in the countryside through attractive interest rates and sovereign guarantee (as most banks were owned by the government).

When the deposit rates were high, maintaining a reasonable margin necessitated levying higher rates of interest on the advances. In view of the government policies the interest rates on the advances coming under priority sector had to be lower than those for other activities like trade and commerce.

The deposit rates ranged between 5 and 12 per cent depending on the duration of deposits. The rates of interest on loans would be anywhere between 11 and 17 per cent.

Only on certain special loans where the government would subsidise, the interest rate would be as low as four per cent.

With the onset of reforms the banks were given freedom to fix the rates of interest on both the deposits and loans. The boards of individual banks were empowered to fix the rates according to their discretion. The consideration would be primarily enhancing the margin between interest cost and interest income.

### *Directional flow of credit*

With the emphasis on efficiency of operation and maximisation of earning the earlier mandate on the flow of credit to certain sectors necessitated by the country's economic needs was set for a change. The concept of priority sector was widened to include lending to units which were only indirectly connected with the objects. The monitoring of advances to priority sector, advances under different schemes of the government and the socially and economically marginalised sections of the society ceased to be rigorous and less frequent.[4]

A new development gave further fillip to this shift. The earlier segregation of development banking and commercial banking was found to be archaic during the era of reforms. The leading term lending institutions like ICICI, IDBI and UTI started their own commercial banks which started advancing on long-term basis for manufacturing and infrastructure activities. There was a reverse merger of ICICI with its offspring. World over the concept of universal banking gained currency with commercial banks going beyond their traditional activities of lending on short-term basis; the wall between commercial lending and development lending almost vanished.

As a fall-out of this development, banks started taking larger exposure to huge advances to industrial houses and corporates to build infrastructure like airports, roads, special economic zones and so on. The net result of these developments was that there was a decisive shift in the directional flow of credit of the banks.

***Disclosure and governance issues***

Along with the aforesaid policy changes introduced, the banks were directed to enhance their standards of disclosure in the annual reports to bring about greater transparency. Simultaneously the issue of corporate governance started getting enormous focus.

As banking involved risks from different sources, the internal supervision was mandated to be linked to defined risks of different kinds in the working of banks.

To face competition and to be on par with international standards these measures were considered critical.

***The Board for Financial Supervision***

In conformity with the recommendations of NC-I the RBI set up an autonomous Board for Financial Supervision (BFS) in 1994. It was a Committee of the Central Board of Directors of the Reserve Bank with the Governor of the Reserve Bank as the Chairman and four non-official directors of the Reserve Bank and the Deputy Governors of the Reserve Bank as members. It was responsible for supervision of banks, financial institutions and non-banking financial companies. In 1995, the RBI set in place the Off-site Monitoring and Surveillance Function. Operationalised in 1997, it was mandated to analyse the position of banks in between the regular inspections (RBI Annual Report 2003-04). Through these steps the regulator could more closely monitor the working of the banks.

***Progressive technology upgradation***

A major thrust was received during the reforms period to the process of computerisation of banking operations. The Rangarajan Committee on Mechanisation in Banking set up by RBI in July 1983 had already set in motion the process of computerising the operations at different levels. There were also agreements with the unions to take them on board.

With the onset of reforms and the exposure to international competition, Indian banks had to adopt higher standards of information technology not only at the back offices but also in front offices while dealing with the customers. This need paved the way for total branch automation in the late 1990's. Technology based facilities like online banking, electronic funds transfer, MICR technology for cheque clearances and anywhere banking were progressively introduced in the industry. Around the same time, automated teller machines (ATMs) to dispense cash were set up by several banks all over the country making cash withdrawals easy and simple for the account holders.

Adoption of advanced technology needed huge resources. This was met through the new capital raised through public issues and internal revenues.

### *Narasimham Committee II*

There were divergent views on the rationale, the strategy and the sweep of reforms introduced during the period between 1991 and 1996. Notwithstanding the divergence and successive changes in the government between 1996 and 1999, the reforms continued unabated. One more committee, the Committee on Banking Sector Reforms, again headed by M. Narasimham was set up in 1998 (NC-II). The new committee advised the government to intensify the process of reforms already in motion from 1992.

As a sequel to these recommendations, the process of reforms was further stepped up. The RBI's action taken report of November 27, 2000 provides a list of important recommendations and the follow up action taken after the report was submitted. Some of them are listed below.

### *Strengthening the capital adequacy*

The view of NC-II was:

> It would be appropriate to go beyond the earlier norms and set new and higher norms for capital adequacy. The Committee accordingly recommends that the minimum capital to risk assets ratio be increased to 10 per cent from its present level of 8 per cent.

The RBI in turn enhanced the capital to risk asset ratio (CRAR) for banks to 9 per cent with effect from March 31, 2000.

To strengthen the capital of the PSBs, the Committee gave two options: funding from the government or from the capital market. As the government had resource crunch, banks were permitted to access the capital market. By November 2000, according to RBI, 12 banks had raised the capital from the market.

### *Prudential norms and disclosure*

As a prudential provision, NC-II had recommended a general provision of 1 per cent on standard assets to be introduced in a phased manner; accordingly, RBI directed the banks to start with a provision of 0.25 per cent effective from March 2000.

To bring about transparency banks were advised by RBI to disclose information on maturity pattern of loans, investments and deposits, movement of NPAs and lending to sensitive sectors (with effect from March 2000).

Banks were required to pay greater attention to asset-liability management and provide for liquidity and interest rate risks. They were also advised to evolve suitable risk management systems.

### *Loan review mechanism*

The NC-II emphasised the need

> ..to institute an independent loan review mechanism especially for large borrowal accounts and systems to

identify potential NPAs. It would be desirable that banks evolve a filtering mechanism by stipulating in-house prudential limits beyond which exposures on single/group borrowers are taken keeping in view their risk profile as revealed through credit rating and other relevant factors. Further, in-house limits could be thought of to limit the concentration of large exposures and industry/sector/geographical exposures within the Board approved exposure limits and proper overseeing of these by the senior management/ boards. (Chapter IV, para 4.12 – 4.16)

Acting on this suggestion the RBI advised the banks in October 1998 to 'put in place an independent Loan Review Mechanism'.

### *Further automation*

Observing that information technology and electronic funds transfer systems had brought about fundamental changes in the global banking scene, the NC-II had recommended a series of measures to be adopted by Indian banks to catch up with banks around the world. The RBI set up a working group to give effect to the recommendations in specific areas spelt out by the Committee. The proposal made by the working group were accepted by the RBI and time bound measures were evolved to accelerate and widen the process of IT adoption in banks.

### *Structural Issues*

In the background of the trend of consolidation and convergence of financial systems around the globe, NC-II had recommended that the financial structure should consist of two intermediaries: banking companies which undertake both term lending (function of a development financial institution-DFI) and commercial banking in the conventional sense and, non-banking finance companies.

While accepting the suggestion of the committee and conceding that the principle of 'universal banking' was a desirable goal the RBI felt that implementing the proposal required further deliberation. In the Monetary and Credit Policy for the year 2000 –2001 it declared that some progress "has already been made by permitting banks to diversify into investments and long-term financing and the DFIs to lend for working capital, etc." The RBI also said "any DFI, which wishes to do so, should have the option to transform into bank" subject to certain conditions.

### *Regulation and Supervision*

The Committee was for greater internal controls, transparency and market discipline which according to the Committee would reduce the supervisory burden on the RBI. It called upon the players to adopt these core principles and implement them. The RBI confirmed that the 'Core Principles for Effective Banking Supervision' were complied with by the banks.

### *Whole time directors and Chairmen*

The Committee had recommended that banks' boards should have two or more whole-time directors. The committee, contending that the tenure of the chairman and chief executive officer should be reasonably long suggested that he/she must have a term of five years (to begin with it suggested at least three years). The compensation package for the CEO and whole-time directors should be delinked from that applicable to civil servants.

Responding to the suggestions, RBI said,

> the recommendation pertaining to reasonable length of tenure for the Chief Executive has been implemented while appointing the new Chairmen of PSBs. As regards the recommendation regarding delinking of pay scales of Chief Executives of public sector banks from

that of the Civil Service, this will have to be considered by the government.

### *Directed lending*

In the background of a perception that directed lending would not be in consonance with commercial lending, the Committee had held a view that

> the banking system should be in a position to equip itself to identify the eligible clients based on prescribed norms in the government sponsored programmes so that the full responsibility for all aspects of the credit decision remains with it.

The government had to take a decision on the recommendation.

### *Reduction in government ownership to 33 per cent*

The Committee recommended that the government holding in the PSBs should be brought down from the current 51 per cent to 33 per cent. This would give the banks necessary autonomy to enhance their effectiveness. According to RBI, this recommendation was accepted by the government and a bill to reduce the government stake in PSBs to 33 per cent was introduced in the Parliament.

The recommendations of NC-II were consistent with the emerging trend of reforms; they provided further reinforcement to the measures till then initiated.

### *Proposal to cut down the staff cost*

The Committee was of the view that the banks should have greater autonomy in recruiting manpower depending on the needs. It endorsed the view of the earlier Committee that the Banking Services Recruitment Board (BSRB) be abolished. Banks should be permitted to undertake campus recruitment to meet the need for skilled and specialised staff.

Contending that there was overstaffing in the PSBs, the Committee recommended introducing a voluntary retirement scheme for the employees so as to cut down staff cost.

The BSRB was abolished in 2002 and PSBs were permitted by the government to recruit manpower directly from campus. The Institute of Banking Personnel Selection (IBPS), set up originally in 1975, started providing assistance to banks in conducting recruitment tests on behalf of PSBs.

In 2000, the government advised the PSBs to introduce a special Voluntary Retirement Scheme with incentives to take an early retirement. About 125000 (14.5 per cent) of the employees at all levels (workmen staff, officers and executives) went out of the banks[5].

## The reforms roll on

The two committees, both headed by M. Narasimham, himself a former RBI Governor, thus provided the rationale and the road map for the transformation of the financial sector during the 15 years following the onset of economic reforms. While the political leadership changed from time to time with four short-lived governments and two with a tenure of five years each and with disparate ideologies, the process of liberalisation started in 1991 continued unhindered.

It is appropriate to quote Rakesh Mohan, a former Deputy Governor of RBI. He had said this in 2005[6]:

> the objective of the banking sector reforms was to promote a diversified, efficient and competitive financial system with the ultimate objective of improving the allocative efficiency of resources through operational flexibility, improved financial viability and institutional strengthening.

What was the impact of these reforms? Did the banks meet the objectives spelt out during the policy pronouncements on different occasions? This issue will be addressed in the next chapter.

## References

1. Government of India, 1991: The Committee on Financial Systems headed by M. Narasimham (NC-I).
2. Bank of International Settlements: 2015: A Brief History of Basel Committee.
3. Evidence is given in the section on review of the reforms.
4. This is elucidated in the section on review of reforms.
5. Independent Commission on Banking & Financial Policy Report, 2006.
6. Rakesh Mohan, address to the 21st Annual General Meeting and Conference of the Pakistan Society of Development Economists, Islamabad, 21 December 2005.

# Chapter - 5

# Impact of Reforms: The Positive Side

## The emphasis on performance

The central theme of the reforms in relation to banking was to make the banks efficient, competitive and sound. The series of measures taken during the period starting from 1991 were designed to meet these goals. The process of reforms triggered after the Narasimham Committee I's report was not only sustained but intensified beyond 1998 when the Narasimham Committee II gave a slew of recommendations to intensify the reforms. Six years later another government led by Manmohan Singh took office in 2004. As the architect of the first phase of reforms and Finance Minister during 1991-96, Manmohan Singh was expected to give a further push to the reforms in the financial sector. But before getting into the changes from 2004 it is necessary to evaluate the performance of banks during the first decade of reforms starting from 1991.

How did the reforms in the financial sector affect the banks more particularly those in the public sector? Did they meet the objectives of reforms namely-to become efficient, competitive and sound? The responses to these questions were mixed: the official version extolled the success of the reforms as evidenced in the pronouncements made by the banks themselves, the RBI as monetary authority, the government as the policy-maker and largest stake-holder in the public sector banks. On the other side of the divide, is found volume of material critical of the policy as well as the after-effects of the radical shift in the banking policy.

## The positive side

To start with, it is instructive to look at different parameters of performance of banks during the relevant period. The parameters selected for this assessment are the overall performance in terms of certain broad macro figures, those related to capital, non-performing assets and performance ratios.

Between 1991 and 2004 the business of the scheduled commercial banks (SCBs) grew by more than seven times: the deposits went up from Rs 2,01,198 crores to Rs 15,42,284 crores. The advances under priority sector increased from Rs 44,572 crores to Rs 3,11,335 crores. The number of branches expanded from 60,220 to 67,188. (For details see Table 1) However, the number of rural branches came down from 35,206 to 32,121. One explanation for this could be that after the publication of population census data what were earlier classified as rural areas were upgraded as semi-urban centres. The issue itself will need greater deliberation and hence more information is provided in another chapter.

**Table 1: Performance of SCBs during 1991-2004**

*Amount in Rs crores*

| | *Parameters* | *1991* | *1997* | *2004* |
|---|---|---|---|---|
| 1. | Number of SCBs | 272 | 297 | 286 |
| 2. | Deposits | 201198 | 505599 | 1542284 |
| 3. | Advances | 121865 | 278401 | 865594 |
| 4. | Credit-Deposit Ratio (as percentage) | 60.6 | 55.1 | 56.1 |
| 5. | Advances to priority sectors | 44572 | 93807 | 311335 |
| 6. | Share of Priority Sector Advances in total credit of SCBs (in per cent) | 37.7 | 34.8 | 37.1 |
| 7. | Number of Bank Offices in India | 60220 | 63550 | 67188 |
| 8. | Out of which, rural branches | 35206 | 32915 | 32121 |
| 9 | Population per office (in 000s) | 14 | 15 | 16 |

*Source:* RBI.

The public sector banks accounted for over 85 per cent of the banking business during the post-nationalisation years. The shortcomings in the financial sector were attributed to them. The reforms were, therefore, primarily addressed at the public sector banks. In this backdrop it is important to look at their performance in terms of the different measures of reforms introduced by both the government and the RBI.

## Capital and Capital adequacy

When the principles of successive Basel accords were to be adopted in the Indian context it was necessary to strengthen the capital adequacy of the banks.

Through the amendment to the Bank Nationalisation Acts of 1970/1980, the government allowed the PSBs to raise capital from the market. After the amendment in 1996, several PSBs came out with initial public offers of their equity shares. The government as owner infused additional capital to these banks. By end-March 1999 it provided an amount of Rs 20,446.12 crore towards recapitalisation of nationalised banks.[1]

There was greater emphasis on building up the internal reserves to augment the owned funds. As a result of these measures PSBs recorded steady increase in their equity and reserves between 1991 and 2004 as seen in Table 2.

**Table 2: Equity and Reserves of PSBs**

*Amount in Rs crores*

| *Bank Group* | *1991* | | *1998* | | *2004* | |
|---|---|---|---|---|---|---|
| | *Equity* | *Reserves* | *Equity* | *Reserves* | *Equity* | *Reserves* |
| SBI group | 313 | 1310 | 1036 | 10999 | 1036 | 26713 |
| Nationalised Banks | 2800 | 1577 | 15035 | 13699 | 13640 | 37835 |
| **Total for PSBs** | **3113** | **2887** | **16071** | **24698** | **14676** | **64548** |

While the equity of nationalised banks (NBs) increased from Rs 2800 to Rs 13640 crores between 1991 and 2004, there was a decline by Rs 1395 crores in their equity between 1998 and 2004. This was because, a few banks returned part of their capital to the government and in respect of a few others the loss incurred by them was set off against government shares which in effect reduced the share holdings.

The RBI had also accepted the recommendation of NC-II to enhance the capital adequacy ratio. Accordingly, the banks were asked in 1998 to achieve a CRAR of nine per cent by 2000[2]. Most PSBs were able to achieve this level so much so that as on March 2004 they reached a level of 13.20. At that time the lowest level of CRAR was 9.48 for Dena Bank whereas Corporation Bank had the highest CRAR at a level of 20.12.

## Deregulation of interest rates and statutory ratios

One major impact of liberalisation was on the interest rate system. Till 1991 the interest rates on deposits and advances were regulated by the RBI and the government. As a sequel to the measures, the banks were permitted to fix the rates of interest on advances and deposits according to the wisdom of the board of directors. The RBI cut its own lending rate to trigger a similar measure from the banks. The interest rates on deposits were also brought down.

Accordingly the bank rate which was at a level of 12 per cent was brought down to 6.5 by 2001. The deposit rates which were around 16 per cent in 1991 came down to around 12 per cent.

As part of liberalisation process, the volume of deposits of banks being pre-empted through statutory cash reserve (CRR) and liquidity ratios (SLR) was brought down. The CRR which was 15 per cent in 1991 came down progressively to 9.5 per cent in 1997 and to 5.5 per cent and SLR from 38.5 to 25 per cent in 2001. To that extent *'financial repression through statutory pre-emptions has been reduced'*[3]. The resources of the banks, thus, became freer for deployment into income yielding assets. (See Table 3)

**Table 3: Interest Rates and statutory ratios (in per cent)**

| *Year* | *Bank Rate* | *Deposit rate (minimum)* | *Cash Reserve Ratio* | *Statutory Liquidity Ratio* |
|---|---|---|---|---|
| 1991 | 12 | 16 | 15 | 38.5 |
| 1997 | 9 | 15 | 9.5 | 25.0 |
| 2001 | 6.5 | 12 | 5.5 | 25.0 |

*Source:* RBI.

## Non-performing Assets

A major thrust of the reform agenda was to address the problem of sticky loans or stressed assets more commonly known as non-performing assets (NPAs). Efforts were on, both internally within the banks and externally through RBI's directions and legislative changes to initiate quick recovery procedure by enforcing securities charged to the banks. The NC-II had given a target of five per cent by 2000 and three per cent by 2002.

In pursuance of this goal RBI had advised the banks to:

(a) Tone up their credit risk management systems.

(b) Put in place a loan review mechanism to ensure that advances, particularly large advances were monitored on an ongoing basis so that signals of weaknesses were detected and corrective actions taken early.

(c) Enhance credit appraisal skills of their staff.

These were intended to be preventive measures. For addressing the stock of NPAs, RBI issued guidelines for one-time settlement in July 2000.[4]

The RBI also permitted the banks to restructure corporate debts (Corporate Debt Restructuring-CDR) which had become overdue. This was what the RBI had said in 2001:[5]

> The process is primarily rescheduling the debt portfolio of the borrowers among its creditors to help the

borrowers in the revival of projects and continue operations through reductions in existing debt burden and establishment of new credit lines with implied assumption that the lender would prefer reduction in risk to optimisation of returns. The objective of the CDR is to ensure a timely and transparent mechanism for restructuring of the corporate debts of viable corporate entities affected by internal and external factors, outside the purview of BIFR, DRT or other legal proceedings, for the benefit of all concerned.

Under the CDR scheme the repayment of instalments and interest due could be rescheduled so that the overdues could be treated as performing assets.

An act to speed up the process of recovery of bad loans was enacted by the government in 2002. Called Securitisation & Reconstruction of Financial Assets and Enforcement of Security Interest Act 2002 (SARFAESI Act 2002), the Act would empower the lending bank to enforce security interest for realisation of dues without the intervention of courts and tribunals.

All these measures did impact the NPA position in banks. The share of NPAs in total advances progressively came down during this period. While in 1993 it was 23.2 per cent of total advances, it declined to 16 per cent in 1998 and to 7.8 per cent by 2004.

The performance of individual banks varied, some of them with a ratio of over 10 per cent and a few with less than or near 5 per cent as illustrated in Table 4. The overall improvement in the NPA position was praiseworthy.

**Table 4: NPAs of selected PSBs as on March 2004**

| ***Name of Bank*** | ***Share of NPAs as percentage of Total advances*** |
|---|---|
| Punjab & Sind Bank | 18.16 |
| Dena Bank | 14.82 |
| Central Bank | 12.55 |

*(Contd...)*

| Bank of Baroda | 10.52 |
|---|---|
| Corporation Bank | 5.03 |
| Andhra Bank | 4.60 |
| Vijaya Bank | 2.94 |
| Indian Bank* | 7.99 |
| UCO Bank* | 6.93 |
| United Bank of India* | 9.07 |

*Source:* RBI Report on Trend 2005-06.
(*banks which were considered weak)

## Performance parameters

On the one side, the business of banks expanded, capital base was strengthened and non performing asscts were brought under control. Simultaneously, there was a qualitative improvement in their efficiency during the reform period. Several authorities confirm this. It is instructive to cite three such views.

Rakesh Mohan, a former deputy governor of RBI had held that reduction in operating expenditure, interest spread and cost of intermediation recorded by the banks was a reflection on the improvements in their efficiency[6]. Speaking about the efficiency in terms of cost reduction Rakesh Mohan said thus:

> The operating cost per unit of earning assets declined from 2.1 per cent in 1992 to 1.8 per cent in 2004; similarly, operating cost per unit of total volume of business declined from 3.4 per cent to 2.6 per cent during the same period.
>
> From the efficiency standpoint, the intermediation cost needs to be viewed in conjunction with non-interest income. Till 2001, the burden (the excess of non-interest expenditure over non-interest income as a percentage to total assets) of commercial banks hovered around 1 to 1.5 per cent. This gap between intermediation cost and income from fee-based activities has narrowed considerably in recent years. For example,

the burden of Indian commercial banks declined from 1.2 per cent in 1992 to 0.2 per cent in 2004.

The cost income-ratio (defined as the ratio of operating expenses to total income less interest expense) of Indian banks showed a declining trend during the post-reform period. For example, Indian banks paid roughly 45 per cent of their net income towards managing labour and physical capital in 2004 as against nearly 72 per cent in 1993. In other words, Indian banks recorded a net cost saving of nearly 27 per cent of their net income during the post-reform period.

D. Subbarao, a former Governor of RBI had, in 2010, appreciated the improvement in the supervisory parameters in the following words:[7]

> There has also been a significant improvement in terms of the standard supervisory parameters: Capital, Asset Quality, Management, Earnings, Liquidity and Systems (CAMELS). Even so, the net interest margin of the Indian banking system is higher than that in some of the other emerging market economies even after accounting for mandated social sector obligations such as priority sector lending and credit support for the government's anti-poverty initiatives.

Using four distinct parameters namely, return on assets, intermediation costs, net interest margin (spread) and cost to income ratio, T. T. Ram Mohan[8] argues that *'it is not just that Indian banks have achieved a turnaround; they have gone on to become among the most profitable in the world'*. The reduction in the NPA ratio and the ability of the banks to attain the prescribed capital adequacy ratio are very positive indicators of the impact of the reforms. He concludes: *'In sum, there has been an improvement on several indicators of efficiency and stability'*.

A table focusing on selected parameters of performance of PSBs between 1992 and 2004 is furnished below:

**Table 5: Selected Financial Indicators of Public Sector Banks between 1992 and 2004**

| Year | Net income spread | Intermediation cost /total assets | Net profit/ Total assets | Cost/ Income | Net NPAs/ Total Assets |
|---|---|---|---|---|---|
| 1992-95 (average) | 2.72 | 2.68 | -0.40 | 68.2 | N.A. |
| 1997-98 | 2.91 | 2.66 | 0.77 | 62.7 | 3.27 |
| 2003-04 | 2.98 | 2.21 | 1.12 | 45.1 | 1.28 |

*Source:* Abstracted from T.T.Ram Mohan.

Professor Ram Mohan also underlines the inner strength of the PSBs and how the reforms process unleashed their potential in these words:

> ....given their formidable distribution strengths, the PSBs had the potential to revitalise themselves when subjected to deregulation, competition and hard budget constraints and given clear commercial objectives. The post-reform record has vindicated the course that India has pursued. Efficiency and stability have improved, going by various parameters; there has been a trend towards convergence in performance between PSBs and private banks. Financial deepening too has also happened although after a pause in the first decade after reforms.

In the backdrop of the global financial crisis that shook the western countries during 2007-2009, what was said by Y.V. Reddy, another Governor of RBI, in 2011 in relation to the contribution of Indian financial sector sums up the robust performance of banks thanks to the reforms. He had said then: *The performance of the financial sector, in terms of its contribution to growth and stability, is rated among the most impressive of all the sectors in India.*[9]

The overwhelming views thus established the internal strength of the PSBs, their ability to change and adapt, their turnaround during the first 12 years after the onset of reforms and their contribution to the strengthening of the financial system of the country.

## References

1. RBI, 2000: *Report on trend and progress of banking in India.*
2. RBI's Action Taken Report on Narasimham Committee II Report- NCII-CC27.11.2000 (ATR, NC II).
3. Rakesh Mohan, 2005: *Reforms, productivity and efficiency in banking: the Indian experience.* Address at the 21st Annual General Meeting and Conference of the Pakistan Society of Development Economists, Islamabad, 21 December published in *BIS Review* 15/2006-7.
4. ATR, NC II, pp. 4 and 5.
5. RBI, 2001: *Report on Trend and Progress of Banking in India.*
6. Rakesh Mohan, 2005: *ibid.*
7. Duvvuri Subbarao, 2011: *Five Frontier Issues in Indian Banking* Inaugural Address at 'BANCON 2010' in Mumbai on December 3, 2010 published in *RBI Monthly Bulletin,* January 2011.
8. T.T. Ram Mohan 2007: *Banking Reforms in India- Charting a Unique Course- Economic & Political Weekly,* March 31.
9. Y.V. Reddy, 2011: *Global Crisis, Recession and Uneven Recovery* Orient BlackSwan (p. 373).

# Chapter - 6

# The Contrarian View

The performance of the financial sector and more particularly PSBs during the 12-year period between 1992 and 2004 was undoubtedly commendable. The official versions uniformly emphasised that Indian banking system had adapted itself well to the changing situation both domestically and internationally. The other side of the story, however, needs focus considering the larger role the financial sector was assigned to, post-nationalisation.

There have been independent surveys, evaluations and studies about the impact of reforms on the financial sector. Some of these studies have figured in the previous chapter where the focus was on the achievements. In fact, Narasimham Committee II itself had made an assessment of the impact of reforms. Its task was however, to suggest measures to accelerate the transformation. It argued for further dilution of the goals of nationalisation to make the banks more competitive, robust and market-responsive.

What were the adverse effects, if any, of the reform process? The adverse impact was in a way in-built in the clutch of measures unleashed. With the new stress on profitability and autonomy in evolving business models, PSBs had to redraw their business goals and the strategies to operationalise the models and achieve goals. The new found autonomy triggered certain malpractices for short-term ends. The most notorious among them was the Securities scandal of 1992-93 followed by a series of other scandals over the first decade of reforms. There were bank failures necessitating forced mergers. The original objectives of nationalisation got diluted inviting serious criticism of the policy shift. There were enduring lessons from these two developments during the reforms era.

In understanding these fallouts, we need to look into an independent study conducted during 2004 and 2006 by a panel headed by S.P. Shukla, a former Finance Secretary and India's official representative for GATT negotiations. Called Independent Commission on Banking and Financial Policy, its report came out in 2006 (ICBP)[1]. Unlike the official panels it had members drawn from diverse fields like banking, academia, management institutes, central bank and civil service. During the course of its work it had extensive public interactions in major cities with multiple stakeholders like farmers' representatives, bankers, legal luminaries, professionals, central bankers of repute, management experts, human resources specialists, economists, researchers, civil servants, union functionaries and political leaders.

The report of the ICBP throws valuable insights into the major failings of the banks during the reform process. Voluminous evidence drawn from RBI and official reports is provided to support the findings of ICBP. Considering its significance the report is discussed at greater length here.

The major findings of ICBP are in the following areas/ issues:

1. Changes in banking practices.
2. Risk aversion of banks impacting distribution of bank credit.
3. Adverse impact on priority sector credit.
4. Entry of micro finance institutions to fill the vacuum created by (3) above.
5. Adverse impact on development banking.
6. Risk of bank fragility.

7. New approach towards human resources management in banks.

### *Decline in CD Ratio*

The banks were given greater choice in their investments to maximise their profits. This freedom resulted in poor outgo of credit and greater investment in securities and financial papers. The release of funds through progressive lowering of the levels of statutory pre-emption did not enhance credit dispensation as reflected by the falling credit-deposit ratios between 1991 and 2004. In contrast, the ratio of investments in government securities continuously climbed during that period. The Table 1 given below is self-explanatory:

**Table1: CD Ratio and Investment Ratio of SCBs between 1991 and 2004**

| *Year* | *Credit Deposit Ratio* | *INVESTMENT IN GOVT. SECURITIES (as percentage to total earning assets)* | *Year* | *Credit Deposit Ratio* | *INVESTMENT IN GOVT. SECURITIES (as percentage to total earning assets)* |
|---|---|---|---|---|---|
| 1990-91 | 60.4 | 22.6 | 1998-99 | 51.7 | 30.9 |
| 1991-92 | 54.4 | 24.3 | 1999-00 | 53.6 | 32.9 |
| 1992-93 | 56.6 | 25.6 | 2000-01 | 53.1 | 33.9 |
| 1993-94 | 52.2 | 28.4 | 2001-02 | 53.4 | 36.0 |
| 1994-95 | 54.7 | 27.0 | 2002-03 | 58.3 | 37.5 |
| 1995-96 | 58.6 | 27.2 | 2003-04 | 55.9 | 40.0 |
| 1996-97 | 55.1 | 29.5 | | | |
| 1997-98 | 54.1 | 29.9 | | | |

### *Small borrowers neglected*

The adoption of Basel norms on capital adequacy, accounting standards and provisioning further affected the credit delivery. The banks preferred risk free or low risk avenues of investment in preference to risky loans to agriculture and small scale industries. The share of advances to these sectors progressively declined during the period 1991-2004. This decline was despite the liberal definition of priority sector to include indirect finance to agriculture, redefining small industry to cover those with much higher capital investment and inclusion of funds contributed by sponsor banks to RRBs. The banks could meet the shortfall by investment in Rural Infrastructural Development Fund of NABARD introduced in1995-96. These options available to the banks worked against the smaller borrowers.

The fallout of this tendency was the sharp decline in the share of small borrowal accounts of banks both in terms of number of accounts and volume of credit given between 1992 and 2003 as indicated in Table 2.

**Table 2: Trends in the Number of Small Borrowal vis-à-vis Other Bank Loan Accounts**

| *Period–ended* | *Total bank borrowal accounts (in lakh)* | | *Small borrowal accounts (in lakh) (Credit Limits of Rs 25,000 and less)* | | *Other bigger accounts (in lakh)* | |
|---|---|---|---|---|---|---|
| | *Number* | *Increase over the previous period* | *Number* | *Increase over the previous period* | *Number* | *Increase over the previous period* |
| *(1)* | *(2)* | *(3)* | *(4)* | *(5)* | *(6)* | *(7)* |
| December 1983 | 277.48 | - | 265.21 | - | 12.27 | - |
| March 1992 | 658.61 | 381.12 | 625.48 | 360.27 | 33.12 | 20.85 |
| March 2001 | 523.65 | - 134.95 | 372.52 | - 252.96 | 151.13 | 118.01 |
| March 2003 | 594.91 | 71.27 | 368.73 | - 3.80 | 226.19 | 75.06 |

*Source: Report of ICBP,* p. 19.

With the perceptible shift from priority sector to more profitable commercial lending there was an increasing vacuum in the institutional credit available to the rural borrowers. To bridge this gap, micro-finance institutions emerged with definite adverse features like higher rate of interest and strong arm tactics in recovery of overdue loans which in turn led to serious agrarian crisis in the early decade of this century. The unending reports of farmers committing suicides in several states necessitated regulatory intervention.

## *Inter-regional disparities*

There were also interregional and interstate disparities in the development of banking facilities during the first 12 years of reforms. Table 3 is instructive.

**Table 3: Credit-deposit ratio of selected states**

| | *C-D ratio as per Sanction of Credit* | | | | *C-D ratio as per Utilisation of Credit* | | | |
|---|---|---|---|---|---|---|---|---|
| ***State*** | ***1980*** | ***1990*** | ***2000*** | ***2003*** | ***1980*** | ***1990*** | ***2000*** | ***2003*** |
| Rajasthan | 67.4 | 57.3 | 46.7 | 50.8 | 72.8 | 61.5 | 50.1 | 55.3 |
| Bihar | 41.2 | 36.8 | 22.5 | 23.1 | 49.3 | 39.0 | 23.2 | 23.7 |
| Orissa | 58.5 | 90.0 | 41.5 | 48.2 | 66.1 | 92.5 | 42.8 | 56.9 |
| West Bengal | 61.4 | 56.8 | 45.5 | 47.9 | 56.1 | 53.9 | 44.9 | 50.0 |
| Madhya Pradesh | 55.2 | 66.1 | 49.1 | 46.6 | 57.6 | 68.1 | 52.5 | 51.7 |
| Uttar Pradesh | 43.2 | 40.0 | 28.2 | 30.6 | 46.7 | 43.1 | 30.9 | 36.0 |

*Source:* ICBP Report, p. 29.

## *Development banking affected*

In the wake of reforms the concept of universal banking became popular. The development finance institutions (DFIs) like ICICI and IDBI set up their own commercial banks. But at a later date through reverse mergers DFIs which had floated the banks got merged with the offsprings. In the process, the commercial lending which yields quick and higher returns on loans received preference over long-term finance. This in turn affected the development banking impacting capital formation necessary for sustained industrial development.

## *Banks become more fragile*

With the shift towards profitability and relaxation of regulatory oversight banks became more fragile and vulnerable, ICBP observed[2]. The failure of the new generation Global Trust Bank was a classic example to support the finding of ICBP. In the summary of its recommendations what ICBP said proved to be prophetic, when we study the problems banks faced later between 2014-17:

One of the consequences of financial and banking reforms is that the structural change it has brought has substantially increased fragility. The processes of liberalisation fundamentally alter the terrain of operation of the banks. One visible impact is the shift in the focus of bank activities away from facilitating commodity production and investment to lubricating trade and promoting personal consumption. There are changes also in the area of operation in the banks, with banking entities not only creating or linking up with insurance companies, say, but also entering into other "sensitive" markets like the stock and real estate markets.

### *Unsatisfactory HR Management*

The extant human resources management strategies of banks also came in for scrutiny by the ICBP. The PSBs had no appropriate HR Policy as documented by the ICBP[3]. This weakness got exposed starkly in 2000 when over 125000 employees out of the total manpower of over 875000 left the banks under a government sponsored voluntary retirement scheme. It was not the package of incentives that made very experienced staff leave the banks but the environment prevailing in the banks which drove them to grab the incentive and leave as reported by ICBP. The massive exodus of trained staff created serious shortage of skilled personnel in the PSBs. There was no attempt to address this weakness either at the policy-makers' level or at the level of PSBs.

The ICBP gave a blueprint for an alternative banking policy with continued public ownership and emphasis on inclusive banking so that the facilities could reach every section and geographical location of the country.

### Other authorities

It is not the ICBP alone which had documented the adverse outcome of the financial sector reforms. Several other authorities shared a similar view. The respected journal, *Economic and Political Weekly* while reviewing the progress of banking in 2002 pointed out a series of shortcomings of the banks after the reforms set in[4]. Four of them were:

1. Narrowing of branch network in the post-reform period.
2. Declining rural credit-deposit ratios.
3. Diversion of deposit resources from backward areas
4. Allocation of credit for agriculture and small-scale industries.

The observations were based on voluminous evidence culled out from RBI's data and published by the journal.

A similar view was expressed in a paper published in the same journal by a group of authorities[5] in regard to directed lending in the following words:

> ......despite the definitional changes for eligibility under priority sector lending that have been effected consistently, the share of priority sector advances in total non-food gross bank credit of scheduled commercial banks (SCBs) has come down from 40.3 per cent in December 1980 to 35.9 per cent in March 2001. The direct agricultural lending accounts of all PSBs also show a declining trend (2.13 crore in 1994 versus 1.59 crore in 2000). The story of regional rural banks (RRBs), a constitution of low-cost banks for rural sector, also paints the same picture. Although during 1993 to 1998, their credit-deposit (C-D) ratio has declined from 67 per cent to 44 per cent (42 per cent in 2001), the share of agricultural loans in total loans has come down from 52.4 per cent to 44.4 per cent during the corresponding period.

The same authorities also pointed out that corporate governance in banks particularly PSBs was another problem area.

The former RBI Deputy Governor, Rakesh Mohan while lauding the positive developments in the post-reforms era, had echoed concern about the exclusion of the underprivileged from the banking system. He had said:[6]

> Although liberalisation of financial services and competition has improved customer services, experience shows that customers' interests are not always accorded priority. More importantly, concerns have been raised with regard to banking practices that tend to exclude vast segments of the population. In this context, the Reserve Bank has announced its intention to implement policies to incentivise banks to provide extensive services responsive to the needs of the under-privileged.

Around the same time a similar view was expressed by two more experts. They focused on three outcomes of the liberalisation process:[7]

1. First, increased financial fragility, which the irrational boom in India's stock market epitomises.
2. Second, a deflationary macroeconomic stance, which adversely affects public capital formation and the objectives of promoting employment and reducing poverty.
3. Finally, a credit squeeze for the commodity producing sectors and a decline in credit delivery to rural India and small-scale industry. The belief that the financial deepening that results from liberalisation would in myriad ways neutralise these effects has not been realised.

In the meantime despite reports, banks continued to move away from financing the underprivileged and the marginal farmers observed by another authority in 2007[8]:

> Official data clearly show that the RBI policy of "social concern" succeeded in forcing the banks to open branches in hitherto unbanked locations. A package of policy initiatives ensured that the share of moneylenders

in rural credit fell from an average of over 75 per cent in 1951-61 to less than 25 per cent in 1991.... Unfortunately though, these gains have been lost in the period after 1991....In the relentless pursuit of profits, banks have forgotten what their primary mandate was and continues to be... The reforms...have reduced both outreach and the human resources capacity of rural banks to deliver high quality credit...

The data circulated by RBI in August 2013 along with a discussion paper[9] on banking structure further confirms the above view. Between 1971 and 1991 the share of institutional agencies in the total rural credit went up from 29.2 per cent to 64 per cent and that of non-institutional agencies had drastically come down from 70.8 per cent to 36 per cent. The banks which had lent just 2.2 per cent of rural credit in 1971 gave as much as 29 per cent at the beginning of reforms. Correspondingly the share of agricultural moneylender had come down steeply from 23.1 to 8.6 per cent.

In contrast, after the reforms began when the banks hesitated to lend, the moneylenders and other non-institutional agencies stepped up their lending in rural areas. Between 1991 and 2002, the share of banks fell from 29 to 24.5 per cent; that of the agricultural moneylender increased from 6.3 to 10 per cent; the share of the professional moneylender jumped up from 9.4 to 19.6 per cent during the same period as shown in Table 4:

**Table 4: Breakup of institutional and non-institutional rural credit (Per cent)**

| | *1951* | *1961* | *1971* | *1981* | *1991* | *2002* |
|---|---|---|---|---|---|---|
| **Institutional Agencies** | **7.2** | **14.8** | **29.2** | **61.2** | **64.0** | **57.1** |
| Government | 3.3 | 5.3 | 6.7 | 4.0 | 5.7 | 2.3 |
| Co-op. Society/banks | 3.1 | 9.1 | 20.1 | 28.6 | 18.6 | 27.3 |
| Commercial banks incl. RRBs | 0.8 | 0.4 | 2.2 | 28.0 | 29.0 | 24.5 |

(*Contd...*)

| Insurance | -- | -- | 0.1 | 0.3 | 0.5 | 0.3 |
|---|---|---|---|---|---|---|
| Provident Fund | -- | -- | 0.1 | 0.3 | 0.9 | 0.3 |
| Other institutional agencies* | - | - | - | - | 9.3 | 2.4 |
| **Non-Institutional Agencies** | **92.8** | **85.2** | **70.8** | **38.8** | **36.0** | **42.9** |
| Landlord | 1.5 | 0.9 | 8.6 | 4.0 | 4.0 | 1.0 |
| Agricultural Moneylender | 24.9 | 45.9 | 23.1 | 8.6 | 6.3 | 10.0 |
| Professional Moneylender | 44.8 | 14.9 | 13.8 | 8.3 | 9.4 | 19.6 |
| Traders and Commission Agents | 5.5 | 7.7 | 8.7 | 3.4 | 7.1 | 2.6 |
| Relatives and Friends | 14.2 | 6.8 | 13.8 | 9.0 | 6.7 | 7.1 |
| Others | 1.9 | 8.9 | 2.8 | 4.9 | 2.5 | 2.6 |
| **Total** | **100** | **100** | **100** | **100** | **100** | **100** |

* includes financial corporation/institution, financial company and other institutional agencies.

**Notes:** Percentage share of different credit agencies to the outstanding cash dues of the households as on 30th June; '–' denotes not available.

*Source:* reproduced from RBI's *Banking Structure in India*-Discussion Paper August 2013).

Former RBI Governor, Y.V. Reddy explains the reduction in bank advances to the priority sectors more clearly in 2011:[10]

> Over a quarter of the asset base of banks in India is earmarked for securities issued by the government. Banks are encouraged by public policy to participate in bond markets, establish private equity or venture capital subsidiaries and step up lending to infrastructure as well as housing. They invest in equity and mutual funds. As a result there is a reduction in advances towards working capital and other funding, especially agriculture, small business and small and medium industry.

In sum and substance, while the reforms brought qualitative changes in the functioning of the banks as explained in the earlier chapter there were serious shortcomings which tantamount to relegating the financial system as an instrument of capital formation and deployment in different sectors of the economy.

While the shortcomings would necessitate a reappraisal of the policy prescriptions and course correction, the new environment of liberalisation brought in its wake serious scandals causing immense loss to the banks and raising fundamental issues of governance in the banks.

These will be discussed in the next chapter.

## References

1. Shukla, S.P., 2006: Report of the Independent Commission on Banking and Finance-(ICBP Report), pp. 17-20 Pub: AIBOC, Bangalore.
2. See pp. 57-63.
3. Chapter XI, pp. 77-88.
4. *EPW,* February 2, 2002: Special Statistics-31: Money, Banking and Finance.
5. M G Bhide, A Prasad, Saibal Ghosh: Banking Sector Reforms-A Critical Overview- *Economic and Political Weekly,* February 2, 2002.
6. Rakesh Mohan: Reforms, productivity and efficiency in banking: the Indian experience, *BIS Review,* 15/2006.
7. C.P. Chandrasekhar, Parthapratim Pal : Financial Liberalisation in India- An Assessment of Its Nature and Outcomes*: Economic and Political Weekly,* March 18, 2006.
8. Mihir Shah, 2007: The crowning of the moneylender- *The Hindu,* September 1, 2007.
9. RBI, DBOD and DEPR (Department of Economic Policy and Research) August 2013: Banking Structure in India - The Way Forward -Discussion Paper.
10. Y.V. Reddy, 2011: Global Crisis, Recession and Uneven Recovery, Orient BlackSwan.

# Chapter - 7

# The Vulnerability of Banks and the Scams

A development of great concern was the financial sector getting increasingly vulnerable to high level scandals resulting in huge financial losses and loss of reputation of the regulators. Scandals were there before the reforms began. But those which hit the banking industry during the first decade of reforms were unique in their methods, pervasiveness and the impact. One cannot directly attribute them to liberalisation, for unscrupulous elements can operate in diverse situations. That they happened during the early years of reforms and thereafter at different times with varied intensity is a reflection on the incapacity of the system to track the signals early and take corrective actions before it is late. They also established once again that both the regulator and the owner had no keenness to learn lessons and take serious preventive actions.

The vulnerability of the financial sector could be examined under three different heads:

1. Systemic scandals
2. Profiteering by individuals
3. Collective abdication (NBI, UCO, IB and UBI).

The story does not end in 2004. But the factors that contributed to them, the nature of the scandals, the failures both systemically and institutionally and the lessons learnt (or not learnt) provide us rich learning experience. The present chapter will focus on three major scandals that exploited the system and the next two will deliberate on individual profiteering and collective abdication.

### *1. The Harshad Mehta scandal*

The basics of what turned out to be a gigantic scandal could be understood from the following passage from the editorials of *Officers' Voice* June and July 1992, written by this author.[1]

> In early 1992 almost every business journal carried a lead article and cover story on the miracle boy of the stock market, Harshad Mehta. A hitherto unknown stockbroker became the darling of the stock markets. The share prices skyrocketed. The prices of shares of companies which were not heard of went up. Almost everyone was caught by the share market bug. Ironically today Mehta occupies the centre stage, this time as a 'villain' for having engineered an artificial boom causing what is now described as securities scandal of the century-involving more than Rs 3000 crores from the financial sector.
>
> Normally when purchase and sale of government securities take place, securities must be with the bank. When selling banks are unable to deliver the securities to the purchasing banks for some reason, the banker's receipts (BRs) are issued. A BR is issued by the bank selling the security to the bank purchasing it confirming that it has received the payment against the sale of its securities and promising that the securities will be delivered in due course.
>
> The statement of accounts pertaining to the transfer of securities is maintained by the Public Debt Office (PDO) of RBI in its Securities General Ledger (SGL). The banks have to send the statements to PDO and an

entry in SGL provides a proof that the securities are delivered by the selling bank to the buying bank.

A broker acts as an intermediary between the buyer and the seller. Until the securities are actually delivered, BRs are issued and when securities are actually delivered the BRs are converted into entries in SGL. The BRs are not transferable or tradable and they must remain with the bank.

In the present scam, it is reported that BRs were freely issued and traded against RBI's own directives. When ultimately the reconciliation of BRs with securities dealt with was taken up, there was a whopping discrepancy of over Rs 600 crores in SBI alone. Several banks, National Housing Bank, foreign banks and a few private banks were involved in it. The money raised through securities deals were used to manipulate the share prices. BRs were pledged to raise loans to finance speculative share transactions. In a nutshell, resources of the financial system were used to speculate in the share market creating an artificial boom with a consequential bust coming too soon.

From all angles, the magnitude of the scandal is gigantic.

The exposure of the banks in the scandal as estimated by Janakiraman Committee was more than Rs 4024 crores; according to the Central Bureau of Investigation it was about Rs 5089 crores.

It was reported that the market capitalisation of equities listed with the Bombay Stock Exchange had reached Rs 2,76,434 crores at the end of March 1992, while it had been a little less than one-fourth of that sum, Rs 75,348 crores, just a year earlier.[2] In the period between April 1991 and April 1992, the Sensex went into a frenzy and returned 274 per cent, moving from 1,194 points to 4,467. That was the highest annual return for the index.

The scam was first exposed by Sucheta Dalal in the daily *Times of India* on April 23,1992 when she broke the news of shortfall in government securities held by SBI. That led to an investigation that later showed that Mehta had manipulated around Rs 3,500 crores in the system. On August 6, 1992, after the scam was exposed, the markets crashed by 72 per cent leading to one of the biggest falls and a bearish phase that lasted for two years.[3]

A number of banks both Indian and foreign, mutual funds, stock broking firms and cooperative banks were involved in the scandal: SBI, State Bank of Saurashtra, SBI Capital Markets Ltd., UCO Bank, Standard Chartered, ANZ Grindlays, Bank of America and Citibank N.A., Bank of Karad Ltd, National Housing Bank, Unit Trust of India, Mumbai Mercantile Co-operative Bank, Canbank Mutual Fund, Canbank Financial Services, Andhra Bank Financial Services and several others. RBI constituted an enquiry committee headed by a Deputy Governor, Janakiraman to investigate the scandal and suggest corrective measures. When the scandal caused public outcry the government set up in August 1992 a Joint Parliamentary Committee under the chairmanship of former minister Ram Niwas Mirdha to go into the whole gamut of the securities scam (JPC-M). In December 1993, JPC-M submitted its report and recommendations for actions against the perpetrators and corrective actions to prevent recurrence of such scams.

A question that plagued the observers of the financial sector was how a scandal of such a magnitude could have taken place without the knowledge of the managements of individual banks and the RBI as regulator. It is instructive to quote from the article in *Officers' Voice* referred earlier[4]:

> It may be recalled that in its circular dated July 26, 1991 RBI had pointed out certain serious failures of banks. Two types of transactions referred to therein are worth recalling:
>
> (a) Sale transactions by issue of BRs/SGL forms

without actually holding the securities and without having sufficient balance in their SGL accounts.

(b) Issuing BRs/SGL forms on behalf of their broker clients without safeguarding the banks' interests.

Regarding BRs, the RBI made a detailed observation:

"...banks have been issuing BRs freely (without regard to whether they will be in a position to deliver the securities there against within a reasonable time) and against an initial outstanding BR, a series of transactions are put through by further issue of BRs and in the final analysis *only the BRs are exchanged and no security is delivered.*" (emphasis added)

After highlighting the malaise, the RBI prescribed, amongst others, the following remedies:

(a) No sale transactions should be put through without actually holding the security in the bank's investment account.

(b) All transactions must be reflected in its investment account on the same day.

Having pinpointed the features and prescribed the remedy why did RBI sleep over it?

The Janakiraman Committee has attributed the situation to the following reasons:

(a) Lack of internal control in banks.

(b) Collusion between the officials and the brokers.

(c) Indiscriminate use of BRs/SGL forms which were not deposited with the PDO of RBI.

(d) Issue of BRs for units.

(e) Issue of BRs at the request of brokers against BRs received and to be received-where banks are neither sellers nor buyers.

(f) Non-reconciliation for long of investment accounts with SGL accounts at PDO.

(g) Absence in the PDO of the system of giving statement of accounts or balance confirmation.

All these failures are not revelations made overnight. When it had known the malaise, was the prescription a mechanical response, as commented by an analyst? Even the Customer Service Committee (Goiporia Committee) has also pointed out that the PDO of RBI is not functioning properly.

RBI directors are on the boards of all PSBs. They are required to ensure that the respective banks comply with RBI guidelines. Interestingly Janakiraman himself is a director on SBI Board. Was he performing his role dutifully? If RBI instructions are not followed by banks, it confirms the observations of several bankers and bank unions that it has ceased to be custodian of the health of the banks. It is not the failure of a system; it is an abdication by RBI of its legitimate and lawful role in safeguarding our monetary system.

As a sequel to the reports of the investigations, criminal actions were initiated against several bankers, heads of many institutions and share brokers. Notable among them as given in the Action Taken Report on JPC-M in December 2001 were: C.L. Khemani, Deputy Managing Director of SBI, R. Sitaraman of SBI, R.Vishwanathan, Managing Director of SBI Caps, Chairman of UCO Bank, K. Margabanthu, and officials of several other banks, V.Krishnamurthy, Member, Planning Commission (formerly, chief of BHEL), S.N. Johri, CMD of NALCO, Harshad Mehta, Bhupen Dalal, A.D. Narottam and other share brokers. In 2003, several officers of banks and NHB were convicted and awarded jail sentences and fines after long and tortuous judicial processes.

JPC-M's observations were very instructive. It had said in para no. 2.7 of its report[5]:

The scam is basically a deliberate and criminal abuse of public funds through various types of securities

> transactions with the aim of illegally siphoning of funds of banks and PSUs to select brokers for speculative returns. The latest irregularities...are manifestations of this chronic disorder since they involved not only the Banks but also the stock market, financial institutions, public sector undertakings, the central bank of the country and even the Ministry of Finance.
>
> The most unfortunate aspect has been the emergence of a culture of non-accountability which permeated all sections of the Government and Banking system over the years. The state of the country's system of governance, the persistence of non-adherence to rules, regulations and guidelines, the alarming decay over time in the banking systems has been fully exposed. These grave and numerous irregularities persisted for so long that eventually it was not the observance of regulations but their breach that came to be regarded and defended as "market practice". Through all these years the ability of the concerned authorities to effectively address themselves to the problems has been tested and found wanting...

The JPC-M focused on several dimensions of the scam which caused grave concern. Four of them are noted here:

1. The largely absent accountability and rarer punishment for a wrong committed.
2. The failure of supervision from top to bottom.
3. Failure to accept responsibility for wrong-doing.
4. Transferring responsibility downwards.

Urging upon the need to build the moral fibre, JPC-M observed in Para 2.8 [6]:

> No system can work through regulations alone; of course, it cannot work if they be flouted; but much more than that, if a system be devoid of the moral quotient, of a common sense appreciation of right from

wrong, of a sense of public duty particularly when entrusted with public funds, then it cannot work.

Did the financial liberalisation sow the seeds of the scam? One authority who has undertaken extensive studies on black money said 'yes' in a paper. These were his words[7]:

> The scam is not just the result of any specific policy in the liberalisation package introduced in July 1991. Policy as a whole enabled the scam to take place on such a large scale and prevented it from being detected early enough. The rising share prices were considered 'good' for the economy. The Finance Minister stated in the Parliament that he would not lose sleep over the price rise. The policy-makers saw it as support for the measures they had initiated. It was taken to indicate the functioning of the free markets. Liberalisation has meant that commercial banks have been under pressure to improve their profitability.

The journal, *Economic and Political Weekly* was forthright in its criticism and it named certain individuals who had scant respect for the system[8].

> After the euphoria over economic liberalisation ....there was a time when the financial system had become the handmaiden of a few individuals like Kamaljit Singh of the Bank of Baroda, (Manohar J.) Pherwani of the UTI (and later Chairman of NHB) and B. Ratnakar of Canara Bank, all of whom showed scant respect for the rules of the game. And they got away with it because they had significant political clout which they used to systematically cock a snook at the RBI. The foreign banks, combined with the Kamaljit Singhs, Pherwanis and Ratnakars, have caused the entire banking system to lose its moorings. The system has forgotten its basic functions of deposit mobilisation and lending; instead bankers have been led to believe that their salvation lies in slick treasury operations—even operations of a completely fictitious nature.

Did the system fail or was it allowed to be subverted? The silence of the RBI as the regulator, when it had information of the goings on inside the banking industry and its failure to intervene decisively to prevent the situation going out of control left the question unanswered. It was the system which was subverted for self-aggrandisement both by the stock broker and the bankers and, the RBI woke up late in the day.

## 2. CRB Capital Markets Scandal

Within five years of the Harshad Mehta scandal hitting the financial sector, CRB Capital Markets scam broke out, again exposing the vulnerability of the system. A chartered accountant by profession, Chain Roop Bhansali (CR Bhansali), hailing originally from Rajasthan had floated a non-banking financial company, CRB Consultancy Private Ltd in 1991 and converted it as CRB Capital Markets Ltd. Next five years saw his net worth jump from Rs 11.65 crores to Rs 436.6 crores. It raised huge deposits from the public offering high returns of 24 to 32 per cent and incentives.

With astounding figures to prove his capabilities Bhansali applied for a banking licence to the RBI. In July 1996, it agreed in principle to grant him the licence to set up what he advertised would be called CRB Global Bank Ltd. Both SBI and Bank of Tokyo lent Rs 1200 crores to Bhansali.

The bubble burst when the claims for refund of deposits could not be honoured. Nearly three lakh depositors and creditors were taken for a ride. He issued fraudulent dividend warrants and encashed them through the banks. There was no guarantee for the deposits, nor did he have real assets to cover the deposits he had received. There was a run on the company to withdraw the deposits.

How the fraud broke out, what was the failing of the regulators and with what consequences were dramatically explained by *Outlook* magazine in the following words[9] :

IT all began with a few cheques bouncing. When some fixed depositors in the high-profile non-banking finance company (NBFC) CRB Capital Markets found that the cheques issued to them by the company were dishonoured, they quickly sat up and took notice. The news spread fast, and with it came panic, as thousands of depositors thronged CRB's offices to withdraw their deposits.

The speed at which things moved thereafter was amazing. CRB's closets, it appeared, stored only skeletons. Within days, the group which claimed a funds' base of more than Rs 1000 crores and which liked to refer to itself as the "complete global financial house", had collapsed, winding-up operations had started, and an international manhunt was on for the "CRB" in CRB Capital: Chain Roop Bhansali.

And what is now clear is that the crash of CRB could have been easily avoided. The Reserve Bank of India (RBI) should have seen it coming months before. Indeed, it did in December 1996, an RBI team wrote a damning report on massive irregularities in the way CRB was using public money, but no follow-up action was taken to save the average investor who had put his savings into CRB. The RBI did put the in-principle approval it had granted CRB for setting up a bank on hold, but it sat and watched as the company collected money from the public, saying, in its prospectus, that it had "promoted its own private sector bank CRB Global Bank Ltd, and is shortly to begin commercial operation....."

The CRB Capital Markets' cash credit account with Bank of Baroda had serious irregularities as pointed out by independent auditors. There was diversion of funds and no operation for a long time. The credit facility was sanctioned during the chairmanship of S.P. Talwar who had now become the Deputy Governor of RBI.

The institutions like CARE and SEBI and also the company's auditors who were required to safeguard the interests of the public obliged Bhansali's companies:

> Every fixed deposit (FD) scheme that is launched in India has to be rated by one of three credit-rating agencies; the aim is to give the potential depositor a clear indication of the safety of putting his money into a scheme. In September 1996, the rating agency, Credit Analysis & Research Ltd (CARE) assigned an A rating to CRB's FD programme, indicating adequate safety. This was after noting in its report that the company had liquidity problems, that it defaulted on loans and that its asset quality was deteriorating. After the RBI stopped CRB from raising fresh FDs, CARE-which claims to have been monitoring the company all through—quickly downgraded its rating to C, denoting high risk. Interestingly, CARE has been promoted by the IDBI, which in turn had given financial assistance to the group.
>
> The Securities and Exchange Board of India (SEBI) watched silently as CRB's merchant banking division handled scores of dubious public issues and went around claiming that it was "the country's No. 1 merchant banker". CRB's auditors would have been blind not to have read the signs of imminent collapse when they checked the company's accounts. But the Calcutta-based D.P. Bhaiya and Company happily gave their seal of approval on CRB's balance sheet without so much as a squeak about its rotten core.

That RBI gave in-principle-approval of a licence to start a bank when applications from bigger companies like Essar, AV Birla and Tatas were pending was inexplicable.

The CBI arrested Bhansali and initiated criminal action against him. But did the banks learn from this scam?

### 3. The pay order and gold trading scandals

In another four years, in 2001 two more scandals hit the financial sector. A share broker, Ketan Parekh and a bullion merchant. K.L. Chokshi by using the medium of pay orders subverted the system for furthering their ends. First, the facts:

Ketan Parekh issued cheques on Bank of India at Ahmedabad and obtained pay orders against them from Madhavapura Mercantile Cooperative Bank (MMCB). These pay orders were discounted by Bank of India's Mumbai Stock Exchange Branch and proceeds were credited to accounts of various front companies of Ketan Parekh like Chitrakoot Computers, Goldfish Computers and Nakshatra Computers. In nine weeks ending March 9, 2001, 248 pay orders worth Rs 2400 crores were discounted. The money was used to play in the stock market. Around that date Reserve Bank returned pay orders worth Rs 137 crores presented for clearing because the co-operative bank did not participate in clearing. By that time the money was already siphoned off by Ketan's Companies. Other banks were also involved - Global Trust, UTI and StanChart to name only three.

Simultaneously, in bullion trading in Ahmedabad, a scandal came to light. The Ahmedabad based Classic Co-operative Bank (CCB) issued pay orders worth crores favouring K.L. Chokshi. Gold was delivered by banks like SBI to Chokshi, before the pay orders issued by CCB were cleared. The pay orders bounced and the banks suffered huge losses.

The estimated loss for banks in the first case was about Rs 270 crores and in the gold scam about Rs 75 crores.

There was share price rigging, insider trading, promoter broker collusion and broker-banker nexus. While criminal actions were initiated against the suspects, a proposed merger of two new generation banks namely, UTI Bank and Global Trust Bank (GTB) was called off as the share prices of the latter were rigged. Several officials of banks, UTI and share brokers were arrested and prosecuted.

Under intense pressure in the Parliament, the NDA I government constituted another Joint Parliamentary Committee under the chairmanship of BJP Member of Parliament, Prakash Mani Tripathi in April 2001(JPC-T) to go into what came to be known as stock market scandal. JPC-T submitted its report in December 2002.

How and why did banks allow this manipulation? There was huge potential for quick earnings in bullion business and large scale credit given to share market operators. The lure of high profits drove the banks to throw caution to winds.

There were warning signals. For example, the internal audit team which went into the bullion trading business of one bank had pointed out the dangers of the dilution of internal systems; but reportedly the lure of quick profit blinded the controller's vision in that bank. If in 1992 bankers' receipts (BRs) were the means through which credit could be generated (without securities having been received), in 2001, pay orders performed the same role.

Ketan Parekh knew that banks would readily respond to proposals that would enhance their profits and profitability. To gain credibility he carefully built an image of highly successful and enterprising financial expert. The image so created would make the senior bankers ignore internal warning signals.

Like all cases of the first decade of financial sector reforms the pay order and gold trading scams took place in spite of rules, systems, regulators and the regulator- and owner- appointed directors on the boards of PSBs.

## Were the lessons learnt?

Every scam was followed by fresh instructions and directions from the RBI and the government of the day.

The very fact that they occurred regularly and continue to occur in the present decade leads to the inference that the objectives of such regulatory interventions have not been fully achieved. But more about this will figure in a different chapter.

## References

1. Bhat, T.R., 1998: *The securities scam,* a two- part article written in *Officers' Voice* June and July 1992, reproduced in *Voice of CBOO,* CBOO.
2. *Economic and Political Weekly,* September 5, 1992: *Securities Scam: The Systemic Origins* -A Special Correspondent.
3. Palande, Pravin, 1998: *Economic Milestone: Stock Market Scam* (1992) *Forbes India,* 22 August, 2014.
4. *Officers' Voice,* June and July 1992, see note in 1 above.
5. Action taken report on the Recommendations of the Joint Parliamentary Committee which enquired into the Irregularities in Securities and Banking Transactions, July 1994, Government of India (p. 1).
6. *Ibid.,* p. 1.
7. Arun Kumar, 1992: *Financial Scam: Wages of Deregulation,* paper published by Public Interest Research Group (PIRG), Delhi.
8. *Ibid.*
9. *Outlook* Magazine, June 11, 1997: *The Anatomy of a Fraud* by Arindam Mukherjee and Shekhar Ghosh.

# Chapter - 8

# The Banks that Forfeited the Trust

The liberalisation of the financial sector gave scope for another kind of malpractice where individuals took advantage of the new found autonomy. The classic case was that of the failure of Global Trust Bank in 2002. A couple of more banks had also collapsed triggering corrective action by the government and Reserve Bank of India. Although these banks were in the private sector, the crisis affected the industry in a large measure. It raised fundamental questions about licensing of new banks, merger of failed banks with public sector banks (PSBs) and the effectiveness of RBI as the regulator. In view of such wider ramifications these cases deserve to be discussed at length. Our study, however, is restricted to three important cases.

### *1. Broker-bank nexus compels merger of Nedungadi Bank with PNB*

Started in 1899 at Calicut (now Kozhikode in Kerala), Nedungadi Bank Ltd (NBL) was an old private bank. In November 2002, RBI placed NBL under moratorium and restricted depositors from withdrawing more than Rs 5,000. As on March 2002, NBL had a deposit base of Rs 1,438 crores and advances of Rs 770 crores and 174 branches spread out mostly in South India. In February 2003 it was merged with PNB.

The RBI's decision was triggered by the fact that NBL had large dealings with three stock broking firms threatening the soundness of the Bank. The broker firms were controlled by Rajendra Banthia, a director of the Bank and who was also a Harshad Mehta protégé. Initially he was the front man for B. Ratnakar, former Chairman of Canara Bank who had floated Fairgrowth Financial Services Ltd with a view to promoting a high-flying financial supermarket. With the untimely death of Ratnakar, Banthia took almost full control of the Bank. A few leading share brokers were also inducted into the board of the Bank. But when the Ketan Parekh episode came to light, RBI swung into action. Chairman & CEO, A.R. Moorthy was sacked by the RBI although until the seat became hot the regulator was supporting the CEO's every action inviting a criticism that it did not act when it should have.

The forced merger of NBL with PNB exposed the nexus between the banking industry and the stock market operators causing serious risk to the stakeholders. While the depositors could get their money from PNB, the shareholders lost out. RBI's delayed action too came in for criticism from an informed commentator[1]. She was unsparing in her indictment of the failure of RBI as regulator. She wrote:

> Rajendra Banthia's influence is neither new nor sudden. He has been consolidating his hold over the bank for an entire decade and there have been several occasions when the alarm bells clanged loudly enough, but the RBI had chosen to ignore them. It similarly ignored letters from depositors and shareholders of the bank detailing its strange policies and practices....
>
> If a regulator will only perform its supervisory duties during a crisis then one can be sure the country will only lurch from one scam to another.

Ironically, sometime before the malpractices came to light, the Bank had engaged the renowned consultants,

Pricewaterhouse Coopers for formulating a five-year business strategy and planning[2].

### 2. Benares State Bank merged with Bank of Baroda

In June 2002, Benares State Bank (BSB), with 105 branches and deposits of Rs 1031 crores was compulsorily merged with Bank of Baroda (BOB). BSB was ailing for sometime; in September 2001 it was brought under moratorium and the initial plan of the government was to close down the bank. While it had an authorised capital of Rs 120 crores its paid up capital was Rs 62 crores. The capital was, however, wiped out due to accumulated losses of about Rs 80 crores as on March 2001.

Although the plan was to liquidate BSB, on account of political implications the government decided that a PSB should take over the sick bank. It was the turn of the BOB to do the salvaging work by absorbing BSB.

### 3. The failure of Global Trust Bank

Global Trust Bank (GTB) was the first of the new generation banks established in the early years of liberalisation of the financial sector. Founded by the high-flying Ramesh Gelli who as CEO of Vysya Bank Ltd had the distinction of being the youngest chairman of any bank in India, GTB was cited as a role model to the PSBs. It was inaugurated by Manmohan Singh as Finance Minister who had declared that it would be the new icon of financial sector. Its techno-savvy branches, ATMs and high profile executives symbolised the success of the reforms. That GTB was the darling of the investors was evidenced by the fact that when it came up in mid-1990's with an initial public offer of equity shares (IPO) to meet the capital adequacy norms, the IPO was oversubscribed by 60 times. Against the target of Rs104 crores planned it collected about Rs 6240 crores of capital. About ten lakh investors had applied for the shares of GTB.

In March 2003 it had a capital of Rs 121.4 crores, reserves of Rs 146 crores and deposit of Rs 6920.90 crores. It had 104 branches, 275 ATMs and 1200 employees. Ramesh Gelli along with his close associates held about 20.5 per cent of the Bank's shares with public owning about 51.28 per cent of shares.

With all these credentials how did the new star in the financial sky fall?

## The problems that surfaced

The first signals of the bank's problems came in the form of an aborted merger with UTI Bank in March 2001. During the second half of 2000, the share price of GTB started moving up. When the price of 10 rupee share reached 114 by January 2001 it was a celebration time for investors. Closely came the announcement of the agreement for merger of GTB with another new generation UTI Bank. The celebration was, however, short-lived. The merger proposal was called off. The reason: with the knowledge of an impending merger Ramesh Gelli and associates had reportedly indulged in insider trading to rig the share prices.

Simultaneously GTB had started lending to share market operators notably Ketan Parekh and his associates. Through key branches in Mumbai, huge credit limits were provided to the brokers. The trouble was not far off. On June 7, 2001 about 40 lakh GTB shares were traded and such activity followed thereafter. It was reported that Ketan Parekh was trying to boost the share price. It transpired that Gelli was hand in glove with the price manipulation when Securities and Exchange Board of India (SEBI) barred him from accessing capital market. He was asked to step down as CEO of the Bank. Later, R.S. Hugar was appointed Chairman of GTB.

## Negative net worth

By March 2002, the failing health of GTB became

evident. While the audited balance sheet showed a net worth of Rs 400.4 crores and a profit of Rs 40 crores, an inspection by RBI revealed that the net worth was negative as on March 2002. The Bank was asked to appoint an independent auditor to reconcile the discrepancies. In February, 2003 the independent auditor confirmed the earlier finding of RBI team about the negative net worth.

Arising out of the findings, RBI gave certain directions to GTB. They pertained to the kind of loans the Bank could give, premature payment of deposits, capital market exposure and declaration of dividend. RBI initiated monthly monitoring of the health of the Bank. The statutory auditors were changed.

By September 2003, GTB continued to suffer overall loss although there was operating profit for the year 2002-03. By that time R.S. Hugar had quit. Sudhakar Gande was appointed CEO of the Bank. In September 2003, GTB declared its plan to cleanse the contaminated balance sheet; RBI welcomed that move. The improvement was however, marginal. According to RBI inspection the net worth had eroded further and Capital Adequacy Ratio (CAR) was negative.

## Audit findings

In November 2003, RBI advised GTB to infuse fresh capital and achieve CAR of nine per cent. This plan also did not bear positive results. In the meantime, the new auditors, Pricewaterhouse Coopers (PwC) submitted their audit report for 2003 with serious qualifications. They opined that the assumption of going concern would be valid only if the management's assessment of business growth was right and if the plans of fresh infusion of capital materialised. They pointed out that the additional provisions were made after the net profit was arrived at by utilising the statutory reserves. They also commented that no provisions were made for restructured accounts aggregating Rs 311 crores and non-banking assets worth Rs 181 crores.

## The moratorium and after

Having been unable to reform GTB and make it stand on its own legs, RBI finally decided to bring it under moratorium through a notification of the central government issued on July 24, 2004. It was to be in operation for three months. The depositors were allowed to withdraw up to Rs 10000 from their accounts. Simultaneously, RBI worked out a plan of forced merger of GTB with PSBs; accordingly the Delhi-based Oriental Bank of Commerce (OBC) was asked to take over the bank. By middle of August, the marriage was solemnised and another private bank started with great fanfare just a decade ago went out of the banking map of the country.

## The losers

The biggest losers in the fiasco were the ordinary shareholders. That the Bank was sinking was already clear to the institutional and foreign investors (FIIs) well in advance. It was reported that FIIs sold almost entire stock of theirs in April-June 2004 itself. Their stake which was at 4.91 per cent in March 2004 came down to 0.98 per cent by June. Goldman Sachs Investment (Mauritius) had brought down its holding from 4.53 per cent in March 2004 to less than one per cent in June. European Investment, a registered overseas corporate body had sold its entire stock of 3.7 per cent during June 2004. A few others had already come out in 2002. As a result of the exit of institutional investors the share of public holding increased from 44.88 per cent in March 2004 to 51.28 per cent in June. It was learnt that the Bank had about 1.60 lakh small share holders who did not get anything as the net worth of that bank was negative.

## JPC's findings

The Joint Parliamentary Committee headed by Prakash Mani Tripathi which went into the Stock Market Scandal had observed that GTB had not ensured the end use of funds it had lent; there was diversion of funds to several companies linked to Ketan Parekh like Zee Telefilms and Himachal Futuristic Communications Ltd. According to the JPC there was a definite evidence of misappropriation of funds.[3]

## The renewed debate

The development had triggered a fresh debate on wider issues. It is instructive to reproduce the observations made by this writer in a paper published in 2004[4]:

> The failure of the high profile GTB raises two substantive issues. One relates to the role of the regulator and the other, to the larger question of privatisation of banks. Both require to be examined dispassionately and objectively.
>
> When the RBI as the regulatory authority considers issue of licence to set up a new bank it should subject the application to critical scrutiny and evaluation. The stake of the promoters, the manner in which the capital will be raised, the management team and the commitment to corporate governance are all the critical factors that should weigh with the RBI. If there are external pressures to bend a guideline it should be resisted in the interest of the bank and the stakeholders. The board of directors need to be kept independent of the influence of the promoters.
>
> Once the licence is given the monitoring and supervision by RBI should be strict. With all the powers it has and access to information about the internal working of a bank, if RBI is not able to evaluate its working, it is a sad commentary on the regulator's efficiency, efficacy and its independence itself. In all the cases of recent failures of banks RBI did have the knowledge of the malpractices indulged in by the promoter groups. Therefore, arising out of the latest case the RBI has to introspect and tighten its supervisory function.
>
> In the larger context comes the question of privatisation of PSBs and opening up the banking sector for more

players. Both the older generation and the new generation banks in the private sector have been in the exit mode at regular intervals. To give succour to the hapless depositors these banks have been forcibly merged with the state owned banks. Despite the losses suffered by some of the PSBs in late 'nineties the depositors never had a problem. These banks continue to enjoy the trust of the people. Through compulsory mergers the interest of depositors may be safeguarded, but the shareholders who are small investors without any decisive say in the running of the banks stand to lose their money. If the bank that takes over the sick bank gets tax benefits the loser is the tax payer.

In the recent years, in the face of competition, radical transformation has been taking place in the work culture and quality of service in the PSBs. The overall efficiency has been consistently improving. Asking such banks to carry the cross of faltering private banks will be unfair. Our emphasis should be on further toning up the government banks rather than privatising them or allowing more operators to start their high profile outfits. If this understanding dawns on the policy-makers and the regulator, that would be the right lesson from the GTB collapse.

## The albatross on the neck of OBC

While the merger of the collapsed GTB with the state owned OBC ensured that the interests of depositors and employees of GTB were protected, it caused a setback to an otherwise well-managed and efficient OBC. Before the forced merger, OBC had earned a net profit of Rs 686 crores as against the loss of Rs 272 crores suffered by GTB. Upon acquisition of the sick bank, OBC had to absorb the loss and the huge NPAs. In 2004, OBC had gross NPA of Rs 1211 crores which jumped to Rs 2513 crores in one year, that was in 2005. The net NPA was nil in 2004 and it shot up to 327 crores in one year. No doubt, it could get tax break but it was at the cost of tax-payers' money. But OBC's CAR was badly hit in as much as it registered a steep fall from 14.47 per cent in 2004 to 9.21 per cent- yet above the prescribed minimum of 9 per cent. It took a little over three years for the bank to recover the lost ground.

## Liquidation vs. mergers with PSBs

GTB was not the last to fail as the mergers of some more banks took place in the later years. In all the cases RBI had, as the regulator access to information about the goings on in the banks. Its actions have almost always been belated. Like the GTB and Nedungadi Bank, the motive of the owners/ promoters was self-aggrandisement at the expense of public institutions. The RBI's actions were belated, as the promoters could bring political pressure to stave off extreme actions. This in turn, always made RBI's decisiveness doubtful.

With all the constraints, the strategy of compulsory mergers in preference to liquidation was intended to safeguard the interest of stakeholders like depositors and employees. That the mergers in most cases were with the PSBs further demonstrated that the government banks had the resilience to carry the baggage with them and help the depositors and other banking public. It also enhanced the role of RBI as the banking regulator.

## References

1. Sucheta Dalal: *Nedungadi Bank and the saga of RBI inaction*, Article in *Rediff.com* May 10, 2001 (downloaded on January 15, 2017).
2. *Rediff.com* report dated February 03, 2003: *Clearance for merger with PNB lifts Nedungadi Bank* (downloaded on January 15, 2017).
3. Sridhar,V: 2004: *The collapse of a bank, Frontline*, Aug. 14-27, 2004.
4. Bhat, T.R., 2004: *GTB Fiasco-The Lessons, Officers' Voice*, November 2004.

# Chapter - 9

# The Case of three 'Weak Banks'

## The case of weak banks

While greed and systemic deficiencies contributed to the scandals in the banking sector and failures of a few banks in the private sector, there was another factor which had not received the attention it deserved. Just at the beginning of the reforms era there was the collapse of Delhi-based New Bank of India which was itself a PSB. As the reforms rolled on, most banks showed substantive qualitative improvement as mentioned in an earlier chapter. Yet, the new-found resilience was not sufficiently strong to make the banks evolve their own strategy to face new challenges. The case of the three banks termed as weak towards the end of the last century is a damning evidence that PSBs were yet to reach a state of robustness to overcome internal weaknesses. A study of these cases becomes important in the backdrop of the problems being faced by the PSBs during the last four-five years (2012-2017).

A major plank of the financial sector reforms was partial privatisation of PSBs with two-fold purposes. One was to meet the demands of restructuring the state owned enterprises including PSBs. The second was the need to find resources to meet the now accepted capital adequacy norms.

Wholesale privatisation of PSBs had political ramifications. The next best was to partially privatise the banks to demonstrate that the government was committed to reforms. But privatisation, fully or partially, would not succeed if the targeted enterprises were incurring losses.

### *New Bank of India*

The first challenge the government faced was connected with the fate of New Bank of India (NBI). NBI was among the six banks nationalised in April 1980. Among them, Andhra Bank, OBC and NBI were, at the time of takeover, much better managed entities than the other three namely, Vijaya Bank, Punjab & Sindh Bank and Corporation Bank. But by the beginning of the 1990's NBI had started its downward slide posting losses continuously. When the reforms began, it had already become sick. By 1993, its accumulated losses were about Rs 450 crores against a capital of Rs 186 crores. The government decided that the bank be taken over by well-managed Punjab National Bank (PNB). Accordingly in September 1993 the merger of NBI with PNB took place. This scheme of merger was termed 'perfunctory' affecting, in the short term, the overall performance of PNB.[1]

### *Three more banks*

The more serious challenge came in 1999, when Indian Bank based in Chennai, and UCO Bank and United Bank of India both based in Kolkata were declared weak in terms of Narasimham Committee-II's recommendations. These three banks were much larger in size and business than the New Bank of India, had been nationalised in 1969 and were incurring huge losses continuously. The RBI appointed a study group under the chairmanship of M.S.Verma, former Chairman of SBI to go into the options available to the government.

The Committee on Banking Sector Reforms (NC-II) had earlier laid down two criteria for a weak bank:

(a) The accumulated losses and net NPAs have exceeded the net worth of the bank, or

(b) Operating profits less the income on recapitalisation bonds has been negative for three consecutive years.

The Verma Committee listed seven additional parameters like capital adequacy ratio, return on assets, net interest margin, ratio of operating profits to average working funds and ratio of cost to income. Applying these parameters the Committee identified Indian Bank, UCO Bank and United Bank of India (UBI) as weak banks.

The figures provided by the Committee about these banks reflect their weaknesses. The following extracts from the summary of the Report of the Working Group on Restructuring Weak Public Sector Banks (M.S. Verma) are instructive:

> Indian Bank continued to incur operating losses in 1998-99 also. The capital adequacy which had turned positive and reached 1.41 per cent in March 1998 with capital infusion of Rs 1750 crores from the Government of India, turned negative again in March 1999. The decline in other income continued during 1998-99 as well. The bank did not make any provision for liabilities arising on account of the proposed wage revision. The deterioration in the NPA front is unabated. Gross NPA went up from Rs 3,428 crores as on 31 March 1998 to Rs 3,709 crores as on 31 March 1999, i.e., 37 per cent of gross advances. This was the highest among public sector banks.
>
> UCO Bank's operating profit improved marginally in 1998-99. However, if the interest income on recapitalisation bonds is excluded, the bank would have incurred operating loss of Rs 91 crores in 1997-98 and Rs 157 crores in 1998-99. Recapitalisation by the government to the tune of Rs 200 crores helped the bank achieve capital adequacy of 9.63 per cent in 1998-99. The bank has not made provision for liability on account of wage revision. Gross NPA as on

31 March 1999 aggregated to Rs 1716 crores (23 per cent). Net NPAs at Rs 715.63 crores were higher as compared to Rs 705 crores as on 31 March 1998. The inability of the bank to register any improvement in the net NPA position is a matter of concern.

United Bank of India's operating profit decreased substantially in 1998-99. Operating income increased mainly on account of extraordinary income by way of interest received on income tax refund. Further, if the interest income on recapitalisation bonds is excluded, the bank would have incurred operating loss of Rs 89 crores in 1997-98 and Rs 117 crores in 1998-99. Recapitalisation by the Government of India to the tune of Rs 100 crores helped the bank achieve capital adequacy of 9.60 per cent in 1998-99. The bank has not made provision during 1998-99 for future pension liability and wage revision. The gross NPAs of the bank as on 31 March 1999 increased in absolute terms to Rs 1,549 crores (32 per cent) from Rs 1,451 crores as on 31 March 1998 (34 per cent). Net NPAs also went up to Rs 573 crores (15 per cent) as on 31 March 1999 from Rs 472 crores (14 per cent) as on 31 March 1998.

### *Causes of weaknesses and remedies*

The Verma Committee's finding was that the weaknesses related to operations, human resources and management.

High level and fresh generation of NPAs, slow decision-making with regard to sanctions of advances, absence of cost control, weak internal control and housekeeping, poor risk management and low level of technology were some of the operational weaknesses of the banks.

In the human resources front, over staffing, low productivity, low levels of skill and motivation of staff and inadequate training facilities were the major weaknesses.

Lack of succession planning, short tenures of and frequent changes in top management and inadequate support from the Boards of Directors were serious management related issues affecting the banks.

After ruling out options like merger, change in ownership and narrow banking, the Committee suggested a comprehensive operational and financial restructuring so as to revive the sick banks. The Committee's proposals included basic changes in the operations, induction of modern technology, resolution of the problem of high non-performing assets and drastic reduction in cost of operations. The financial restructuring of the three banks would need additional resources of about Rs 5500 crores.

### *CII's Task force advises liquidation*

In contrast with the proposals of Verma Committee, the Task Force on Non-Performing Assets of Banks, appointed by Confederation of Indian Industry (CII) and headed by K.V. Kamath, Managing Director & CEO (as he then was) of ICICI Bank Ltd., recommended, in December 1999 that the weak banks be closed down[2]. There was a sharp reaction to this suggestion from both the employees and the management personnel. The primary reason for the reaction was that many companies who were members of CII had been chronic defaulters of the loans borrowed from these banks and recovery proceedings were pending before different fora against the companies. Had these companies cleared their defaulted loans the sick banks would not have had problems, contended the unions. The government, however, did not act on the CII's recommendation.

### *Unions' stand*

As the operational restructuring advised by Verma Committee involved proposals to cut down on staff cost through different methods, there was resistance from the unions in these banks supported by the national level bank unions. The All India Bank Officers' Confederation (AIBOC), the largest bank officers' union of the country submitted a separate note to the government in early 1999. The note contained a number of suggestions to revive these banks through additional capital, strong measures to recover NPAs, changes in business strategies and professionalising the top management teams[3]. As stakeholders the reactions of the employees were expected.

### *The path chosen*

The government and the RBI were, perhaps, more inclined to revive the banks, rather than closing them or even merging them with stronger banks. The earlier merger of NBI with PNB had caused considerable disruption of the working of the PNB. What a former Governor had said at that time is worth recalling[4]:

> Mergers have often been suggested as a way out. To merge a healthy bank with a weak bank will only expose the former to contagion. Merger is not a panacea, except at the cost of widespread disruption in the system.

The later merger of the new generation private bank, namely, Global Trust Bank with Oriental Bank of Commerce in 2004 (as explained in an earlier chapter) had adversely affected the working of the latter which was a healthy and efficient PSB.

On the strategy required, D.N. Ghosh, who was once the Chairman of SBI had stressed on a team effort[5]:

> Government and Reserve Bank have to decide to entrust the responsibility of governance in the hands of persons who have the credentials and capability to provide leadership, to integrate the employees with a common vision and commitment and to evolve and enforce the discipline of a new strategy.

The government and the RBI decided to revive the banks by adopting the strategy recommended by M.S.Verma Committee.

Belying the prognostication of the soothsayers of the doomsday the three 'weak' banks made a remarkable turnaround during the next five years as demonstrated in their performance under several parameters. The Tables 1, 2 and 3 furnished here speak eloquently. In an effort to cut down on cost, a number of branches were rationalised and through voluntary retirement scheme offered to the employees the staff strength was also cut down. It is to the credit of these banks that despite being branded as weak and 'fit to be liquidated', the banking public continued to have faith in them as confirmed by the sustained increase in their business from the early part of this century.

## Performance of 'Weak banks' between 2000 and 2005

(**Note:** Figures relating to items 1 to 6 in the tables 1 to 3 are in Rs crores)

**Table 1: Indian Bank**

| | *Parameters* | *1999-2000* | *2002-2003* | *2004-2005* |
|---|---|---|---|---|
| 1. | Capital | 2504 | 4574 | 4574 |
| 2. | Reserves and Surplus | 390 | 556 | 1362 |
| 3. | Deposits | 19114 | 27016 | 34808 |
| 4. | Advances | 8203 | 12275 | 18380 |
| 5. | Operating Profit | 24 | 590 | 958 |
| 6. | Net Profit | -427 | 189 | 408 |
| 7. | Staff Strength | 26259 | 22045 | 21567 |
| 8. | No. of Branches | 1496 | 1378 | 1382 |
| 9. | Return on Assets (%) | -1.81 | 0.53 | 1.08 |
| 10. | Business Per Employee (Rs. In Lakhs) | 104.03 | 178.23 | 246 |
| 11. | Capital Adequacy Ratio (%) | -12.00 | 10.85 | 14.14 |
| 12. | Net NPAs to Net Advances (%) | 16.18 | 6.15 | 1.35 |

**Table 2: UCO Bank**

| | *Parameters* | *1999-2000* | *2002-2003* | *2004-2005* |
|---|---|---|---|---|
| 1. | Capital | 2504 | 4574 | 4574 |
| 2. | Reserves and Surplus | 390 | 556 | 1362 |
| 3. | Deposits | 19114 | 27016 | 34808 |
| 4. | Advances | 8203 | 12275 | 18380 |
| 5. | Operating Profit | 24 | 590 | 958 |
| 6. | Net Profit | -427 | 189 | 408 |
| 7. | Staff Strength | 26259 | 22045 | 21567 |
| 8. | No. of Branches | 1496 | 1378 | 1382 |
| 9. | Return on Assets (%) | -1.81 | 0.53 | 1.08 |
| 10. | Business Per Employee (Rs. In Lakhs) | 104.03 | 178.23 | 246 |
| 11. | Capital Adequacy Ratio (%) | -12.00 | 10.85 | 14.14 |
| 12. | Net NPAs to Net Advances (%) | 16.18 | 6.15 | 1.35 |

**Table 3: United Bank of India**

| | *Parameters* | *1999-2000* | *2002-2003* | *2004-2005* |
|---|---|---|---|---|
| 1 | Capital | 1811 | 1811 | 1811 |
| 2 | Reserves and Surplus | 159 | 151 | 146 |
| 3 | Deposits | 16788 | 21031 | 25348 |
| 4 | Advances | 4563 | 7352 | 11390 |
| 5 | Operating Profit | 84 | 556 | 689 |
| 6 | Net Profit | 31 | 305 | 300 |
| 7 | Staff Strength | 21316 | 17745 | 17493 |
| 8 | No. of Branches | 1331 | 1299 | 1310 |
| 9 | Return on Assets (%) | 0.16 | 1.26 | 1.04 |
| 10 | Business Per Employee (Rs. In Lakhs) | 100.16 | 159.95 | 208 |
| 11 | Capital Adequacy Ratio (%) | 9.60 | 15.17 | 18.16 |
| 12 | Net NPAs to Net Advances (%) | 12.70 | 5.50 | 2.43 |

*Source:* Database on Indian banking 2000-2003, IBA Bulletin Special Issue, January 2004.

### *The questions*

The failure of NBI and its merger with PNB in the early years of reforms and the serious weaknesses of three banks demanding a different strategy during the first decade of reforms raised some fundamental questions related to the role of the regulator and the owner.

In the wake of the financial sector reforms, apart from capital infusion by government as the owner, several measures were initiated to make the PSBs healthier and efficient. As indicated earlier, the performance of most banks measured in terms of quantitative parameters was creditworthy. There was qualitative improvement as well, thanks to the series of measures on risk management, supervision and control, adoption of advanced technology, better customer orientation and greater operational freedom to bank boards.

In spite of these measures if large banks like UCO Bank, Indian Bank and United Bank of India suffered heavy losses and were on the brink of either closure or merger what went wrong?

One would attribute this to collective failure at three levels: at the levels of individual bank's management, the RBI as regulator and the government as owner.

The major areas of management failures were failures of the top management in providing the leadership, bringing in new technology and managing human resources efficiently.

According to the Verma Committee, 'absence of dynamic leadership for long period has been a major contributor to the consistent deterioration in the functioning of the three banks'. Leadership was lacking in the middle levels of the banks because of inadequacies in skills related to both conventional and new areas of banking. The training facilities were also inadequate to meet the needs of the times.

The failure of the top managements of the banks was further evident from the inability of the CEOs to resist political pressures on sanction of loans. For example, with regard to the affairs of Indian Bank the following observation made by this writer in September 1996 is instructive[6]:

> It is stated that during the chairmanship of M. Gopalakrishnan, the (Indian) Bank had granted loans to certain companies without following the lending norms. It is also reported that the Bank had violated several regulations of the RBI which were pointed out by the RBI inspectors in their reports...
>
> For quite some time it was a matter of common knowledge that the former Chairman of Indian Bank had a lot of political clout giving him immunity against any probe by either the RBI or Central Vigilance Commission.

It was not the management alone which was at fault. The conduct of the RBI as the regulator was also open to criticism for its failures. A similar failure on the part of the government as the owner was noticed during the time. The following observations made by this author on the same occasion raise certain pertinent questions:

> When the RBI has its nominee on the board of the bank, when it has access to all information regarding the business of the bank and when it can conduct periodic inspections how is it that RBI did not take corrective action at the right time?
>
> Is blacklisting of the statutory auditors as the RBI has done recently an answer to the question relating to the failure of the RBI?
>
> Why did the government which has its nominee on the board of the bank keep quiet when through the RBI it could get all the relevant information from the bank?

That the three banks in question recovered and had a turnaround as revealed by the statistical data or that the

PNB was able to overcome the cost of absorbing NBI does not mitigate the basic questions of the roles of the regulator and the owner. Have the lessons been learnt from such setbacks experienced during the first 12 years of reforms? The answer to this crucial question requires a more elaborate analysis.

## References


1. Kurup, N.P., 1994: *Muddle of Partial Privatisation of Banks, Economic and Political Weekly,* September 10, 1994.
2. *Frontline* Magazine: *January 8, 2000: Banking-A controversial report* by V. Sridhar.
3. AIBOC's Study of PSBs sought to be termed as 'Weak' with specific reference to UCO, UBI and Indian Bank, 1999, AIBOC-(This author was part of the study group constituted in 1998 by AIBOC to evolve remedial measures to turn them around. See his notes dated October 14, 1998 on UCO Bank, October 29, 1998 on Indian Bank and November 24, 1998 on United Bank of India submitted to the group).
4. S.Venkitaramanan, 1999: *Cure For The Sick, The Telegraph,* Kolkata May 31.
5. D.N. Ghosh 1999: *Weak Banks: A Strategy for Self-Renewal, Economic and Political Weekly,* January 29, 2000.
6. Bhat, T R., 1996: *Indian Bank: What next? Voice of CBOO,* collection of editorials pub. by CBOO, pp. 242-244.

# Chapter - 10

# How did Banks become Fragile?

### *A bag of mixed results*

While the first 12 years of financial sector reforms witnessed radical changes in the banking industry, the period saw many shortcomings which led to major scams, bank failures and forced mergers; there were also basic weaknesses as documented by both the official committees namely, Narasimham Committee-II and M.S.Verma Committee. As explained in the preceding chapters, it was a bag of mixed results.

These developments raised one fundamental question namely, how sustainable was the process of reforms? A corollary of this was if they were not sustainable what were the factors responsible for the situation? A detailed examination of these issues assumes significance in the light of the fresh problems faced by the banks in the current decade.

### *The weaknesses*

Although the reform process was all-pervasive and helped the PSBs to record both quantitative and qualitative growth during the period under review, many shortcomings continued to dog them. In fact, these weaknesses came to be focused periodically by different committees, RBI in its annual reports, independent analysts and, the employees as well. The weaknesses could be grouped as under:

1. Corporate governance issues
2. HR management issues
3. Owner related issues
4. Regulator related issues.

These are dwelt upon more extensively in the following sections.

### *Corporate governance issues*

Until the reforms began, the concept of corporate governance was hardly ever heard in the banking sector. This was natural because an overwhelming majority of banks were owned by the government and they functioned more as appendages of the banking division in the Ministry of Finance with hardly any autonomy to the boards and the top managements of the PSBs. They were vulnerable to political influence as well. These had adversely affected the working of the banks for quite long.

When the financial sector reforms were unleashed, a major thrust was in the area of operational autonomy. The success of reforms was dependent upon adoption of corporate governance principles in running the affairs of the banks. Unfortunately this did not happen for many years after 1991. The security scam of 1991-92, the Ketan Parekh imbroglio of 2002, the problems faced by Indian Bank, UCO Bank and United Bank of India and the collapse of Global Trust Bank repeatedly exposed the absence of corporate governance in the Indian banks.

This experience should be related to the good governance practices indicated by the Basel Committee on Banking Supervision in 1999. A few of them are listed below:

(a) Establishing strategic objectives and a set of corporate values that are communicated throughout the bank.

(b) Setting and enforcing clear lines of responsibility and accountability throughout the bank.

(c) Ensuring that board members are qualified for their positions, have clear understanding of their role in governance and are not subject to undue influence from management or outside concerns.

(d) Ensuring that there is appropriate oversight by senior management.

(e) Effectively utilising the work conducted by internal and external auditors in recognition of important control function they provide.

In paper, the system in vogue in the banks was elaborate and streamlined as spelt out by the Basel Committee. As owner, the government had enormous control over the PSBs. As regulator, the RBI was the authority to issue licences to open new banks and regulate their working. The banks were under constant oversight of Reserve Bank of India and the Ministry of Finance, Banking Division, Government of India (GoI) in formulating various banking policies. The Governor and senior RBI functionaries and the Minister of Finance and his officials would regularly meet the CEOs of banks to review, advise and guide the banks on almost all matters regarding the working of the banks. Although the term corporate governance was rarely used those days, the underlying principles were set to be carried out by banks under the dual supervision of the government and the RBI.

The reality, however, was different. The banks regularly faced problems of different kinds. A few of them are worth recalling in this context:

(a) Increasing vulnerability of banks to both white collar and corporate frauds.

(b) Increasing incidence of loan losses and mounting volume of nonperforming assets.

(c) Absence of accountability for non-performance at the top level.

(d) Unsatisfactory levels of disclosure and transparency.

(e) An audit mechanism which is strong in form but unsatisfactory in substance.

(f) Lack of professionalism on the part of the directors.

It was in this background that M.S.Verma Committee found that accountability for non-performance at any level including that of the board was nearly absent and it would end up with efforts to fix accountability at the management level for loans and advances that go bad. The standards of corporate governance in state owned banks were poor compared to international standards. The group also called for more transparency, a greater accountability and streamlined process of induction of directors.

An issue related to the governance was the appointment and working of the boards of PSBs. The chairman, the whole-time directors and other directors had been government appointees for a long time. The process of their selection, the terms of their appointment, the levels of accountability for non-performance or failures were not above demur. In the conduct of the board meetings too the principle of equality of all directors was seldom in practice; the government and RBI directors would always dominate the board proceedings.

Although in the early years of reforms the share of NPAs came down substantially, the improvement was apparently superficial as the second decade of this century established. A major part of the blame for this was laid on the doors of the boards of the PSBs. In a workshop for officer directors organised by All India Bank Officers' Confederation (AIBOC) in 2000, the feedback received was instructive. Among other issues, the functioning of the management committees of the boards came up for scrutiny by the participants. They had shared the following information[1]:

> When we come to the decision-making in respect of large advances, in almost all banks the Management

> Committee of the Board (MCB) disposes off most of the loan papers. It is learnt that working of the MCB leaves much to be desired. Every note on a loan proposal runs into 50 to 60 pages. Often supplementary agenda is given to the directors at the last minute. Apart from loan papers several other subjects are put up for its consideration. The meeting itself takes place in two hours. Will it really be possible to study each agenda properly and decide objectively?

The top executives of PSBs were themselves vulnerable to external pressures in granting of loans as commented by a former RBI Governor[2]:

> Rare is the Chief Executive Officer (CEO) who can resist the blandishment of a minister or his panjandrum who asks that a particular loan be expedited. The CEO exists at the sufferance of the government and has at least to consider their requests even when they are unreasonable...Behest will be behind many of the loans that have turned sour in the latest saga of Indian banks.

For better governance, transparency is essential. The banks, however, were bogged down by the archaic law of secrecy regarding their borrowers. The critical stakeholders of the banks, namely the shareholders of private banks and partly privatised PSBs and, the depositors of the banks had no clue of the names of the large borrowers who had defaulted in the payment of interest and instalments. There would be no way by which these stakeholders could pierce the veil of secrecy. That handicap denied them the opportunity to demand action against specific delinquents.

Effective governance demands that another group of stakeholders, namely, the employees were taken on board in matters affecting the functioning of the individual banks. Although PSBs had the scheme of appointing directors representing the interests of workmen and supervisory staff they were less than equal to the other directors. They were excluded from certain crucial sub-committees of the board. As people from within, the employee directors could have worked as eyes and ears of the boards if they were treated on par with their peers on the boards. Whistle blowing which the employees could have utilised to bring malpractices to the attention of the boards or the CEOs was not encouraged. Individually, as employees they were bound by the oath of confidentiality and if any employee disclosed the name of a defaulting borrower it would be treated as an act of indiscipline triggering disciplinary proceedings from the bank management.

A function that did not live up to the levels expected of it was the internal and external audit. For effective governance a capable internal audit department was necessary. The internal auditors suffered from serious complex of superior-subordinate relationship which cramped their independence. As a result internal audit was unable to point out serious irregularities involving senior executives of the banks as revealed during the security and pay order scandals. Where the aberrations were pointed out the management team responsible to act upon them would shut their eyes. Commenting on the gold and pay order scandal of early 2000, this was what this author had written in a paper[3]:

> For example, the internal audit team which went into the bullion trading business of one bank had pointed out the dangers of the dilution of internal systems; but reportedly the lure of quick profit blinded the controller's vision in that bank.

... Like all cases of the first decade of financial sector reforms the latest scam took place in spite of rules, systems, regulators and the regulator and owner appointed directors on the boards of PSBs.

The external audit firms appointed by the regulator or the banks' boards were also vulnerable. Their certificates in the annual reports had helped conceal the shortcomings in the accounts rather than reveal the true state of affairs. If they were truly professional how did the financial irregularities associated with the scams of 1992, 1997 and 2001 go unnoticed by them? This shortcoming strengthened the inference that corporate governance was wanting in the banks.

In early 2002 the RBI, while appointing a Consultative Group of Directors of banks and financial institutions on the issue of corporate governance had confirmed that there was 'ample evidence that inadequate corporate governance standards in certain banks and financial institutions could contribute to their financial fragility'. Commenting on the state of affairs a leading journal editorially observed[4]:

> Poor corporate governance is reflected basically in ineffective risk management, poor quality lending and fudging of accounts. Managements' attempt to conceal the actual state of affairs through creative accounting could eventually lead even to systemic instability.

It was not the problem with the PSBs alone; the problems in the newly established private banks were worse, commented the same paper.

Analysing the factors that led to certain PSBs being branded as weak, a former RBI governor had this to say about the internal reason for failure[5]:

> A different category of sick banks is typified by the Indian Bank, where over lending and errors of the top management had led to problems.

Chastened by such experience and guided by the recommendations of different study groups, in the beginning of this century the RBI as regulator started emphasising on better corporate governance practices as evidenced from its following statement[6]:

> As part of the ongoing financial sector reforms, the Boards of banks and FIs have been given greater

autonomy to lay down guidelines and procedures to enhance transparency and disclosure, to contain risk and for asset-liability management. The Consultative Group of Directors of Banks and Financial Institutions (Chairman: Dr. A. S. Ganguly), set up by the Reserve Bank, reviewed these aspects and recommended measures to make the supervisory role of the Boards of Banks and FIs more effective. These recommendations have been benchmarked against international best practices as enunciated by the Basel Committee on Banking Supervision. In June 2002, a list of actions to be undertaken by banks was indicated to banks. These included due diligence procedures for appointment of directors on the boards of private sector banks, and role and responsibilities of independent/non-executive directors.

As a sequel to these measures, the banks started disclosing, under the chapter 'Report on corporate governance' in their annual reports, more information about the directors, board meetings, composition of different committees of the board etc. These measures, it was expected, would bring about substantial qualitative improvement in the governance of both public and private sector banks with constant monitoring by RBI.

### *HR management issues*

The second and equally critical issue related to the management of human resources in the PSBs. For long, management of human resources (HRM) was a low priority issue in banks. The department handling HRM was called 'Staff Department', 'Establishment Department', 'General Administration Department' or 'Personnel Department'. There was hardly any attempt to study the issues connected with HRM. The wages and the service conditions of the workmen employees were governed by the provisions of industry level bipartite settlements starting from the first one signed in 1966. In the aftermath of nationalisation the government had appointed a Committee headed by V.R. Pillai to examine the issue of standardisation of pay scales for the officers. But the larger issues of training, skill building, deployment, empowerment, motivation, succession planning did not get the importance they deserved.

In the 1980's the government as owner imposed a restriction on fresh recruitment under the notion that the PSBs were over-staffed. It had also made service in rural and semi-urban branches mandatory for the supervisory staff. While the business grew and the network of branches expanded rapidly, the cap on recruitment hamstrung the bank managements in building up trained manpower over time. In the next twenty five years the adverse fallout of this on the calibre of the staff was experienced by most PSBs.

The Narasimham Committee-II (NC-II) had, in fact, noted that the delay in recruiting skilled manpower had an impact on the competency levels of public sector banks in some areas and they had consequently lost some ground to foreign banks and the newly set up private sector banks. The Committee had recommended lateral recruitment of skilled manpower to augment the human resources.[7] Considering the newer kind of services being offered by the PSBs to keep pace with demands of changing generation of clientele it was imperative for the banks to build up a complement of adequately trained and skilled staff.

Skill building was essential for efficient banking operations which involve public money. The fundamental work of sanctioning loans to clients, for example, needs minimum skill of appraising the loan proposal and the capability of the loan applicant. The PSBs did not pay adequate attention to such skill development as illustrated below[8]:

> At the branch level in many banks the lending powers have been enormously enhanced without corresponding

skill upgradation or support of trained personnel. When a branch head sanctions a credit limit of say Rs 25 lakhs to a firm, does he prepare self-explanatory process note or get it prepared? Very little attention is given to the method of appraisal, processing, documentation and post-sanction monitoring.

For some time, even after NC–II, the belief that the PSBs were overstaffed continued. It was, therefore, suggested by S.S. Kohli Committee appointed by the government in 2000 in its interim report that a voluntary retirement scheme (VRS) be introduced for the staff to reduce the staff strength. The scheme was launched in 2000 in all banks except one. Although unions opposed it, the response from the staff, both workmen and officers, was overwhelming. As much as 14.24 per cent amounting to over 125,000 employees opted for VRS. A larger percentage of officers (about 62000 amounting to 25.40 per cent) went under VRS. No attempt was made to study why such a large section of senior employees preferred to go out of an otherwise well-paying service industry.

Although it facilitated a trimming down it was at a heavy cost. There was a drain of experienced and knowledgeable officers many of whom were re-employed by private financial institutions. There was very little infusion of fresh blood into the system. At the time of Kohli Committee Report itself about 160,000 out of 233,000 were above the age of 35 years. This was likely to create serious shortage of skilled and experienced manpower unless timely infusion of fresh talent was made. The banks could not fill the vacuum as the government had mandated that such vacancy should not be filled. In the meantime the number of branches and business were growing with no sufficient manpower.

Sometime later, in 2006, the S.P. Shukla Committee extensively dealt with the issues connected with the HRM in the banks and made a series of recommendations to address the problems.

The banks in the state sector were pioneers in introducing the concept of participative management, although mandated by Bank Nationalisation Acts of 1970/ 1980. In terms of these acts one representative each of workmen employees and officer employees were required to be appointed by the government on the boards of PSBs. As usual with the owner, in the 1980's the government gave a go-by to the representative character of such appointment and introduced the system of appointing employees of the top management's choice. It was with the intervention of the Supreme Court in 1990 that the government restored the system of appointment of the nominees sponsored by the recognised unions of workmen and officers as directors on the boards of PSBs. The institution of employee directors gave room for some element of participative management. Even here, over years, the top managements of PSBs would expect the employee directors to toe the official line in every matter that came up before the board; this attitude would make the concept dysfunctional and go against the much needed empowerment of the human resources. What S.Venkitaramanan, former RBI Governor had said was an eloquent testimony to this[9]:

> There should be empowerment of staff and officers, many of whom know more about and advise on the causes of the malady. If they are allowed to speak freely, many of the arbitrary decisions of CEOs would have been exposed long ago.

While the issue related to the manpower dogged the PSBs, the appointment of the Chairmen and executive directors who would be in charge of the day-to-day operations of PSBs invited adverse comments from different quarters. There were also recommendations from some of the study groups to make the banks' boards autonomous. More about this will be said in the next section.

### *Owner related issues*

A major problem of the PSBs during the pre- and post-reform period was the inability of the government as owner to keep an arm's distance from the management of the banks. As owner, the government had a legitimate claim to run the enterprise as it deemed fit, though. But a commercial organisation like a bank required autonomy in the matter of its functioning. The government should have limited itself to laying down the broad policy framework and guidelines; the responsibility of implementing them and meeting the policy objectives should have been left to the top management of the organisation. While during early years of nationalisation which was triggered more by political considerations it was natural for the ruling dispensation to treat the banks as departmental undertakings, with the increasing stress on governance reforms it was imperative for the government to free itself from the conflicting role of the owner and the manager. That the government was unwilling to understand the role differential was evident in many of its actions both before and after the reforms began.

The owner related problems were as follows:

1. Appointment of the top executives of the banks.
2. Appointment of the directors to the boards.
3. Working of the boards.
4. Internal working of the banks.
5. Fixing accountability.

Before dwelling upon these issues it is relevant to examine the role of the chairman and managing director of a PSB. Until 2015, in PSBs the posts of chairman and managing director were clubbed into one. The chairman and managing director (CMD) would be the chief executive officer (CEO) of the bank and the link between the board and the operational staff. In SBI, the practice of appointing separate chairman and managing directors was in vogue much before the reforms began. The chairman of SBI, however, was and continues to be the CEO on a full time basis; s/he is supported by many full-time managing directors who are also members of the central board of the SBI. Till 2015, the chairman and managing director of the PSB was the CEO.

The leadership provided by the CEO to a PSB is critical for the bank as observed by this writer in a different occasion[10]:

> Time and again it is proved that the leadership of the organisation is a decisive factor in its performance. The banks with a track record of good performance suddenly start experiencing setbacks under a new CEO. In contrast, there are instances of a CEO causing turnaround in a bank which is almost written off. In both the occasions the structures and the people were the same. His experience, professional skills, a proven record of performance and his value system have a direct influence on the overall performance of the bank.
>
> His role is not limited to measurable performance alone. The leadership provided by him can have an enduring impact on team building, on developing second line and succession plan and promoting a value system to be imbibed by everyone in the organisation. He can help strengthen a sense of belonging and a work culture that makes everybody down the line proud. His contribution should be such that the legacy he leaves behind when he departs from the scene should be continued.

The appointment of the chairmen, managing directors and executive directors of the PSBs was within the power of the government as the owner or, after the reforms, as a majority shareholder. A lot of questions were raised at different quarters about the mode of selection, the caliber of selected personnel, the tenure of their appointment and the standard of accountability applicable to the executives appointed.

As early as 1991, the Narasimham Committee-I had opined that the appointment of CMDs should be based on the recommendation of a "group of eminent persons who could be invited by the governor of the Reserve Bank" for this purpose. But it had left the issue of transparency in selection unaddressed.

The Narasimham Committee-II recommended that the CEO of a PSB should have a tenure of five years. A similar term was recommended for the executive directors[11]. The RBI in its Action Taken Report confirmed that the recommendation was implemented. The later evidence, however, showed that the CEOs continued to have shorter terms, sometimes even for one year or 13 months contrary to the confirmation by the regulator!

There were several cases of questionable selections made by the government. That a couple of chairmen of PSBs were criminally prosecuted for misdemeanors, dismissed for misconduct or asked to go on leave during the reforms era provokes the questions on the selection process itself.[12]

A corollary of this state of affairs was the inability of the government to seek accountability from the appointees for failure to perform or for misconduct. As appointments were linked to proximity to political masters, the accountability for performance was also deflected. Non-performing executive director of one PSB or one against whom there would be serious allegations of corrupt practices could be elevated as CEO of another bank. When there was poor performance, the CEO was never made answerable; he would comfortably demit his office on superannuation. Worse still was the virtually absent accountability for patently colourable exercise of powers causing losses to the bank. The instances of dismissal, compulsory leave or prosecution were triggered by public outcry made through the media or people's representatives. Such absence of prompt action had telling effect on the health of PSBs in the years to come as evidenced by the unabated growth of loss making advances granted at the behest of influential persons in the industry and political patrons.

To an extent there was a conflict of interest in the role of government as owner and as guardian of the public interest. As owner it appointed its officials as directors on the boards of PSBs. How did they discharge their role as members of the boards? If they had done a good job, the failure of New Bank of India and the successive scams would not have occurred or could have been preempted; the rapid decline in the health of three banks threatening their continued existence could have been diagnosed in time.

The ownership-related problems were summed up succinctly by Bhide, M. G. and others in 2001 itself while evaluating the reform process in the following words[13]:

> Multiple layering of 'principal-agent' chains in the case of PSBs by virtue of Government holding creates unauthorised power centres outside the chain of command. The government ownership also creates problems for the RBI as regulator/supervisor of the financial system, since it acts as a 'quasi-regulator'.

The government as owner had a decisive role in both appointment and fixing accountability on the selected officials. In discharging this critical role the successive governments did not inspire confidence about their conviction to bring about a qualitative change in the PSBs' top management teams.

### *Regulator related issues*

The Reserve Bank of India as the guardian and regulator of the country's financial system had evolved a new regulatory culture during the reform era. It had received, on many occasions, accolades from different quarters for its sterling performance. Simultaneously there were failures attracting critical observations from learned bankers and analysts.

In understanding the regulator related issues, it is appropriate to take a look at the relationship of RBI with the banks. It has four dimensional role in dealing with the PSBs. *One*, a nominee of the RBI is appointed by the government to a bank's board as director. Depending on the size of the bank the status of the RBI nominee would vary. For instance, during the Harshad Mehta scandal, R. Janakiraman, a deputy governor of RBI was on the board of SBI and in a small bank like Corporation Bank an official of the regional office of RBI was the nominee.

*The second* role is in its capacity as regulator. In this role RBI would regularly inspect the banks in the normal course. When circumstances warranted RBI could conduct special audits. The reports of inspection would always be discussed with the top executives of the bank concerned and they would be placed before the Audit Committee of the Board (ACB) for consideration and follow up action.

*The third* role of RBI is that of an advisor under which it can initiate institutional mechanism to monitor the working, give policy directions to the banks collectively and advices separately to individual banks. During the reforms era there were a number of measures initiated by the RBI in this role.

For example, in 1994, in the wake of Narasimham Committee-I's recommendations, the RBI set up the Board for Financial Supervision (BFS). It was mandated to supervise banks, financial institutions and non-banking financial companies. It was to be a Committee of the Central Board of the RBI with Governor as the Chairman[14]. During 2002-03, the RBI adopted the system of Macro-Prudential Indicators (MPI) for studying the macro level data and suggesting measures in the desired direction. At the individual bank level, the system of Prompt Corrective Action (PCA) was also introduced simultaneously to identify signs of financial vulnerability and initiate pre-emptive actions[15].

Two instances, out of many, of the RBI giving advice and directions to the banks could also be cited here to highlight the advisory role. In its *Report on Trend and Progress of Banking in India for 2001*, the RBI elaborated on the new Basel Accord on Capital Adequacy brought out by BIS in 2000 and indicated the time schedule for its adoption by Indian banks (by 2005). In the same Report, the regulator spelt out the purpose and modalities of Corporate Debt Restructuring to enable the banks to reduce the incidence of overdue of corporate debts. RBI regularly invoked this power to guide the banks on important operational issues like risk management, asset liability management, corporate governance and control over frauds. Banks were required to heed the advice of RBI.

*The last* mode of its supervision over the banks is through the complex set of periodic returns and statements on diverse issues the banks would be required to send to the RBI as the monitoring authority. In fact much of the management information system in operation in the banks was and is intended to provide vital information to the apex bank on the working of every bank.

Having such clearly spelt out responsibility and role, did RBI live up to the task entrusted to it? The views are mixed, some adulatory, others critical.

In the early years of reforms when the securities scandal rocked the country, the role of the Governor came in for praise for sensing the brewing irregularities. He was credited for diagnosing it and setting the investigation through Janakiraman Committee in motion. The RBI was able to establish the link between the various chains in the fraudulent securities transactions. It was felt that but for the intervention of the then Governor, the fraud would have been hushed up between Harshad Mehta and SBI[16].

The contrary perception also deserves to be recalled. The industry witnessed successive scams like Harshad

Mehta, CRB Capital Markets and Pay Order scams; New Bank of India failed in 1993; Global Trust Bank had to be bailed out by compulsory merger with Oriental Bank of Commerce. How could all these have taken place if the RBI had discharged its role as regulator effectively? While scams could have taken place by suborning the system, did RBI as licensing authority issue banking licences to persons without adequate background check? The conduct of Ramesh Gelli, the promoter-cum-CEO of GTB and of Chain Roop Bhansali, the promoter of CRB Capital Markets deserved more objective scrutiny by the regulator before issuing licences[17].

Both the Securities scam and Pay Order scam revealed the deficiencies in the regulatory system; the JPC on the latter scam was of the view that the regulatory agencies had not been watchful.[18]

There was another issue related to RBI's reluctance to promote transparency in releasing the list of loan defaulters particularly those belonging to the corporate sector. In fact, after the Task Force appointed by CII recommended the liquidation of UCO Bank, United Bank of India and Indian Bank, the transparency issue came to public scrutiny. The national level employees' unions reacting to the suggestion of the CII Task Force pointed out that many of the large loan defaulters causing losses to the weak banks were members of CII and called upon RBI to publish their names.[19]

In handling the problem of the sinking GTB, the RBI's response was also subjected to criticism. A leading national daily had pointed out that the Bank was in trouble was known for three years, but the regulator had 'frowned' upon the suggestions to set the house in order.[20] During the second half of the 1990s there was a serious financial crisis in the East Asian countries affecting the economies of the so-called 'Asian Tigers'. India was insulated from its adverse impact. But the lessons were worth imbibing to pre-empt a similar set back in India. Indian financial sector too needed an efficient regulatory and supervisory mechanism[21].

It could thus be seen that the functioning of the RBI during the first decade of financial sector reforms left much to be desired. While its limitation was understandable, the recurrence of scams, the inability to act promptly on definite signals and the reluctance to stand up for its autonomy as guardian of the financial sector did not strengthen RBI's image. Apparently there was greater emphasis on the form rather than the substance of regulation and supervision. The cost of such failure was heavy.

### *Conclusion*

The period from 1991 to 2004 was one of achievements and failures. As the developments of the second decade of this century corroborated, the reforms were yet to address the inherent weaknesses of the PSBs. The PSBs, the regulator and the government were still away from evolving a robust and healthy financial system which could self-regulate in the face of unforeseen challenges.

With all these shortcomings, both the policy-makers and the monitoring authority deserve praise for the serious attempt to put the financial system into a new trajectory of sustainable growth. Another creditworthy achievement was through conscious strategy Indian banks could tread their own path of banking which would continue to meet the community's needs in a large measure.

## References

1. *Officers' Voice*, Edit., August, 2000 *The loan portfolio of banks*
2. S.Venkitaramanan, (1996): *Bankers and their dilemma, Times of India,* August 25, 1996.
3. *The Gold And Pay Order Scams - Business Sans Values, Officers' Voice.*
4. *Governance in Banks: Cleaning the Augean Stables, Economic and Political Weekly,* April 20, 2002.

5. S. Venkitaramanan *The Telegraph*, Kolkata *May 31, 1999:The cure for the Sick.*
6. RBI Annual Report 2002-03 (p. 163) *Current Issues in Corporate Governance.*
7. NC-II, Chapter IV, para 4.21 – 4.23.
8. *Officers' Voice*, Edit., August 2000 *The loan portfolio of banks.*
9. S.Venkitaramanan (1996): *ibid.*
10. *Corporate governance principles in banks: Need for a new approach*: Paper presented by T.R. Bhat, President, CBOO to BECON 2002 held in Bangalore on 27th and 29th December.
11. NC-II, Chapter IV, para.4.29 – 4.30.
12. See examples given in Chaps 7, 18 and 19.
13. M.G. Bhide, A.Prasad and Saibal Ghosh: Stanford University Working Paper No. 103, June 2001: Emerging Challenges in Indian Banking.
14. Reserve Bank of India 2000, Communication numbered NCII-CC and dated 27 November.
15. RBI Annual Report 2002-03 (p. 163): Box X.6 p. 169.
16. Securities Scam: The Systemic Origins, A Special Correspondent, *Economic and Political Weekly*, September 5, 1992.
17. Arindam Mukherjee and Shekhar Ghosh, *The Outlook*- The Magazine p. 11 June 1997.

    -The CRB Scam The Anatomy of a Fraud
18. D N Ghosh: *Economic and Political Weekly,* May 17, 2003 p. 1916 Market Scandals and Regulatory Governance.
19. Frontline: *January 8, 2000: A controversial report V. Sridhar.*
20. *The Hindu*, Editorial: Jul 27, 2004: The crisis of Confidence.
21. M.G. Bhide and others, Stanford University Working Paper No. 103, June 2001: Emerging Challenges in Indian Banking.

# SECTION - III

# Further reforms (2004-2014)

# Chapter - 11

# 2004 and Beyond

## The changing political scenario

The period from 1991 to 2004 witnessed wide ranging changes in the banking scenario of the country in furtherance of the declared policy of the government. The period saw several governments headed by parties of different ideological dispensation. The reforms started when a government led by Congress Party was in power at the centre with P.V. Narasimha Rao as Prime Minister and Manmohan Singh as Finance Minister. Although it was a minority government the reforms initiated by it continued unabated till the end of its term in 1996. The next two years saw emergence of coalition governments headed by three prime ministers, A.B.Vajpayee of the Bharatiya Janta Party (BJP) and H.D. Deve Gowda and I.K. Gujral of Janatha Dal, all of which had short tenures. In 1998, a new coalition government of National Democratic Alliance led by A.B. Vajpayee of BJP came to power which ruled for 13 months. In 1999, after fresh general elections, a stable government headed by Vajpayee himself assumed office; it lasted till 2004. The changes in the government, however, did not affect the process and the pace of reforms as documented earlier. This could be because of the apparent consensus among the ruling establishments about the compulsions of the changes taking place the world over and the belief that India could not remain insulated from the influence.

In fact, the Narasimham Committee-II (Committee on Banking Sector Reforms) and the M.S.Verma Committee on Weak Banks were set up during this period of non-Congress governments and the follow up on the recommendations was carried out by these governments notwithstanding their divergent political background.

In 2004, the Congress Party leading a coalition government came back to power. The person known as the architect of the first phase of economic reforms as Finance Minister between 1991 and 1996, Manmohan Singh headed the new government as Prime Minister signalling the continuation of the process of reforms. The reforms in the financial sector had already continued beyond 1996 till 2004. There was no reason, at least from the official side, to relook at the reforms.

## The vision of the bankers 2010

In early 2004, the Indian Banks' Association (IBA), the national level bankers' body brought out a document titled *Banking Industry: Vision* 2010[1]. It was a wish list of what the industry should strive to achieve by 2010 in the short turn. After reviewing the progress achieved by the Indian banking sector during the period 1992-2003, the document envisioned the industry's role in enabling the country to reach the *'India Vision:2020'* unveiled earlier by the Planning Commission, Government of India. As 2020 was a long way, the IBA team gave a shorter vision for banks to be realised 10 years ahead of *India: 2020*. It enlisted the challenges ahead and suggested certain action points. A few of them are quoted below:

1. Banks will have to adopt global standards in capital adequacy, income recognition and provisioning norms.
2. Risk management set-up in banks will need to be strengthened.

3. Regulatory set-up will have to be strengthened in line with the requirements of a market-led integrated financial system.
4. Banks will have to adopt best global practices, systems and procedures.
5. The skills of bank staff should be upgraded continuously through training.
6. Banks will have to set up Research and Market Intelligence units within the organisation, so as to remain innovative, to ensure customer satisfaction and to keep abreast of market developments.

As representative body of the banks in India, IBA was familiar with the ground realities and the practical course of action to consolidate the gains made till then.

## The focus of reforms

During the first phase of reforms, as elaborated earlier, the banking sector was opened up for competition, the government ownership in public sector banks was progressively reduced, the interest rates were freed from controls, the cash reserve and statutory liquidity ratios were brought down, greater autonomy was given to the bank boards in the matter of branch opening; accounting standards and classification of assets were changed, better disclosure norms were introduced and emphasis was laid on building up capital. As pointed out by earlier studies and reports, public sector banks still had many issues to be addressed if the financial system were to meet the requirements of the agenda of economic liberalisation pursued further by the new government. These issues related to capital adequacy, performance efficiency, competitive capability and soundness. The principal attention of both the government and the RBI during the next six years was focused on these issues. Simultaneously, on the basis of the experience of the preceding years, the regulator's role was further streamlined so as to address periodic vulnerabilities.

## Progression from Basel I to II to III

During the first phase of reforms as recommended by Narasimham Committee-I, Indian banks were mandated to move towards- what till then was unheard of- the capital adequacy standards suggested by the Basel Committee. By 1999, the banks were moving towards a level of nine per cent Capital Adequacy Ratio (CAR) prescribed in the early years of reforms. The Narasimham Committee- II (1999) desired the CAR, which was by then around eight per cent, to be increased to ten per cent. The RBI, however, preferred to peg it at nine per cent from March 2000. According to RBI's own report, by March 2004, most PSBs attained a CAR level of 13.20 per cent, well over the level of nine per cent prescribed by the regulator. It ranged between 9.48 for Dena Bank and 20.12 for Corporation Bank.

By the end of the first phase of reforms, the Basel Committee released, in 2004, a new framework of capital adequacy. Commonly known as 'Basel II' the framework had, what the Committee called, three pillars as under[2]:

I. Minimum capital requirements, which sought to develop and expand the standardised rules set out in the 1988 Accord;
II. Supervisory review of an institution's capital adequacy and internal assessment process; and
III. Effective use of disclosure as a lever to strengthen market discipline and encourage sound banking practices.

During 2007-08, there was a serious financial crisis in the U.S. consequent upon the reckless lending by US banks for mortgages of poor quality. Federal government had to intervene through bailout packages at the cost of the exchequer. Called the 'Sub-prime crisis', it did not affect Indian financial sector[3]. In September 2008, Lehman Brothers, one of the oldest and biggest financial institutions collapsed sending shock waves around the globe. These developments brought into focus the inadequacy of the Basel II. Too much leverage and inadequate liquidity buffers on the one hand and poor governance and risk management standards on the other hand, had to be addressed.

The existing capital and risk assessment standards had to be revisited. As a sequel to the exercise, a new set of proposals was firmed up and adopted in December 2010. Known as Basel III, the proposals covered liquidity risk, risk measurement, standards and monitoring and a regulatory framework for creating more resilient banks and banking systems in the world.

Committed as the government was to consolidate the gains made during the period 1992-2004, it mandated the regulator to continuously address the issue of capital standards and gradual transition towards Basel II during the first decade of this century.

## The Committee on Fuller Capital Account Convertibility 2006

In 2006, the Committee on Fuller Capital Account Convertibility headed by S.S.Tarapore submitted a road map for capital account convertibility of Indian rupee. Among other recommendations the committee suggested a series of measures relating to the banking sector with a view to facilitating convertibility. These included enactment of a comprehensive single law covering banks, registration of banks under Companies Act, reduction of government holding below 51 per cent and consolidation of banks. The banks were to be governed by market forces.

## Independent Commission on Banking and Financial Policy 2006

In late 2006 the Independent Commission on Banking and Financial Policy (ICBP) headed by S.P. Shukla came out with a report more in the nature of a critique of the gamut of reforms from 1992 along with an alternative banking policy. It had observed that the reforms had enhanced the fragility of the financial institutions in the following words:

> One of the consequences of financial and banking reforms is that the structural change it has brought has substantially increased fragility. The processes of liberalisation fundamentally alter the terrain of operation of the banks. One visible impact is the shift in the focus of bank activities away from facilitating commodity production and investment to lubricating trade and promoting personal consumption. There are changes also in the area of operation in the banks, with banking entities not only creating or linking up with insurance companies, say, but also entering into other "sensitive" markets like the stock and real estate markets.

While giving a blueprint for an alternative banking policy it said:

> The analysis of outcomes of the liberalisation strategy and the dangers involved in adopting it in the banking sector, suggest that what is necessary is an alternative banking policy tied in the final analysis to an alternative strategy of development. *While the long-term objective of such an alternative would be to raise the rate of growth and make it more broad-based, equitable and inclusive, the immediate concern should be to restore social banking as one of the means to deal with the agrarian crisis and acute agrarian distress facing the country and the farming community* (emphasis added).

The panel advocated restoration of social banking to make the economic growth more equitable and inclusive. The need for financial inclusion as a strategy for growth was underscored by the panel.

## The Committee on Financial Sector Reforms 2008

In 2008, a new committee on financial sector reforms under the chairmanship of Raghuram G. Rajan (CFSR) was set up to take stock and suggest the way forward for the Indian banking sector. (Rajan later became the Governor of RBI in 2013). Unlike the two Narasimham Committees, the CFSR focused on financial stability and on protecting the economy from the kind of turbulence experienced by the Asian countries in 1990s and by the western world during 2007-08. Improvement in the performance efficiency of banks and innovation were emphasised upon. The CFSR advocated more effective regulatory regime to ensure better performance by the banks.

## The measures taken by RBI

RBI's strategy for reforming the banks further was two-fold. One was to promote effective internal systems to enhance the efficiency of operations. The other was through systematic monitoring by RBI as the regulator. In fact after the Narasimham Committee II, it had started laying greater emphasis on regulation through series of guidelines to the banks.

The Board for Financial Supervision (BFS) set up in the early years of reforms (1994) with the Governor as the chairman had the responsibility to undertake supervision over the working of banks. More structured inspection, off-site surveillance, better corporate governance and internal controls were the strategies adopted by the BFS. Through the acronym CAMELS specific areas deserving consideration were identified for focused attention. Capital adequacy, Asset quality, Management, Earnings, Liquidity and Systems became the key parameters for assessment of performance.[4]

As a follow up to the recommendations of NC-II the RBI in 1998 had taken a few specific measures to bring about qualitative changes in the banks' approach to handling their loan portfolio. The banks were advised against the tendency to resorting to 'ever-greening' the loans so as to show them as performing assets. Ever-greening involved granting fresh loans to the delinquent borrower to enable him to settle the interest outstanding so that the loan would not be classified as NPA. RBI mandated the banks to follow the prudential norms on asset classification. Banks were advised to bring out operational manuals for adherence by the field staff and also to set up independent loan review mechanism. The RBI urged the banks to enhance the quality of corporate governance in banks.

The concept of assessing the soundness of banks through a structured set of Macro-Prudential Indicators (MPI) was developed and put into operation around 2003. The RBI said in its Annual Report 2002-03 (p. 169):

> The ability to monitor financial sector soundness presupposes the existence of valid indicators of the health and stability of financial systems. These macro-prudential indicators (MPIs) matter for several reasons. They allow assessments to be based on objective measures of financial soundness. Publicly available MPIs enhance disclosure of key financial information to the markets. Moreover, MPIs adhering to internationally agreed standards facilitate monitoring of the financial system at the global level, especially in view of the magnitude and mobility of international capital, and the risk of contagion of financial crises. MPIs, in essence, comprise both aggregated micro-prudential indicators of the health of individual financial institutions and macroeconomic variables associated with financial system soundness. Financial crises often occur when both types of indicators point to vulnerabilities.

With a view to simplifying the legal recourse for recovery of bad loans, the government enacted in 2002 the Securitisation and Reconstruction of Financial Assets and Enforcement of Security Interest (SARFAESI) Act. It would empower the lenders to enforce the securities charged for the bank loan without the interference of the courts or tribunals.

## Corporate Debt Restructuring

Bank lending to large corporate borrowers was emerging as a major channel of deployment of credit. But when due to factors beyond the control of the borrowing companies if they were not able to honour the credit repayment schedule the loan would run the risk of being treated as NPA under the new classification norms. Security enforcement against the borrower under the prevailing laws would also cause difficulties in sustaining its activities. To help both the banks and the corporate borrowers a scheme called Corporate Debt Restructuring (CDR) was introduced in August 2001. CDR was applicable to viable units and the loans outstanding in their accounts could be restructured with new terms of repayment. It was further revised after a committee headed by an RBI deputy governor Vepa Kamesham submitted its recommendation during 2002-03. CDR became a key strategy to contain the NPA; but more importantly it was intended to help the borrowing units to tide over their short-term difficulties. During the early years of this millennium this mechanism was used frequently by the banking industry initially with good intentions but later to help even wilful defaulters[5].

Through such measures, the RBI was able to promote self-sustaining internal systems of control, monitoring and corrective intervention. This in turn contributed to better efficiency and productivity in the PSBs.

The measures were further pursued during the second phase of reforms. The next chapter will elaborate these measures.

## References

1. Indian Banks' Association: *IBA Bulletin,* January, 2004.
2. Bank for International Settlements, Basel Committee on Banking Supervision : A brief history of the Basel Committee, October 2015.
3. For details see chap.14 on Global Financial Crisis.

4. M.G. Bhide, A. Prasad and Saibal Ghosh: Emerging Challenges in Indian Banking, Stanford University Working Paper No. 103, June 2001.
5. During the tenure (2013-16) of Raghuram Rajan as Governor, the issue was given a fresh look with serious consequences to the banks as explained in chaps.16 and 17.

# Chapter - 12

# Sustaining the Momentum

As the changing political dispensations were committed to sustain the financial sector reforms and as advised by different official committees, both the government and Reserve Bank of India (RBI) continued their emphasis on making the banks stronger, healthier and more efficient. In realising these goals five thrust areas were given the main attention. These areas were:

1. Capital adequacy-Basel II and beyond
2. Risk based supervision
3. Higher disclosure norms
4. Asset classification and provisioning
5. Corporate governance.

The process of reforms during the preceding years did lay considerable stress on these issues. The new grounds already broken in the banking sector had to be sustained with greater vigour. Logically, therefore, the emphasis now was on qualitative reforms to enhance stability of and insulate the banks from external shocks.

## Capital adequacy-Basel II and beyond

As mentioned in an earlier chapter, Indian banks had substantially improved their capital base during the first phase of reforms and moved in the direction of achieving the capital adequacy ratio prescribed under Basel I norms. By March 2005, banks were already compliant with these requirements[1].

In 2005, the new capital accord known as Basel II was adopted. Basel II attempts to link the risks in the different operations of a bank with its capital requirements; it also takes into account the modern risk management techniques. These norms are supported by what the BIS calls the 'Three Pillars'. A little more elaboration on these pillars is critical in understanding the logic of RBI's actions during the II phase of reforms. A simplified explanation as provided by a former Deputy Governor of RBI throws better light on these concepts[2].

> The Pillar 1 stipulates the minimum capital ratio and requires allocation of regulatory capital not only for *credit risk* and *market risk* but additionally, for *operational risk* as well, which was not covered in the previous Accord. The Pillar 1...provides a menu of approaches, from the simplified to the advanced ones, for determining the capital charge for each of the three categories of risks. The credit risk mitigants used by the banks have been specifically recognised to provide appropriate capital relief.
>
> The Pillar 2 of the framework deals with the '*Supervisory Review Process*' (SRP)... In fact, this is the element which makes the revised framework very comprehensive in its sweep by addressing the entire risk domain of the banks. It requires the banks to develop an Internal Capital Adequacy Assessment Process (ICAAP) which should encompass their whole risk universe – by addressing all those risks which are either not fully captured or not at all captured under the other two Pillars – and assign an appropriate amount of capital, internally, for all such risks, commensurate with their risk profile and control environment. Under the Supervisory Review, the supervisors would conduct a

detailed examination of the ICAAP of the banks, and if warranted, could prescribe a higher capital requirement, over and above the minimum capital ratio envisaged in Pillar 1.

The Pillar 3 of the framework, *Market Discipline*, focuses on the effective public disclosures to be made by the banks, and is a critical complement to the other two Pillars. It recognises the fact that apart from the regulators, the banks are also monitored by the markets and that the discipline exerted by the markets can be as powerful as the sanctions imposed by the regulator. It is premised on the basic principle that the markets would be quite responsive to the disclosures made and the banks would be duly rewarded or penalised, in tune with the nature of disclosures, by the market forces.

The minimum level of capital required under Basel II continued to be nine per cent. But the new requirements, linked to different risks the banks were exposed to, demanded greater ability to manage them; this in turn would enhance their ability to adopt international standards of risk management. The new standards were required initially to be attained by March 2007 and later put off to March 2009. In addition to the credit and market risks, banks were required to provide capital for operational risks as well. In other words, capital required would be aligned with the risks the banks would be exposed to in undertaking their business. This requirement, in turn, would encourage stronger risk-management practices in banks. The core issue shifted from capital adequacy to capital efficiency so as to make the banks stronger and more stable. Indian banks were mandated to progressively adopt the standards prescribed under Basel II.

In 2007-08, the financial crisis in the western economies and the collapse that year, of Lehman Brothers triggered a further study of the shortcomings of the extant norms. By 2010, after fresh rounds of discussions among the group of governors and heads of supervision, Basel III standards were evolved bringing in, leverage and liquidity issues as equally critical to strengthening the banks.

One would observe that from the quantitative parameters of capital adequacy based on risk weights given to different assets on the banks' portfolio adopted in the early years of reforms, efforts shifted to qualitative and issue based measures to enhance the financial soundness of banks during the second phase. This in turn was expected to contribute to the stability of the financial system.

## Risk based supervision

A corollary of the progressive changes in the Basel standards was the renewed but more focused emphasis on risk based supervision (RBS) in banks. RBI as the regulator desired the banks to link their capital to credit risk, market risk and now operational risk in conformity with Basel II. Through the institution of Board for Financial Supervision (BFS) set up in 1994, the RBI was able to put into operation the new supervisory regime.

The Basel Committee had listed seven kinds of risks coming under operational risks. They were: (i) internal fraud, (ii) external fraud, (iii) employment practices and workplace safety, (iv) clients, products and business practices, (v) damage to physical assets, (vi) business disruption and system failures and (vii) execution, delivery and process management. These risks were primarily associated with the normal operations of the banks. To address them, banks were required to strengthen their risk management techniques and enhance the skills.

The supervisory review in relation to risk assessment and capital requirements would, according to the Basel Committee, be based on four principles[3] :

(a) Banks should have a process for assessing their overall capital adequacy in relation to their risk profile and a strategy for maintaining their capital levels. The fundamental elements of this assessment include policies and procedures designed to ensure that the bank identifies, measures, and reports all material risks - a process that relates capital to the level of risk.

(b) Supervisors should review and evaluate banks' internal capital adequacy assessments and strategies, as well as their ability to monitor and ensure their compliance with regulatory capital ratios. Supervisors should take appropriate supervisory action if they are not satisfied with the result of this process. The supervisors should assess the degree to which internal targets and processes incorporate the full range of material risks faced by the bank.

(c) Supervisors should expect banks to operate above the minimum regulatory capital ratios and should have the ability to require banks to hold capital in excess of the minimum. Pillar I capital requirements will include a buffer for uncertainties surrounding the Pillar I regime that affect banks. Bank-specific uncertainties will be treated under Pillar II.

(d) Supervisors should seek to intervene at an early stage to prevent capital from falling below the minimum levels required to support the risk characteristics of a particular bank and should require rapid remedial action if capital is not maintained or restored.

These measures were intended to enhance the internal supervisory systems with complementary monitoring by the regulator.

As the risks of banks would vary, the system of risk based supervision (RBS) could be bank-specific. The regulator's words are instructive[4] :

> The RBS approach is based on the principle of differentiated supervision. Banks are differentiated on

the basis of their risk profiles and the risks posed by them to the stability of the financial system. Banks with high risk, and within the banks, critical areas with high risk, receive more supervisory attention. The RBS thus helps in allocating supervisory resources more efficiently and focusing supervisory attention according to the risk profile of each institution. Evaluation of risk management systems in banks is the essence of the RBS.

During the first decade of this millennium credit expansion was of a high order particularly in certain sectors like housing and real estate. The period saw rapid escalation in the prices of the assets related to these sectors. To address this kind of credit risk the measures had to be related to the specific context and counter the cyclical variation in asset prices. RBI Governor Y V Reddy elaborated on the kind of measures initiated by the central bank during this period[5]:

> In June 2005, the RBI advised banks to have a board mandated policy in respect of their real estate exposure covering exposure limits, collaterals to be considered, margins to be kept, sanctioning authority/level and sector to be financed. In view of the rapid increase in loans to the real estate sector raising concerns about asset quality and the potential systemic risks posed by such exposure, the risk weight on banks' exposure to commercial real estate was increased from 100 per cent to 125 per cent in July 2005 and further to 150 per cent in April 2006. The risk weights on housing loans extended by banks to individuals against mortgage of housing properties and investments in mortgage backed securities (MBS) of housing finance companies (HFCs), recognised and supervised by National Housing Bank (NHB) were increased from 50 per cent to 75 per cent in December 2004. However, on a review, banks were advised to reduce the risk weight in respect of exposures arising out of housing

loans up to Rs 30 lakh to individuals against the mortgage of residential housing properties from 75 per cent to 50 per cent, in view of the lower perception of risks in these exposures.

To a large extent these measures helped the banks to emerge stable and stronger. The transition to the Basel II framework was incremental making it smoother.

## Asset classification and provisioning

With a view to enhancing the quality of the loan assets, the existing norms for classification of assets into standard, sub-standard, doubtful and loss assets were made more rigorous effective from March 2005. For example, a sub-standard asset if it continued in that category beyond 12 months would now be degraded as doubtful asset whereas till then there was a longer duration of 18 months for such reclassification. This would necessitate higher provisioning. In respect of assets which continued to remain 'doubtful' beyond three years the provisioning was fixed at 100 per cent effective from April 2004. Another example was the new norm for classifying advances guaranteed by the state governments. Similar refinements in the classification of advances and provisioning norms were put through during the first decade of this millennium.

## Higher disclosure norms

Till the financial sector reforms began the banking industry was almost entirely dominated by the public sector banks with a small share of business being handled by a few small private banks and a few foreign banks. With the gradual opening up of the sector, more players entered the scene; government also progressively divested its shareholdings in PSBs as permitted by the amended Banking Companies (Acquisition & Transfer of Undertakings) Acts 1970/1980. Once the shares in the PSBs were open to the public and the banks' shares were listed in the stock exchanges these listed banks had to be governed by the minimum standards of disclosures as prescribed under the listing requirements. In pursuance of the Narasimham Committee-I's recommendations partially privatised PSBs and other banks had to adopt certain standards of disclosure. In 1991, the formats of the banks' balance sheets were changed to make way for greater transparency. Banks were also required to disclose their accounting policies along with the notes on accounts in their balance sheets and conform to the disclosure norms prescribed by the Institute of Chartered Accountants of India.

With the progress in reforms the standards of disclosure were further enhanced. The Basel II parameters had underlined the need for subjecting the banks to market discipline. This necessitated more detailed disclosures about the banks' operations. Accordingly, in addition to the 16 schedules attached to the balance sheets they were required to disclose information on several issues. Some of them are related to capital adequacy ratios, composition of Tier I and Tier II capital, share of NPAs, amount of write offs and provisioning for stressed assets, details of provisions and contingencies, details of debts restructured, exposure to sensitive sectors, depreciation on investments, asset-liability management with maturity pattern of advances, deposits and investments, details about the efficiency ratios and details of single/group borrower's limits and the cases of exceeding such limits.

As a sequel to this new discipline, the balance sheets of PSBs have since become more transparent with voluminous information critical to evaluating their performance being published for public scrutiny.

## Corporate governance

Financial institutions operate in a fiduciary capacity. There are multiple stakeholders whose interests have to be safeguarded by the institutions. Their operations are directed and monitored by the boards of directors at the top and carried out by different levels of management and the operating level staff. This necessitates that there are, adequate checks and balances, transparency and accountability. Corporate governance essentially is the framework which lays the guidelines for ensuring these requirements. When the PSBs were wholly owned by the Government of India, in principle they were accountable to the government. But given the political compulsions, banks as public corporations were seldom held accountable for failures or non-performance. With the onset of reforms came the need to subject the banks to the discipline of corporate governance. During the first decade of reforms the level of governance was far from satisfactory.

The series of scams in the financial sector, the continued losses of three banks threatening their existence, the criminal actions against some bank officials and the failures of the government owned New Bank of India and the privately owned new generation Global Trust Bank raised fundamental questions on the standards of governance in banks. In 2000, the RBI-appointed Advisory Group on Banking Supervision headed by M.S.Verma had found that accountability for non-performance at any level including that of the board was nearly absent and it would end up with efforts to fix accountability at the management level for loans and advances that go bad. The group also called for more transparency, a greater accountability and streamlined process of induction of directors.

Commenting on the issue, *Economic and Political Weekly* observed editorially as follows[6]:

> Corporate governance in Indian banks has suffered because the boards are really not in charge of governance. The problem starts with the manner in which the boards are constituted. In public sector banks there is political interference in the appointment of the chief executives and the other directors. Aspiring candidates invariably lobby influential industrial groups and/or politicians, opening the way for quid pro quo deals. Matters are made worse by the government's

detailed administrative control of the banks. In the private banks the promoter groups keep tight control of all important business decisions, bypassing the boards. Though RBI rules do not allow the main promoter group to nominate the chairman, the supposedly independent chairman is invariably obliged to fall in line with the group's wishes.

Poor corporate governance is reflected basically in ineffective risk management, poor quality lending and fudging of accounts. Managements' attempt to conceal the actual state of affairs through creative accounting could eventually lead even to systemic instability.

The Joint Parliamentary Committee on Stock Market Scam had underlined the need for effective corporate governance. The RBI appointed Consultative Group of Directors (CGD) of Banks and Financial Institutions headed by A.S. Ganguly on Corporate Governance in Banks recommended in 2002 a number of measures to make the supervisory roles of the boards more effective. The regulator documented the follow up action it had taken on the CGD in its report of 2002-03:

> These recommendations (of CGD) have been benchmarked against international best practices as enunciated by the Basel Committee on Banking Supervision. In June 2002, a list of actions to be undertaken by banks was indicated to banks. These included due diligence procedures for appointment of directors on the boards of private sector banks, and role and responsibilities of independent/nonexecutive directors.
>
> Other corporate governance measures to be taken by banks relate to strengthening of the risk management framework, review of connected lending and constitution of various committees in conformity with corporate governance standards. They are also required to develop mechanisms to ensure percolation of their strategic

objectives and corporate values throughout the organisation.

In fact, the Basel Committee had, in 1999, reiterated certain practices to be followed in the following words:

1. Establishing strategic objectives and a set of corporate values that are communicated throughout the bank.
2. Setting and enforcing clear lines of responsibility and accountability throughout the bank.
3. Ensuring that board members are qualified for their positions, have clear understanding of their role in governance and are not subject to undue influence from management or outside concerns.
4. Ensuring that there is appropriate oversight by senior management.
5. Effectively utilising the work conducted by internal and external auditors in recognition of important control function they provide.

In the background of all these, RBI called upon the banks to further improve their governance standards. Although it did not have the power to appoint the board-which was with the government with regard to PSBs-RBI gave periodic guidelines to them to enhance corporate governance in banks. The banks were required to publish reports in their annual reports with details about the background of directors, the meetings of boards and the sub-committees, disclosures, shareholding patterns and many other issues.

As compliance function is a critical area of corporate governance, in April 2007, RBI issued detailed guidelines to the banks for strengthening their compliance standards in conformity with the Basel Committee's paper on *'Compliance and the Compliance Function in Banks'*. Each bank was required to set up a separate Compliance department with a top level executive as Chief Compliance Officer reporting directly to the CEO.

Did these measures bring about qualitative changes in governance of PSBs? That question defies a simple answer as elaborated in a later chapter. It is, however, to the credit of RBI that it ensured incremental but sustained improvements in the performance efficiency of banks during the next couple of years.

## Autonomy package

In 2005, the government took a policy decision to give managerial autonomy to PSBs. Banks which fulfilled the following norms as on March 2004 were eligible for the autonomy:

(a) Earned net profits over the last three years,
(b) Capital adequacy ratio of nine per cent or more,
(c) Net NPAs of less than four per cent, and
(d) Minimum owned fund of Rs 300 crores.

The government professed that the bank boards would have the freedom and responsibility for deciding managerial issues with a clear demarcation of the roles of the owners, board of directors and the management team. The objective, claimed the government, was to ensure that the PSBs function on sound principles of corporate governance. It also declared that while exercising its ownership rights it would not transgress into the management functions.

Accordingly the government retained the power to appoint the Chairmen, Managing Directors, executive directors and non-official directors by adopting 'fit and proper' criteria in consultation with RBI. The bank boards were given the freedom to evolve business strategies, human resources policies, fixing accountability etc. This package was, an expansion of the earlier plan formulated by the government during the 1990's which contained the freedom to open and close branches.

## Legal reforms

The success of financial sector reform necessitated complementary reforms in the legislations applicable to the banks. The issues addressed since the beginning of the reforms could be grouped under the following heads:

(a) Establishment of new banks, dilution of government ownership in PSBs, composition of the boards and mergers of banks.
(b) The loan recovery process.
(c) The regulatory powers of RBI.
(d) Technology related legislation.
(e) Prevention of crimes through banking sector.

To facilitate the entry of new banks, the Banking Regulation Act, 1949 was amended during the early phase of reforms. To reduce the government ownership in PSBs, the Banking Companies (Acquisition & Transfer of Undertakings) Acts 1970/1980 were also amended. Through the amendments the government could divest its share holdings in PSBs to a level not less than 51 per cent of the total capital. With part ownership vested with the private shareholders the amended act provided for share holder directors to be elected at the general body meetings. The State Bank of India Act, 1955 and State Bank of India (Subsidiary Banks) Act 1959 were amended in 2007 for augmenting their capital. The banks came out with public issue of shares during this period. As a result by March 2004, the government holding in the share capital of PSBs including SBI group declined to varying levels as shown in the Table 1; out of 27 PSBs, four nationalised banks and three subsidiaries of SBI still continued as wholly owned by the Government of India:

**Table 1: Ownership Structure of Public Sector Banks as on March 2004 (in per cent)**

| | *Name of Bank* | *Share of government* | *Share of others* |
|---|---|---|---|
| 1. | Vijaya Bank | 53.9 | 46.1 |
| 2. | Corporation Bank | 57.2 | 42.8 |
| 3. | Union Bank of India | 60.9 | 39.2 |

*(Contd...)*

| | | | |
|---|---|---|---|
| 4. | Indian Overseas Bank | 61.2 | 38.8 |
| 5. | Andhra Bank | 62.5 | 37.5 |
| 6. | Oriental Bank of Commerce | 66.5 | 33.5 |
| 7. | Bank of Baroda | 66.8 | 33.2 |
| 8. | Bank of India | 69.5 | 30.5 |
| 9. | Dena Bank | 71.0 | 29.0 |
| 10. | Allahabad Bank | 71.2 | 28.8 |
| 11. | Canara Bank | 73.2 | 26.8 |
| 12. | Syndicate Bank | 73.5 | 26.5 |
| 13. | UCO Bank | 75.0 | 25.0 |
| 14. | Bank of Maharashtra | 76.8 | 23.2 |
| 15. | Punjab National Bank | 80.0 | 20.0 |
| 16. | *Central Bank of India* | 100.0 | - |
| 17. | *Indian Bank* | *100.0* | - |
| 18. | *Punjab & Sind Bank* | *100.0* | - |
| 19. | *United Bank of India* | *100.0* | - |
| 20. | State Bank of India | 59.7 | 40.3 |
| 21. | State Bank of Bikaner & Jaipur | 75.0 | 25.0 |
| 22. | State Bank of Travancore | 75.0 | 25.0 |
| 23. | State Bank of Mysore | 92.3 | 7.7 |
| 24. | State Bank of Indore | 98.1 | 2.0 |
| 25. | *State Bank of Hyderabad* | *100.0* | - |
| 26. | *State Bank of Patiala* | *100.0* | - |
| 27. | *State Bank of Saurashtra* | *100.0* | - |

Recovery of overdue loans had been a major problem for the banks till the reforms era. In 1993, the Recovery of Debts due to Banks and Financial Institutions Act was enacted to facilitate setting up of Debt Recovery Tribunals. The purpose was to expedite the recovery proceedings against the borrowers who had defaulted their repayments. The Act was further amended in 1999 to strengthen the efforts in realisation of overdues.

In 2002, the Securitisation and Reconstruction of Financial Assets and Enforcement of Security Interest (SARFAESI) Act was passed. The intent was to facilitate enforcement of banks' interests on the securities charged for the loans for realising the dues without the intervention of courts. Under the simplified procedure incorporated under the Act authorised officials of the banks could enforce the securities and take steps to recover the dues.

To strengthen the regulatory powers of the RBI certain measures were taken during this period. The RBI Act was amended in 2006 for giving regulatory powers to the RBI over derivatives and money market instruments. Through an amendment in 2007 to the Banking Regulation Act, 1949 the lower limit to the Statutory Liquidity Ratio was removed but wider powers to regulate the liquidity in the financial sector were given to the RBI.

By an amendment in 2002 to the Negotiable Instruments Act 1881 the definition of 'cheque' was expanded to include electronic cheque and cheque truncation. The Government Securities Act, 2006 was enacted to consolidate and amend the laws relating to the government securities and their management by RBI. The Act made computerised information as admissible evidence.

As money laundering became an issue of international concern and as a follow-up to a 1998 resolution of the United Nations General Assembly, the Prevention of Money-Laundering Act was passed in 2002. It contained specific mandate to the banks to keep track of the movement of unaccounted money through banking channels.

The process of legal reforms in banking was an ongoing process with further changes in the relevant laws applicable to banking sector. In 2013, the Financial Sector Legislative Reforms Commission (Chairman: Shri B.N. Srikrishna) had proposed a comprehensive Indian Financial Code to replace a major part of the existing legislation related to the financial sector.

## Frauds in Banks

A financial institution is vulnerable to frauds. Banks' credit portfolio was more prone to frauds. In bill finance and cheque discounting, hypothecation of assets, creation of mortgage on property offered as security for housing loan, discounting and credit and debit cards fraudulent transactions could be more common. According to an RBI report during 2005-06, commercial banks had reported 13,914 cases of frauds involving a sum of Rs 1,381 crores.

The Basel Committee had identified internal and external frauds as risks coming under operational risks. As part of risk-based supervision banks are required to take appropriate safeguards to reduce the incidence of frauds. In 1999, a special chapter on vigilance management in PSBs was brought into force which would govern the authority, method and acts that would come under vigilance scrutiny, the power of the Vigilance Department of the Bank and the procedure that should be followed in handling cases with vigilance angle. In 2004, RBI set up a separate Fraud Monitoring Cell attached to the Department of Banking Supervision of the RBI. Banks were mandated to take preventive measures through better credit appraisal, timely follow up after sanction of loans, and through internal checks and controls.

As a preventive measure and as a source of early detection of frauds involving higher level officials, the government introduced, in May 2004, a scheme called Public Interest Disclosures & Protection of Informer. Known as whistle blowers' protection policy in the common parlance, this action was triggered by the Supreme Court advice in the case of the murder of Satyendra Dubey, a whistle-blower of Bihar. Under the scheme, CVC could receive complaints in the nature of whistle blowing from the employees about suspected misdemeanors of the senior officials of the PSBs. On receipt of the complaint in the form prescribed by the CVC it would initiate its own investigation safeguarding the identity of the complainant-whistle blower and take suitable action.

## Attempts to restructure PSBs

The Narasimham Committee-II had recommended restructuring of PSBs through mergers and consolidation.

The suggestion was to build a three-tier structure with 2-3 mega banks of international character, 8-10 national banks and a number of local banks. It was on the premise that size was an important determinant of a bank's strength. There were mixed reactions to this proposal. The government was for building size so as to enable the Indian banks to face international players; however, it did not proceed with the idea of merger of PSBs. With the existing sizes, most of them registered sustained growth with better parameters of efficiency during the period from 2004 to 2010 indicating that performance is not linked to size.

In the private sector, where new banks came into existence post-1991, there were mergers and takeovers. There were reverse mergers too: the private sector development financial institution (DFI), ICICI Ltd, set up in 1955, which in turn had promoted ICICI Bank, a new commercial bank in 1994, merged itself with the offspring in 2002 to create what was claimed to be a universal bank performing both development and commercial banking functions. In 2004, another premier DFI, Industrial Development Bank of India (IDBI) , established in 1964 by an Act of Parliament, was corporatised by repealing the act of incorporation and registering it as a government company under the Companies Act. Next year, its focus shifted to commercial banking and it was renamed as IDBI Bank Ltd; it continued to perform both the roles as DFI and commercial bank. Attempts were also made to convert the oldest DFI of the country, Industrial Finance Corporation of India (IFCI) established in 1948 into a bank or merge it with another PSB. These changes marked the extinction of specialised development financial institutions which had promoted industrial development during the 1950's and 1960's. These had far reaching implication on capital formation in the economy during the post-liberalisation era.

Among the new generation private banks there were voluntary mergers. For instance, Times Bank and Centurion Bank of Punjab had merged respectively in 2000 and 2008 with HDFC Bank Ltd. Some of the old generation banks either voluntarily or by force merged with new generation banks and PSBs. For instance, in 2001 Bank of Madura Ltd merged with ICICI Bank; in 2003, Nedungadi Bank Ltd merged with Punjab National Bank. Between 1994 and 2008 about 20 banks lost their identity through such mergers. Through this process and organic growth, ICICI Bank Ltd emerged as the largest bank in the private sector.

Among the PSBs, the first land mark merger was that of two subsidiaries of SBI namely, State Bank of Saurashtra and State Bank of Indore with SBI itself in 2008 and 2009 respectively. Until 2016 there were no further mergers of PSBs.

While these measures were intended to sustain the process of reforms so as to make the PSBs robust and efficient, there were policy changes relating to lending, interest rates and the kind of services offered to the public. These will be deliberated in the next chapter.

## References

1. V.Leeladhar, 2007: *India's Preparedness for Basel II Implementation*- Special Address delivered at the Panel Discussion during "FICCI-IBA Conference on Global Banking: Paradigm Shift", held on September 13, 2007, Mumbai.
2. V. Leeladhar, 2007, *ibid.*
3. RBI, 2005, *Report on Trend & Progress of Banking in India* (RTPBI).
4. RBI, 2005, *ibid.*
5. Reddy, Y.V., 2008: *Global Financial Turbulence and Financial Sector in India: A Practitioner's Perspective* Address at the Meeting of the Task Force on Financial Markets Regulation organised by the Initiative for Policy Dialogue at Manchester, United Kingdom, on July 1, 2008.
6. *Economic and Political Weekly,* April 20, 2002: *Governance in Banks-Cleaning the Augean Stables.*

# Chapter - 13

# The Renewed Emphasis on Social Banking

During 2004 and 2010 the reforms addressed the issues primarily of efficiency and stability of the public sector banks (PSBs). In the operations, however, the early days of reforms had seen steady erosion of the share of lending under social banking. There were many geographical areas in different states still without banking facilities. There were criticisms of the failures of the banking sector in these areas. Consequent upon the demise of development banking, commercial banks were increasingly involved in funding industrial activity on a long-term basis exposing them to new kind of risks. With further strides in information technology, banks had to introduce more IT enabled services to meet the expectations of a new kind of customers conversant with technology. These developments triggered changes in the business strategies of the banks in general and PSBs in particular. The key issues in this new strategy were the following:

(a) Renewed emphasis on social banking through 'financial inclusion'.

(b) Lending to education and housing.

(c) Providing term finance to industry.

(d) Introduction of newer IT enabled services.

## The concept of 'financial inclusion'

A major after-effect of financial liberalisation was on social banking. Driven by the mandate to improve efficiency and profitability, the PSBs steadily shifted their priorities from being 'instruments that subserve national priorities and objectives' as contemplated in the 1969 Bank Nationalisation Act to activities that would maximise their income. The dangers of such a shift were echoed by many authorities, the latest being the Independent Commission on Banking & Financial Policy (ICBP). After a thorough analysis of the developments in the financial sector it recommended an alternative model of banking linked to a strategy of inclusive development. The panel had said in November, 2006:

> The analysis of outcomes of the liberalisation strategy and the dangers involved in adopting it in the banking sector, suggest that what is necessary is an alternative banking policy tied in the final analysis to an alternative strategy of development. While *the long-term objective of such an alternative would be to raise the rate of growth and make it more broad-based, equitable and inclusive*, the immediate concern should be to restore social banking as one of the means to deal with the agrarian crisis and acute agrarian distress facing the country and the farming community (emphasis added).

Although the panel was unofficial, its recommendation for restoration of social banking through the alternative strategy of inclusive banking gained currency during the period following the report. Several central bankers of the country echoed the need for financial inclusion in their discourses in different platforms.

In fact in 2004 itself a deputy governor had conceded that the direct advances to socially disadvantaged sectors like agriculture and small industry had declined[1].

While addressing the Annual Washington Conference in 2007 another deputy governor said this[2]:

> While banks are focusing on the methodologies of meeting the increasing demands placed on them, there are legitimate concerns with regard to the banking practices that tend to exclude rather than attract vast sections of population, in particular pensioners, self-employed and those employed in unorganised sector.

In its *Report on the Trend & Progress of Banking in India* for 2007, the RBI acknowledged the problem of exclusion especially in the rural areas. It said:

> Despite widespread expansion of the banking sector during the last three decades, a substantial proportion of the households, especially in rural areas, is at present outside the coverage of the formal banking system.

The data provided in the All India Debt and Investment Survey confirmed that the share of institutional agencies in the rural credit which had improved from 29.2 per cent in 1971 to 64 per cent in 1991 had declined to 57.1 per cent one decade after the financial sector reforms began. Correspondingly the non-institutional agencies led by the moneylenders stole a march over the institutions: their share which had progressively declined from 70.8 per cent in 1971 to 36 per cent in 1991 again went up to 42.9 per cent in 2002. The traditional moneylenders continued to dominate the scene as indicated in the accompanying Table 1. The agrarian crisis faced in major agriculture dominated states like Maharashtra, the undivided Andhra Pradesh, Karnataka and Tamil Nadu which witnessed thousands of farmers committing suicide unable to repay the usurious debts they had to borrow from moneylenders was an indictment on the failure of the institutional agencies to meet the financial needs of a large section of the society.

**Table 1: Breakup of institutional and non-institutional rural credit (Per cent)**

| | *1951* | *1961* | *1971* | *1981* | *1991* | *2002* |
|---|---|---|---|---|---|---|
| **Institutional Agencies** | **7.2** | **14.8** | **29.2** | **61.2** | **64.0** | **57.1** |
| Government | 3.3 | 5.3 | 6.7 | 4.0 | 5.7 | 2.3 |
| Co-op. Society/banks | 3.1 | 9.1 | 20.1 | 28.6 | 18.6 | 27.3 |
| Commercial banks incl. RRBs | 0.8 | 0.4 | 2.2 | 28.0 | 29.0 | 24.5 |
| Insurance | - | - | 0.1 | 0.3 | 0.5 | 0.3 |
| Provident Fund | - | - | 0.1 | 0.3 | 0.9 | 0.3 |
| Other institutional agencies* | - | - | - | - | 9.3 | 2.4 |
| Non-Institutional Agencies | 92.8 | 85.2 | 70.8 | 38.8 | 36.0 | 42.9 |
| Landlord | 1.5 | 0.9 | 8.6 | 4.0 | 4.0 | 1.0 |
| Agricultural Moneylender | 24.9 | 45.9 | 23.1 | 8.6 | 6.3 | 10.0 |
| Professional Moneylender | 44.8 | 14.9 | 13.8 | 8.3 | 9.4 | 19.6 |
| Traders and Commission Agents | 5.5 | 7.7 | 8.7 | 3.4 | 7.1 | 2.6 |
| Relatives and Friends | 14.2 | 6.8 | 13.8 | 9.0 | 6.7 | 7.1 |
| Others | 1.9 | 8.9 | 2.8 | 4.9 | 2.5 | 2.6 |
| **Total** | **100** | **100** | **100** | **100** | **100** | **100** |

* *includes financial corporation/institution, financial company and other institutional agencies. Note Percentage share of different credit agencies to the outstanding cash dues of the households as on 30th June. — denotes not available.*

*Source:* All India Debt and Investment Survey, Various Issues.

(Data reproduced from RBI's *Banking Structure in India*-Discussion Paper August 2013)

In 2008, the Committee on Financial Sector Reforms headed by Raghuram G Rajan (CFSR) observed in its draft report that banking services were not reaching the majority of Indians who continued to depend on the money lender.

It is pertinent to note that RBI openly admitted in 2008 that growth by itself does not enhance the living conditions of those who are at the bottom of the economic pyramid. The following observations of a deputy governor made in 2008 were very clear[3].

> ...there is growing realisation that the 'trickle down' effect of economic growth, while no doubt works, takes too long a time and hence there is a need to focus on inclusive growth. "Inclusive growth", is a little more

> than just the benefits of growth being distributed equitably and evenly; it is the participation of all sections and regions of society in the growth story and their reaping the benefits of growth.

The RBI Governor himself conceded that the data on the magnitude of exclusion was staggering[4]:

> Out of the 600,000 habitations in the country, only about 30,000 have a commercial bank branch. Just about 40 per cent of the population across the country have bank accounts, and this ratio is much lower in the north-east of the country. The proportion of people having any kind of life insurance cover is as low as 10 per cent and proportion having non-life insurance is an abysmally low at 0.6 per cent. People having debit cards comprise only 13 per cent and those having credit cards only a marginal 2 per cent.
>
> The National Sample Survey data reveals that, in 2003, out of the 89.3 million farmer households in the country, 51 per cent did not seek credit from either institutional or non-institutional sources of any kind.

In 2008 Dr C. Rangarajan Committee set up by the government on 'Financial Inclusion' had submitted its interim report. It had recommended setting up of two funds. One was Financial Inclusion Fund. It was to meet the cost of development and promotion of financial inclusion. The other was, Financial Inclusion Technology Fund which was to meet the cost of technology adoption. They were later set with a corpus of Rs 500 crore each shared by the government, RBI and NABARD and under the supervision of NABARD.

It was not that the RBI or the government as the owner of PSBs had ignored the marginalised sections. In fact as enumerated in an earlier occasion the post-nationalisation era witnessed a conscious attempt to promote inclusive banking. The measures included both obligatory targets to banks to lend to certain targeted beneficiaries and promoting institutional structures to establish linkages between the lending institutions and the borrowers. The lead bank schemes, integrated rural development programmes, setting up of rural development and agricultural branches of banks, linkage through self-help groups (SHG) and the institutions of regional rural banks (RRBs) promoted by the governments and with institutional backing by PSBs – all these in no small measure enhanced the availability of funds to the lower strata of the economy. What happened was that with the onset of reforms the priorities changed with serious fall out crying for immediate attention.

Responding to this perception, the regulator initiated a series of measures to promote financial inclusion. Financial inclusion according to the RBI meant 'delivery of banking services at an affordable cost to the vast sections of disadvantaged and low-income groups who tend to be excluded from the formal banking channel'. The idea was to connect people with the banks, rather than dispensing credit. It also necessitated sensitising bankers to the needs of the ordinary people of the country living on the margin.

To translate this plan into concrete action, the scheme of 'zero balance' or 'no-frills' accounts was introduced in 2006.[5] A pilot project for 100 per cent financial inclusion was launched by RBI to popularise the system. In every state and union territory one district was to be selected for 100 per cent financial inclusion. They were advised to provide no-frills accounts with simpler KYC (Know Your Customer) norms and issue general purpose credit cards. Under the credit cards, credit facility up to Rs 25,000 was to be provided. Over a period of time the project was to be extended to cover all districts. By 2007, the RBI said, all districts of Himachal Pradesh had achieved financial inclusion targets.

It was indeed a unique scheme to bring those who were excluded from the modern banking into the financial sector.

Around the same time the RBI permitted banks to appoint business correspondents (BCs). The BCs, with appropriate technology support were expected to make banking service accessible at lesser cost. They would be the new agents of banks' outreach, like banking outposts. The RBI encouraged the banks to take the help of non-governmental organisations (NGOs), SHGs and micro-finance institutions (MFIs) to act as intermediaries between the banks and the customers. The MFIs, according to RBI, had provided *access to finance to an entire sector of people left behind by the formal financial sector demonstrating that the low income proposals were bankable. It was their cost which ranged between 20 and 24 per cent that was a matter of concern although compared to the indigenous moneylender they were still cheaper.*[6] (emphasis added)

The RBI also desired the banks to adopt technology based solutions for intensifying financial inclusion with minimum cost. It said in its report for 2006-07 on the banking trends:

> The Reserve Bank has been encouraging banks to use technology-based solutions for increased financial inclusion. Credit delivery in rural areas has often been expensive for banks with large number of small loan accounts to be serviced. Information Technology (IT) enabled methods are being looked into as the best alternative for rural credit delivery that can increase outreach and reduce cost of delivery.

As late as 2011, the Finance Minister in his budget speech reiterated the resolve to strengthen the government's commitment to financial inclusion through the institution of business correspondents and technology upgradation. The government launched a financial inclusion campaign known as *Swabhiman* to reach out to the people through branchless banking. The Finance Ministry in a statement noted[7]:

> Inclusive growth as a strategy for economic development aims at making products and services, including

financial services, available to those who for various reasons stand excluded. Financial Inclusion is important as it provides an avenue to the poor for bringing their savings into the formal financial system, an avenue to remit money to their families in villages besides weaning them away from the clutches of the usurious money lenders. It is thus essential to extend banking services to the rural hinterland at the earliest in order to include these regions in India's growth story. The provision of banking and financial services to the rural hinterland would be an enabler for inclusive growth.

The focus area during the second phase of reforms was, thus making bank finance accessible to all with reduced cost, simpler procedure and trustworthy agents. This strategy of course correction was a conscious response to the well-founded criticism of the failure of reforms to reach all sections of the society.

Simultaneously, the guidelines related to the advances to priority sector were also modified to enhance the flow of credit to this sector. Steps were taken to strengthen the rural cooperatives and restructure the regional rural banks. The RBI advised the banks to simplify the processes and procedures governing the appraisal, sanction and disbursement of credits to agriculture and micro, small and medium enterprises.

## Educational loans

With the liberalisation of the economy and the consequent need to invest in human capital, professional education received tremendous importance. But at the level of higher education the government support was minimal and the aspiring students had to find their own means of financing their studies. As the amount involved was higher than that needed for conventional courses banks had a higher element of risk. The rate of interest would logically be higher and securities would otherwise be necessary for loans. The intervention both by the state and the regulator was necessary to make loans for education cheaper and hassle free.

Accordingly banks were called upon to extend cheap loans for pursuing higher studies without security with easy repayment schedule. The availability of bank finance with reasonable conditions provided considerable relief to the parents of lower income groups and helped the upward mobility of the student community.

## Loans for housing

The development of real estate sector and the increased involvement of financial institutions in extending finance to that sector coupled with the importance of housing in a developing economy necessitated liberalisation of the personal housing loan schemes of banks. The government through income tax rebates for interest and repayment of loans provided incentives to home loans particularly those with assured income. The terms of housing loans were also simplified with cheaper rates of interest, long repayment schedules and quicker processing and sanction of loans. Banks had benefits in terms of assured interest and repayment apart from little follow–up depending upon the kind of beneficiaries. If the real estate industry thrived during the post-reforms era, a major factor was the rapid expansion in the housing loan portfolio of the banks.

The spurt in housing loans created problems for the lenders in terms of delayed projects, cost escalation, slow repayment and greater risk of default. Although the banks could invoke the provisions of SARFAESI Act to initiate recovery proceedings in the event of chronic defaults, such acts particularly against the common man would trigger adverse publicity to the banks.

## Preference for term lending

With the merger of development finance institutions (DFIs) and emergence of commercial banks as 'universal banks', the banks were required to provide term finance to industry. Sectors like infrastructure (construction of roads, airports, ports and special economic zones), power generation, oil, steel, airlines and hospitality needed huge capital. Individual banks by themselves could not meet the volume of finance required by a borrower as it was huge running into thousands of crores; the exposure would have been too large. Through consortium of lenders the banks would provide the loans required to such projects which had long gestation period.

From the point of view of the banks, lending to giant corporations of industrial houses which were involved in the projects was simpler: the project appraisal, terms of sanction and follow-up would all be the primary responsibility of the consortium leader. The participating bank had only to take its share of commitment and release the funds as prescribed in the sanction letter.

In the background this development, the period witnessed huge spurt in term loans, both medium and long term. For instance between 2006 and 2009 the gross bank credit to small, medium and large scale industry jumped from Rs 5,50,444 crores to Rs 10,54,390 crores. The advances to the infrastructure sector more than doubled from Rs 1,12,853 to Rs 2,69,972 crores; those for basic metals and metal products from Rs 65,896 to Rs 1,28,763 crores, for construction nearly trebled from Rs 13,303 to Rs 38,505 crores and for cement and cement products from Rs 7,799 to Rs 19,220 crores.[8]

## IT enabled services

To meet the rising expectations of the customers and to face the competition more effectively banks under the direction of RBI evolved several services based on information technology like electronic funds transfers, more ATMs, credit and debit cards and internet banking facilities. Banks also started changing their IT platforms from stand alone system prevailing at the beginning of the millennium to core banking solution (CBS). Under CBS environment transactions in different branches could be integrated and bank accounts accessed anywhere and at any time. By 2008 around 67 per cent of the bank branches had migrated to CBS platform.

In 2005, RBI set up the Board for Regulation and Supervision of Payment and Settlement Systems (BPSS). As a committee of RBI's Central Board it was mandated to give policy direction in the area of payment and settlement systems. In 2004, real time gross transfer settlement (RTGS) was operationalised and with BPSS in place the transfer of large value amounts could be streamlined to protect the interest of the customers.

## Customer oriented facilities

With rapid expansion in business and kind of services offered by the banks it was natural that the grievances of customers would also grow. To address this in 1995 RBI had introduced the Banking Ombudsman Scheme (OBS). It was further revised in 2002 and again in 2006. Under the scheme customers who had grievances against their banks on the services could refer the complaint to the designated Ombudsman. It was a time bound and inexpensive mode of grievances redress available to the customers and monitored by RBI offices. To ensure fair treatment to customers, an Independent Banking Codes and Standards Board of India was also set up.

## The global financial crisis

While banking industry in India was trying to consolidate the gains made during the first phase of reforms, the financial sector in the world was in a major crisis. Indian banks largely remained unaffected by the turmoil and they demonstrated greater stability. Before analysing the performance of Indian banks it is appropriate to study the causes, nature and impact of the financial sector crisis. A question relevant is what was its impact on them. In the next chapter an attempt is made to throw some light into the financial crisis of 2007-08 experienced by major countries.

## References


1. Rakesh Mohan, 2004 : *Financial Sector Reforms in India: Policies and Performance Analysis,* RBI Bulletin, October 2004.
2. Vittaldas Leeladhar, 2007: *Indian Financial Sector Reforms,* Address to Annual Washington Conference 2007, RBI Bulletin, April 2007.
3. Usha Thorat, 2008, *Inclusive Growth - The Role of Banks in Emerging Economies,* RBI Bulletin, March 2008.
4. Duvvuri Subbarao, 2009, *Financial Inclusion: Challenges and Opportunities,* RBI Bulletin, January 2010.
5. In 2015, repacked with a new nomenclature as *Pradhan Mantri Jan Dhan Yojana*-PMJDY; PSBs were mandated to open a targeted number of accounts.
6. Duvvuri Subbarao, 2009. *ibid.*
7. Statement dated February 20, 2011 issued by the Ministry of Finance.
8. The problem of a sharp spurt in NPAs in next decade could be linked to this as will be seen in a later part of this book

# Chapter - 14

# The Global Financial Crisis of 2007-08 and its Impact on Indian Banking*

While the banks in India, particularly those in the public sector, were on the path of evolving themselves as efficient and stable purveyors of financial resources for the economic development during the second decade of reforms, their counterparts world over were heading towards serious turmoil. During 2007-2008, banks in the western world experienced their severest crisis in seventy years. How did it originate, what was its dimension and impact and the lessons learnt (or missed?) provide a fascinating drama in an otherwise drab evolution of the financial sector.

## The origin of the crisis

The immediate reason for the crisis was the housing loan bubble that burst starting from late 2007. Known as subprime loans, the housing loans granted to borrowers who were strictly not eligible to avail the loans had a major impact on the earnings of the lenders. When the property prices were rising continuously, further loans were given

---

* *This was originally published in* Officers' Voice, *in its issue dated February, 2009, under the caption* The Global Financial Crisis: What Went Wrong, Why And What Are The Lessons? *It has been refined here to provide greater clarity in the present situation.*

against the same property, sometimes for consumption also. Related to such loans were certain complex derivatives held out as "innovative products" created by the financial sector. It is not only commercial banks, which dealt with such loans and instruments; many insurance corporations and investment banks freely circulated them so as to maximise short-term earnings. When the crisis hit, every institution was at the receiving end.

## The instruments

What were these financial instruments created at that time?

Derivatives were in simple words, financial instruments deriving their value from the assets to which they were related. The assets might be mortgaged property, shares, bonds or commodities. They would help reduce risk.

Related to housing loans was the Collateralised Debt Obligation (CDO), which was issued by the lender on the basis of the mortgage, created in his favour. They were pools of loans bundled for investors. CDOs were rated by the rating agencies and sold in the market for a commission. They could also assume the name of Mortgage Based Securities (MBS). Another popular instrument was Credit Default Swap (CDS). It was a kind of guarantee an insurance company issued against the possible default of bonds including CDOs. With the help of credit rating agencies these instruments were rated.

These were the principal instruments extensively used in the US financial market during the years preceding the crisis. While they helped the players reap huge profits, hidden in them was a grave risk of loan default. When the sub-prime loan defaults began as a result of a steep fall in property prices, the CDOs started losing their value even if they were 'AAA' rated. When CDOs lost their value CDSs ceased to be of any value. The resulting hole was too big to be filled and it started destroying one institution after another. No wonder, therefore, that the famous investor,

Warren Buffet had said, "Derivatives are financial weapons of mass destruction." The magnitude of the destruction could be assessed from the fact that CDSs accounted for roughly $60 trillion worldwide.

## Why it happened

There are a number of factors that contributed to the crisis. Divergent views were expressed at different quarters. Broadly, the following reasons were behind the whole problem:

(a) The urge to earn profit by any means and poor internal risk management,

(b) The removal of the firewall between investment banking and commercial banking,

(c) The regulator's inability to foresee the risk in new, exotic products, and

(d) The policy-makers' belief that free enterprise is self-regulatory.

## Profits and risk management

Towards the end of the last century and the beginning of the current one, the financial sector attracted the best of the management graduates from the top ranking business schools of the world. What attracted them was the compensation package, which included huge bonus (generally to the top bosses). There was also movement from one institution to another. Firing was also common if the chief executive officer failed to deliver on a targeted earning. How were these profits earned?

American International Group (AIG) was the biggest insurer with assets over $1 trillion before the crisis. It had a reputation of a well-run insurer. But its investment division at one time contributed more than 25 per cent of its profits through CDS. This was, however, covered under its insurance business. As at June 2008 it had an exposure of $441 billion; out of this $58 billion was exposed to sub-prime securities.

Merrill Lynch was the most famous brokerage house not only of USA but in the World. Its performance in 2006 was said to be 'breathtaking with revenue and earnings soaring. Its decision to invest heavily in MBSs was paying off handsomely'. In its hunt for profits, it increased its exposure to complex and poorly regulated financial products linked to mortgages. Simultaneously, the risk management department loosened internal controls making the company vulnerable to the risk. At the end of the first half of 2008, it came to light that with record number of mortgage defaults Merrill Lynch was carrying $71 billion eroded mortgage based assets in its books. It was forced into a merger with Bank of America.

Citibank was for long considered the biggest bank in the world in terms of assets and world's smartest financial services group. Its urge to increase earnings made it go for high level of trading activity without proper risk management and supervision. It took greater trading risks to enhance its business. The CEO Vikram Pandit had said in an interview, "We got here by lending money, and putting money to work in the US real estate market, in a size that probably was larger than what we ought to have done on a diversification basis." But before long the bubble burst and as per the reports it suffered more than $65 billion in losses, provision for bad mortgages and future losses. It was reported that more than half this amount came from mortgage related securities.

Lehman Brothers Holdings was the fourth largest investment banker in USA. Established in 1850, it had only $30 billion in equity but as much as $639 billion in assets as of August 2008. Most of these were related to mortgages; a five per cent fall in the value of the assets would wipe out its equity. Its loss was to the tune of $13.8 billion and in September 2008 it filed for bankruptcy.

These were only examples. There were many others who merrily indulged in sub-prime lending and trading activity without risk assessment and actual supervision.

Further, with a view to increase the returns on equity the banks resorted to leveraging heavily *(Leverage ratio is total debt divided by equity; using borrowed funds would help raise the return to equity).* So long as the divisions generated fat revenue, the systems were not meant to be enforced. At one time or the other the lid was bound to come off with dire consequences. The same thing had happened with Barings Bank a few years ago whose trader Nick Leeson earned huge profit to the bank without questions being asked.

Adding to this problem was the absence of any regulatory oversight by the authorities believe as they did in an unregulated economy.

## Firewall between investment banking and commercial banking

A major contributory factor for the crisis was the removal of the traditional distinction between investment and commercial banking. During the Great Depression of the 1930's, the US government had enacted the famous Glass-Steagall Act, which paved the way for separation of commercial banking from investment banking. In the years preceding the Depression, banks indulged in all kinds of business ranging from pure banking to dealing with insurance and other financial products. There was a conflict of interest and, the regulatory oversight became light. The Glass-Steagall Act was a landmark legislation to build a firewall between investment banking and commercial banking.

During the last two decades of Twentieth Century the financial sector had expanded so rapidly that finance capital became the major player in the global financial market and it accounted for a staggering 40 per cent of corporate profits at one time. Banks, insurance companies, mutual funds and brokerage houses started dabbling in each other's business. The concept of universal banking steadily emerged. A universal bank was conceived as a financial super market where different financial products would be available. Term finance, working capital finance, insurance, mutual funds, derivatives, bonds etc. would be sold by a single agency. While such diversification would help spread the risk associated with the economic fluctuations, concentrating excessively on one activity, which earned quick profits, was the risk these companies ran.

This development had official blessings too. For instance, in August 2008 Alan Greenspan, former Chairman of Federal Reserve Board said, "The past decade has seen mounting global forces quietly displacing government control on economic affairs." Two years earlier Ben Bernanke, the Chairman of Fed had said, "America became an attractive destination for capital from the east that had savings glut (after the 1997 crisis). US was attractive because of the depth and sophistication of the country's financial markets." It was during the tenure of Robert E. Rubin as Treasury Secretary in Clinton Administration that the controls of the 1930's were relaxed. That allowed the banks to move beyond their conventional roles. Incidentally, Rubin was earlier senior advisor and director of Citibank who along with Chuck Prince encouraged the bank to deal with exotic financial products.

In an interview to a radio, Paul Krugman the celebrated Nobel Prize winner for Economics 2008 had said in October 2008:

> We created a financial system that basically outgrew the defence we created way back in the 1930s to protect against the crisis. We should have understood that because the system had outgrown those defences there was possibility of another one.

## Some banks weathered the storm

Amidst the crisis there were stronger banks that stood undisturbed. Notable among them were HSBC in England, JP Morgan Chase and Wells Fargo in US, Nomura and

Mitsubishi in Japan, Banco Santander in Spain, BNP Paribas in France and Intesa Sanpaolo in Italy. They survived and grew stronger. How did they ensure this? They followed the conservative business model without going for the new financial architecture. For example, HSBC went by the rule book evolved over its years in Hongkong. Its deposits always exceeded its loans. Santander CEO, Emilio Botin gave a simple recipe for succeeding in this new financial world: "If you don't understand an instrument don't buy it. If you don't know your customers very well don't lend them any money." With 13500 branches it had the biggest international retail network with virtually no exposure to investment banking and 84 percent of its earnings were generated from retail banking.[1]

## The magnitude of the crisis

At this stage it is necessary to understand the magnitude of the crisis faced by US, Europe and Asia. It is easier to appreciate this by looking at the fate of the gigantic financial institutions.

In July 2008 Bear Stearns, a big investment bank merged with J P Morgan Chase. The US government facilitated this. In August, the giant mortgage institutions, Fannie Mae and Freddie Mac were nationalised. They had private debts of over $5 trillion. Next month, Lehman Brothers Holdings went for bankruptcy. It had assets worth $639 billion. (That distinction was earlier held by WorldCom, which with an asset base of $103 million went bankrupt in 2002, the biggest in US till then.) In the same month that is September 2008, the world's largest insurance company, AIG burdened by its toxic assets running into $441 billion sought emergency help from the government. Earlier in the same month Merrill Lynch, the most famous brokerage house was forced to merge with Bank of America.

Around the same time, Goldman Sachs (founded in 1869), saying that it needed the stability of large deposit base to compete with the likes of JP Morgan Chase and Bank of America, decided to become a bank, instead of investment bank. In October 2008, Wachovia was taken over by Wells Fargo based in San Francisco.

## The bailouts

In October 2008, the US government announced a huge bailout plan under which banks and institutions under distress would get various kinds of support amounting to $700 billion. The biggest six of them would get $120 billion in equity injection as under:

| *Name* | *Amount in $ billions* |
|---|---|
| JP Morgan Chase | 25 |
| Wells Fargo | 25 |
| Bank of America/Merrill Lynch | 25 |
| Citibank | 25 |
| Morgan Stanley | 10 |

The support given should be seen in the background of the losses suffered by them. Some of the banks/ institutions with their losses and write-downs are given below:

| *Name* | *Amount in $ billions* |
|---|---|
| Wachovia | 96.5 |
| Citi Bank | 67.2 |
| AIG | 60.9 |
| Freddie Mac | 58.4 |
| Fannie Mae | 56.0 |
| Merril Lynch | 55.9 |
| UBS | 48.6 |
| Washington Mutual | 45.6 |
| HSBC | 33.1 |
| Bank of America | 27.4 |

East of the Atlantic, in Europe also banks suffered heavily needing government support. In France,

BNP Paribas took control of Fortis of Luxembourg and Belgium through a $19.7 billion deal.

In Germany, the state rescued Hypo Real Estate, the second biggest property lender with a package of $68 billion. It also guaranteed all savings accounts in the German banks. The governments in Ireland, Greece, Denmark and Austria gave similar guarantees. Britain guaranteed savings banks accounts up to £50,000. The government doled out about £50 billion to the biggest four banks namely, RBS, Barclays, Lloyds TSB and HBOS (Mortgage bank); it could in turn get ownership of those banks up to 30 per cent. The government also guaranteed their loans to the extent of £250 billion.

Banks in Korea too suffered. They had inadequate funding structure, inflated loan books and heavy exposure to uncertain real estate and construction industry apart from struggling SME Sectors. The banks there lent excessively with CD ratios reaching as high as 181 per cent! In Russia there was a bailout package of $86 billion.

According to an estimate of Bank of England the global bailout figure might reach $8 trillion (equivalent to eight times India's GDP!).

## The implications

The turmoil in the financial sector had far reaching implications. They related mainly to health and survival of the banks, the economic activities, the direct and indirect job losses and the social cost.

One direct result of the problems in the financial sector was on the health of the banks. The erosion of the strength of the banks with the sub-prime lending was very fast. Many banks had built up huge non-performing assets, particularly in home loan portfolio. Provisioning had been in billions of dollars and consequent losses huge. Unable to bear the losses, they needed bailout or where it was not there, they got merged with others or went for bankruptcy.

The huge losses and the need to regain health compelled the banks to go slow in financing economic activities. The governments and central banks everywhere thought of providing financial relief or stimulus to rejuvenate the economies and avert a recession.

An equally serious fallout was mounting job losses in financial institutions. For example, Citigroup as of end November 2008 reduced its manpower by 20 per cent from its December 2007 level of 375,000 and Commerzbank by 9000. American Express reduced the staff by 7000. The estimated job losses in the financial sector during 2008 were about 250,000. At one time, financial sector was the most attractive destination for the best of business school graduates.

In terms of social cost it was reported that the crisis took heavy toll in the form of declining health, higher mortality and stressed marriages.

For many years now, two emerging features of the financial sector were considered noteworthy. One was the increasing stress on universal banking as a better model than pure commercial banking. In the process the financial institutions started working as financial supermarkets. Even Indian commercial banks steadily started emulating this model. In the process the banks, in the absence of proper regulatory surveillance, became vulnerable.

Over years mergers and acquisitions had been advocated as a strategy to face competition and provide strength. The fallacy in this argument was also exposed by the crisis. Citigroup and AIG are among the biggest institutions, which suffered heavily. A failure of these giants would have sent shock waves not only in US but also in the entire global economy. They had to be bailed out by government support.

## The economic model

The 2007-08 financial sector crisis and its fallout on the economies of different countries brought into sharp focus the efficacy of capitalism as a model suitable for economic development and stability. It was the famous Austrian economist Friedrich Hayek who advocated free market economy in 1944 in his *The Road To Serfdom.* According to him, free market capitalism would be self-regulating and there should not be interference by the State in the economic matters. Although free market capitalism gave birth to fascism in 1930's, in 1970's and 1980's, Hayek's theory found favour with US and British governments. Former Federal Reserve Chairman, Alan Greenspan was an ardent champion of non-interference by governments in economic affairs. The policy was in favour of low taxes, light regulation and minimum government intervention. These were expected to be self-regulating and at the same time spur economic growth. But many economic thinkers felt otherwise and saw the inability of markets to provide stability to the economy. Many years ago, John Kenneth Galbraith had argued that unfettered, competitive capitalist system operating on pure free market principles was inherently cyclical and unstable. It would drive to accumulate excessive wealth and make the financial system fragile.

Unregulated capitalism may create wealth, but it does not distribute it effectively. It does not take into account social or community relationship or the environment, which are necessary to human well being. According to another eminent economist and Nobel laureate, Joseph Stiglitz, Americans had lost faith not only in the administration, but also in its economic philosophy.

Even the financial model came for criticism from different quarters. Niall Ferguson, a Harvard economics historian felt that over-reliance on computer models led to failure to predict the current financial crisis. The models were disconnected from reality and history, he said. Paul Krugman said that USA created a financial system that basically, outgrew the defence which were evolved way back in the 1930's.

## Impact on the Indian financial sector and the economy

Initially every one felt that Indian economy would not be affected by the sub-prime crisis that hit USA. But several actions and pronouncements of the regulators, the problems faced by certain sectors of the economy, the demands made by the captains of the industry on the government and the government responses - all indicated that the Indian economy and its financial sector were not entirely immune to the crisis sweeping across the world.

In September 2008, there was a panic among the customers of the new generation ICICI Bank arising out of a perception that the Bank was not safe. Depositors had queued up before its branches and ATMs to withdraw cash causing an alarm. The RBI promptly intervened with a statement: "The RBI has arranged to provide adequate cash to ICICI Bank to meet the demands of its customers at its branches and ATMs". The Union Finance Minister P.Chidambaram also made a statement to assure the market: "We are suffering the consequences of turbulence around the world. Basically, the Indian market is a sound, attractive and well-regulated market." With the timely intervention of the government and the RBI the confidence was restored without any bruises on the Bank concerned.[2]

The ICICI Bank came out with series of press statements and media announcements about its soundness. The Bank took the help of matinee idol, Shah Rukh Khan to reassure the depositors about its soundness. (Contrast this with three government owned banks, which had serious losses in the late 1990s. They did not need a new brand ambassador nor repeated public statements. The depositors continued to have faith in them as evidenced by the fact that their deposits continuously grew during the period.)

It was reported that the banks in India had lost around Rs 410 crores due to exposure to Lehman Brothers and AIG. Apart from the direct financial loss there would be downsizing of the staff by the foreign banks based in India.

Indian exports were under serious threat. The inflow of capital was affected. According to Punjab and Haryana Chamber of Commerce and Industry, there would be large-scale lay-offs. The textiles sector had already laid off 5, 00,000 workers. Leather industry was expected to be hit. IT and BT sectors were on a downsizing mode. These developments were expected to affect the financial sector.

There was, however, an overwhelming view that RBI Governor, Dr. Y.V. Reddy had saved the Indian banks through proactive steps to ensure the stability of India's financial sector. He had foreseen the risks in real estate loans, derivatives and securitisation and took steps to curtail excessive exposure of banks to such sectors. While periodically raising interest rates to curtail inflation he would insist the banks put more capital for additional loans. RBI as well as Government of India's emphasis was on financial stability.

With recession looming large in US and elsewhere the RBI and Government of India initiated a series of steps intended to stimulate the economic activity. The reduction in cash reserve ratio and statutory liquidity ratio, the government and the RBI advice to increase advances to housing and the reduction in the rate of interest for advances etc. were calculated to boost the disposable funds with the banks and enhance the volume of loans. In the result, the Indian banks remained largely unaffected by the global financial meltdown.

## Lessons for Indian banks

There were many lessons for the Indian banks from the global meltdown. Broadly they were at the government and regulator's level, at the policy level and at the individual bank's level.

Time and again it had been proved that market would not regulate itself. In the financial sector, with the stakes being very high, the impact of crisis was far reaching. Therefore, the government and the regulator were required to keep their eyes and ears open about the happenings in the institutions. There was a need for stringent regulatory oversight on the banks to prevent malpractices. In spite of the demands of many industrialists and recommendations of official committees, the government had preferred to retain the majority holding in the banks. This approach had to continue for, banks owned by the public were (and are) accountable to the society. The government had to lay emphasis on efficient working of banks through better corporate governance and autonomy rather than dilution of ownership or mergers.

Further, despite pressure from different quarters, the Indian financial sector was not opened up for foreign banks; it would have been a foolish decision according to Joseph Stiglitz. The government did not succumb to pressures.

At the policy level the authorities did not emulate the western model blindly. There was a felt need to separate investment banking activity from commercial banking activity. In fact, this was recommended by Independent Commission on Banking and Financial Policy (ICBP) in its report submitted in October 2006. ICBP in its analysis had forewarned the danger of removing the Chinese walls between investment and commercial banking. It may be remembered that in the wake of the reverse merger of ICICI Ltd. with ICICI Bank, there was a demand to popularise the concept of universal banking where all financial services and products would be available under one single vendor. Abroad, the gigantic Citigroup, once the largest (in terms of assets) financial service provider and the trend setter in universal banking but now unable to bear the burden of the mounting losses of successive quarters decided to split into two smaller functional units. These developments proved that size and the model of financial supermarket were no guarantee of efficiency and success; rather they would expose the banks to greater risks. As a policy, therefore the demand to separate investment banking from commercial banking stood vindicated.

At the individual bank level, there were a few lessons to be learnt. One was that over leveraging should be avoided. No doubt, the regulator would keep a vigil on the banks and give direction on the capital adequacy. Yet the banks should work within the capital adequacy norms. The second lesson was that the risk assessment of investments should be guided by long-term interests of the banks and not by the scope of quick returns. Further, the assessment should be system based and not dependent on an individual employee's decision. For, however efficient an individual might be, beyond a stage profits would override all other considerations as it happened in case of the failed Barings Bank where a single trader Nick Leeson brought huge profits but caused the collapse of the bank.

## Conclusion

In the ultimate analysis the financial crisis to which the US economy was exposed was primarily man-made. As a risk manager wrote around that period in *The Economist*: 'no crisis comes completely from the blue; there are always clues and advance warnings if you can only interpret them correctly.' The fact that the failed institutions or those troubled ones suffered because of the management failures made the observation of Walter Bagehot, a famous editor of that magazine long ago true and irrefutable. He had said: "A well-run bank has no need for capital while no amount of capital can save a badly run bank." It has relevance even today both in India and abroad.

## References

1. Reported in *Newsweek* October 27, 2008.
2. ENS Economic Bureau, Delhi, September 30, 2008.

# Chapter - 15

# Performance between 2004 and 2010

Between 2004 and 2010, scheduled commercial banks consolidated the gains made during the early years of reforms. This trend was reflected in the statistical and performance data related to relevant parameters. It is also to the credit of banks in India and the Reserve Bank of India as regulator that during the financial meltdown which affected different economies world over India largely remained unaffected. There were, however, signals of certain weaknesses which could, if not addressed in right earnest, affect the health of the banks, particularly those in the public sector.

## Performance of banks

The banking industry recorded further growth during the period. With the merger of regional rural banks the total number of scheduled commercial banks came down from 291 to 169. There was further expansion of the branch network in the urban and metropolitan areas whereas the growth of branches in rural areas was sluggish causing concern particularly in the backdrop of the challenge of financial inclusion. The aggregate deposits increased almost three times from Rs 15,42,284 crores in March 2004 to Rs 44,92,826 crores in March 2010; the advances shot up nearly three times from Rs 8,65,594 crores to Rs 32,44,788 crores. With the credit deposit ratio going up from 56.1 to 72.2 and the percentage share of deposits in the national income going up from 68.5 to 86.6 financialisation of the economy further intensified. Table 1 gives the details.

**Table 1: Progress of commercial banking at a glance 2004-2010**

| *Sl. No.* | *Parameter* | *As on March 2004* | *As on March 2010* |
|---|---|---|---|
| 1. | Number of commercial banks | 291 | 169 |
| 2. | Number of branches:<br>out of which: | 67188 | 85393 |
| | *Rural* | 32121 | 32624 |
| | *Semi urban* | 15091 | 20740 |
| | *Urban* | 11000 | 17003 |
| | *Metropolitan* | 8976 | 15026 |
| 3. | Population per office (in thousands) | 16 | 13.8 |
| 4. | Deposits of banks in India (`Rs Crore) | 1542284 | 4492826 |
| 5. | Credit of banks in India (Rs Crore) | 865594 | 3244788 |
| 6. | Deposits Banks as percentage of National Income (at current prices) | 68.5 | 86.6 |
| 7. | Credit Deposit Ratio | 56.1 | 72.2 |

*Source:* RBI BSR

## Thrust to advances to industry

During this period the advances to industry recorded much larger increase than those to other sectors. For example, the total advances to medium and large industry in March 2004 were of the order of Rs 2,47,210 crores; in March 2010 the figure was Rs 13,11,451 crores. The loans to infrastructure industry were at a level of Rs 56,709 crores and they shot up to Rs 3,79,888 crores in 2010. This thrust to industry advances was, as explained earlier, on account of merger of development finance institutions with commercial banks and also the emphasis the government was laying on development of infrastructure in the country. While this development was a logical outcome of the policy changes, its impact on the profitability and the health of the banks during the current decade was a matter of serious concern.

## Priority sector advances

The Advances to Priority Sector (PSA) increased in absolute terms from Rs 3,11,335 crores in March 2004 to Rs 11,40,406 crores in 2010. But expressed as percentage share of total bank advances, it declined from 37.1 to 35.1 during the same period. The advances to agriculture, however recorded an increase both in absolute and relative terms. From a level of Rs 86,187 crores (15.4 per cent) in 2004 it went up to Rs 3,72,463 crores (17.9 per cent). The advances to small scale industry also recorded increase from Rs 58,278 crores in 2004 to Rs 2,76,319 crores; in terms of percentage share it went up from 10.4 to 13.3. (In terms of the revised guidelines on lending to priority sector, loans to small enterprise sector, retail trade, microcredit, education and housing are treated as PSAs.)

## Soundness Indicators

Further to the Basel framework for capital adequacy and consequential follow up action by the regulator the Indian banks continuously augmented their capital adequacy ratios. Despite the global financial crisis, Indian public sector banks were able to maintain their internal strength as reflected by the steady improvement in CRAR. From a level of 13.2 per cent in 2004 it declined to 12.2 in 2006; but recovered to reach 13.2 again in 2008. There was further improvement in the ratio as reported by the RBI[1]:

> The CRAR of Indian banks under Basel I framework, which had been on a steady rise since 2007, posted a marginal increase during the crisis year, from 13.0 per cent at end-March 2008 to 13.2 per cent at end-March 2009. At end March 2010, there was a further rise in the CRAR to 13.6 per cent.

> Under Basel II, CRAR of Indian banks as at end-March 2009 stood at 14.0 per cent, far above the stipulated minimum ratio of nine per cent. This signified that Indian banks successfully managed to meet the increased capital requirement under the changed framework. Moreover, between end-March 2009 and 2010, there was an increase by about 0.5 percentage points in the CRAR of SCBs reflecting further strengthening of their capital adequacy under the new framework.

RBI also confirmed that the banks in India had 70 per cent of their capital as the core capital:

> Core CRAR reflecting the paid up capital and reserves generally forms the prime measure of the financial strength of any bank. In the case of Indian banks, core capital (measured by Tier I capital) made up about 70 per cent of the total capital at end-March 2010. Core CRAR ratio of SCBs at end-March 2010 stood at 9.4 per cent and 10.1 per cent under Basel I and II frameworks, respectively, again much above the Reserve Bank's stipulation of six per cent as under the Basel II framework, underlining the core capital strength of the Indian banking system.

## Efficiency parameters

During this period the PSBs further improved their efficiency as indicated by the data in Table 2. The cost of funds although increased steadily to a level of 5.35 by 2010, it declined to 4.89 the next year. The return on funds increased from 7.5 in 2006 to 8.34 in 2010 with a further increase to 8.41 in 2011. The spread reflecting the difference between the cost of, and return on funds steadily came down to reach to 2.99 in 2010 but in 2011 it was up at 3.52.

**Table 2: Some efficiency parameters**

| | *Parameter* | *2005-06* | *2006-07* | *2009-10* | *2010-11* |
|---|---|---|---|---|---|
| 1. | Cost of funds | 4.2 | 4.4 | 5.35 | 4.89 |
| 2. | Return on Funds | 7.5 | 7.6 | 8.34 | 8.41 |
| 3. | Spread (2-1) | 3.3 | 3.2 | 2.99 | 3.52 |

**Note 1:** Cost of Funds = (Interest Paid on Deposits + Interest Paid on Borrowings)/(Deposits + Borrowings)

**Note 2:** Return on Funds = (Interest Earned on Advances + Interest Earned on Investments)/(Investments + Advances)

*Source:* RBI Reports.

The returns on equity and assets of PSBs showed marginal decline during 2004 and 2010. The return on equity (net profits/average total equity) which was at 19.8 per cent in 2004 declined to 17.47 in 2010; the return on assets (net profits/average total assets) too declined though marginally from 1.2 to 0.97. According to a former governor of RBI 'Indian banks have typically posted higher earnings than those of other leading Asian economies as measured by return on assets and return on equity'.[2]

## The NPA phenomenon

Through the persistent direction and follow up of RBI the banks were able to further bring down the volume and share of NPAs in their balance sheets thereby contributing to the better health of the banks. As indicated in Table 3 the share of NPAs in the total advances declined from 7.8 per cent in 2004 to 2.1 in 2010.

**Table: 3: Volume of Non-performing assets of PSBs**

*In Rs crores*

| *Year* | *Total advances* | *NPAs* | *Percentage of NPAs to Total advances* |
|---|---|---|---|
| 2004 | 6,61,975 | 51,541 | 7.8 |
| 2007 | 14,64,493 | 38,968 | 2.6 |
| 2010 | 27,01,019 | 57,301 | 2.1 |

*Source:* RBI Reports.

Arising out of the strategy adopted by the banks and the need to follow better standards of classification of advances the internal composition of different categories of loan assets underwent substantial improvements as shown in the Table 4. While the volume and share of standard assets grew, the volume and share of doubtful and loss assets declined during the six years period underscoring more effective control over the loan portfolios of the banks.

**Table 4: Classification of Loan Assets of PSBs**

*(Amount in Rs crore; figures in bracket represent percentage of total advances)*

| *Year ended March* | *Standard* | *Sub-standard* | *Doubtful* | *Loss* |
|---|---|---|---|---|
| 2004 | 6,10,435 (92.2) | 16,909 (2.5) | 28,756 (4.4) | 5,876 (0.9) |
| 2007 | 14,25,519 (97.3) | 14,275 (1.0) | 19,873 (1.4) | 4,826 (0.3) |
| 2010 | 26,73,534 (97.8) | 28,791 (1.0) | 25,383 (0.9) | 5,750 (0.2) |

## Further computerisation

The period also saw major developments in adoption of advanced IT into the banks' operations to make them more customer oriented and competitive. According to RBI reports, by 2010, 97.8 per cent of the branches were fully computerised. The PSBs had incurred a cumulative expenditure of Rs 22,052 crores between 1999 and 2010 on adopting IT into their operations.

A major improvement brought about was adoption of Core Banking Solutions (CBS) by banks. CBS would, to quote the regulator, *enable banks to offer a multitude of customer-centric services on a continuous basis from a single location, supporting retail as well as corporate banking activities thus making "one-stop" shop for financial services a reality*. By March 2010 the share of branches brought under CBS reached about 90 per cent.

Simultaneously, there was further expansion of Automated Teller Machines (ATMs) installed by banks. The emphasis was also laid on off-site ATMs which could provide means of withdrawing cash anywhere and anytime. The PSBs had 29,795 on-site and 19,692 off-site ATMs by March 2011.

Banks increasingly promoted electronic modes of funds transfer like National Electronic Fund Transfer (NEFT) for retail payments. Large value payments were encouraged to be settled through Real Time Gross Settlement (RTGS).

These measures were undertaken on a sustained basis so as to enable the PSBs to face competition from more IT-savvy new generation private banks and foreign banks. The rapidly widening base of new generation customers necessitated more IT enabled services from the PSBs.

## The issues of concern

While recording the fairly good performance of the PSBs during this period it is also important to note certain developments of concern.

One major failure of the banks was their reluctance to lend to small borrowers who till the reform process began, were getting much better attention than after reforms. For long, loan up to Rs 25,000 was treated as small loan by RBI. The number of such loan accounts in terms of percentage in total loan accounts came down from 55.4 in 2004 to 38 in 2010; the amount of loans outstanding increased from Rs 38,555 crores to Rs 43,389 crores but in percentage terms it fell down from 4.4 to 1.3. With regard to the funds given under the next higher band of loans namely, between Rs 25,000 and up to Rs 2 lakhs, although the absolute amount of loans increased, their share substantially declined as detailed in Table 5.

**Table 5: Loans to small borrowers upto Rs 2 lakhs**

| *Credit range* | *March 2004* | | *March 2010* | |
|---|---|---|---|---|
| | *No. of accounts* | *Balance outstanding in Rs. crores* | *No. of accounts* | *Balance outstanding in Rs. crores* |
| With limits upto Rs 25,000 | 3,67,66,092 (55.4%) | 38,555 (4.4%) | 4,51,79,809 (38%) | 43,589 (1.3%) |
| Limits above Rs 25,000 upto 2 lakhs | 2,51,33,746 (37.9%) | 1,24,144.38 (14.1%) | 5,74,52,043 (48.4%) | 3,17,,156.04 (9.5%) |

**Note:** Figures in brackets represent share in total number of loan accounts/outstanding balance.
*Source:* RBI-BSR.

Related to this was also the slow process of financial inclusion. There were still pockets in the central, eastern and north-eastern regions of the country where the population served by bank branch was higher in the range of 18,000 to 19,000. In the allocation of credit, the top 100 centres accounted for over 78 per cent of the total bank credit as on 2010 although they mobilised about 69.4 per cent of the bank deposits. Credit was concentrated more in western, northern and southern regions as explained by RBI in its report for 2009-10:

> The amount of credit per capita in the western region was about 11 times the corresponding amount in the north-eastern region and about six to eight times the amount in the central and eastern regions at end-March 2010. The differential was less wide in the case of deposits per capita; the amount of deposits per capita in the western region was about four to five times the corresponding amount in the north-eastern, central and eastern regions.

Another major cause for concern was the increasing NPAs of PSBs. The share of NPAs had shown continuous decline starting from the early reforms' period till almost the end of the first decade of this century; but towards 2010-11 the strains were visible. Both in volume and share in total credit, the NPAs had started looking up causing concern. A corollary of this was the stress on the earning capacity of the banks leading to the erosion of their profits.

While summing up the challenges before the industry at the end of 2010, RBI made a very pointed statement:

> To sum up, in the near future, banking sector needs to support the growth momentum in the economy while giving due attention to the asset quality and prudent provisioning to balance emerging returns and risks. Further, banks need to step up efforts towards financial inclusion using the instrument of scale-neutral technology as this would help in bringing the vast population into the ambit of formal finance and also boost future economic growth coupled with equity.

How would the banks meet these challenges in the second decade? What measures did the government and the regulator initiate to overcome the threats faced by them? These will be examined at length in the ensuing chapters.

## References

1. RBI, 2010: Report on Trend and Progress of Banking in India, Chap 4.
2. D. Subba Rao 2011: Five Frontier Issues in Indian Banking: *RBI Monthly Bulletin,* January.

# SECTION - IV

# Towards the turmoil (2014-17)

# Chapter - 16

# Beyond 2010-emphasis on Efficiency

## Focus on efficiency

The period from 1992 to 2010 saw fundamental changes in the banking scenario of the country but thereafter, the pace of reforms slowed down and the focus shifted to governance issues to make the banks more efficient. The Committee on Financial Sector Reforms headed by Raghuram G. Rajan had in 2008 suggested certain measures to enhance the banks' efficiency. Beyond 2010 the symptoms of downslide started emerging. At the political level after a decade of rule by Congress-led United Progressive Alliance at the centre, in May 2014 the Bharatiya Janatha Party led National Democratic Alliance came to power with Narendra Modi as Prime Minister and Arun Jaitley as Finance Minister. The new government declared its commitment to continue the reforms in the financial sector. The measures undertaken by two different governments during 2010-15 were intended to enhance the performance efficiency and the health of the banks and bring in greater financial inclusion. The actions taken were interlinked. The range of measures could be listed under the following heads:

1. Adoption of Basel III norms
2. Deepening financial inclusion

3. Regulation and supervision
4. Restructuring of standard advances
5. Better corporate governance
6. Cleansing the contaminated loan portfolios
7. Institutional structure
8. Recapitalisation of PSBs.

## Basel III norms

Banks had been strengthening their capital position in accordance with the schedule prescribed by the RBI while implementing the Basel II norms. According to the RBI, the CRAR of all bank groups under Basel I and II had remained well above the stipulated regulatory norm of 9 per cent in 2010-11[1].

The financial crisis of 2007-08 and the collapse of Lehman Brothers in September 2008, necessitated a relook at the banking standards. The need for the fresh look was summed up by the Bank for International Settlements as follows[2]:

> Even before Lehman Brothers collapsed in September 2008, the need for a fundamental strengthening of the Basel II framework had become apparent. The banking sector had entered the financial crisis with too much leverage and inadequate liquidity buffers. These defects were accompanied by poor governance and risk management, as well as inappropriate incentive structures. The dangerous combination of these factors was demonstrated by the mispricing of credit and liquidity risk, and excess credit growth.

After further deliberations the Basel Committee on Banking Supervision (BCBS) evolved fresh set of guidelines to strengthen the three pillars established under Basel II along with certain innovations as explained below:

(a) an additional layer of common equity – the capital conservation buffer – that, when breached, restricts payouts of earnings to help protect the minimum common equity requirement;

(b) a countercyclical capital buffer, which places restrictions on participation by banks in system-wide credit booms with the aim of reducing their losses in credit busts;

(c) a leverage ratio – a minimum amount of loss-absorbing capital relative to all of a bank's assets and off-balance sheet exposures regardless of risk weighting (defined as the "capital measure" (the numerator) divided by the "exposure measure" (the denominator) expressed as a percentage;

(d) liquidity requirements - a minimum liquidity ratio, the liquidity coverage ratio (LCR), intended to provide enough cash to cover funding needs over a 30-day period of stress; and a longer term ratio, the net stable funding ratio (NSFR), intended to address maturity mismatches over the entire balance sheet; and

(e) additional proposals for systemically important banks, including requirements for supplementary capital, augmented contingent capital and strengthened arrangements for cross-border supervision and resolution.

The new framework which came to be known as Basel III was issued by the BCBS in December 2010 for adoption by the member countries. The RBI after due consultation issued new guidelines in May 2012 to be operational from January 2013 and to be complied with by Indian banks by March 2018.

As per the Basel III norms prescribed by RBI, Indian banks should have a total capital equivalent to at least nine per cent of the Risk Weighted Assets (RWA) with Tier I capital at a minimum level of seven per cent and Common Equity Tier 1 of 5.5 per cent (as against 8, 6 and 4.5 respectively prescribed by BCBS). The banks were also required to maintain what was known as capital conservation buffer (CCB) in the form of common equity to the extent of 2.5 per cent of RWA. Accordingly the total capital with CCB would be 11.5 per cent (9 per cent CRAR+2.5 per cent CCB) of RWAs [as against 10.5 per cent (8 per cent CRAR +2.5 per cent CCB) prescribed by BCBS]. The RBI further advised the banks to maintain a leverage ratio of not less than 4.5 per cent and those banks which had a lower ratio were asked to strive to reach that level as early as possible.[3]

In 2011 itself, the regulator had expressed its confidence in the ability of the Indian banks to adjust to the Basel III framework, 'both in terms of quantum and quality'[4]. The actions that followed thereafter were in conformity with this exuberance.

## Deepening financial inclusion

Considering the criticality of inclusive banking the thrust given to financial inclusion during the first decade of the current century was continued. Both the regulator and the government through regular communications and interactive meetings with the bankers laid greater stress on extending banking facilities to unbanked centres, opening no-frill accounts, strengthening the concept of banking correspondents (BCs) and promoting financial literacy so that progressively banks could reach out to hitherto inaccessible areas.

As a practical strategy a two-phase Financial Inclusion Plan was launched by RBI in 2010. In the first phase spread from 2010 to 2013, over 74,400 unbanked villages with population of above 2000 were allotted through the State Level Bankers' Committees (SLBCs) for extending different forms of banking facilities like branches, BCs, satellite branches or ATMs. In phase II, between 2013 and 2016, another 4,90,000 unbanked villages with population of less than 2000 were required to be similarly covered.

According to RBI's report[5], by March 2014 substantial progress was made in moving towards greater financial inclusion. The figures are instructive:

(a) About 1,15,350 banking outlets were opened during 2013-14.

(b) About 5300 rural branches were opened in 2013-14; out of these, 4,600 were in unbanked centres.

(c) Over 60 million basic savings bank deposit accounts (BSBDAs) were added during 2013-14 taking the total number of BSBDAs to 243 million.

(d) About 6.2 million small farm sector credit accounts were added during 2013-14, taking them to 40 million accounts as on March 31, 2014.

(e) With the addition of 3.8 million small non-farm sector credits during 2013-14, there were 7.4 million such accounts as on March 31, 2014.

However, RBI observed that the accounts opened and the banking infrastructure created had not seen substantial operations in terms of transactions. The emphasis, therefore, had to be given to utilising the infrastructure built.

In August 2014, the new government launched *Pradhan Mantri Jan Dhan Yojana (PMJDY).* The erstwhile 'no-frills' BSBDAs were remodelled with additional benefits like accident and life insurance covers and overdraft facility (after satisfactory conduct of the account for six months). The government had proposed to route the direct financial subsidies of the eligible beneficiaries through these accounts. Banks were given massive targets to open accounts under PMJDY scheme.

## *Financial Inclusion Advisory Committee (FIAC)*

To monitor the measures to promote financial inclusion the RBI had, in 2012, set up Financial Inclusion Advisory Committee (FIAC); it was reconstituted in June 2015 with additional responsibilities. A major task was to evolve a national strategy for financial inclusion.

The financial inclusion fund (FIF) and the financial inclusion technology fund (FITF) set up in 2007-08 were merged into a single FIF in July 2015 with a corpus of Rs 20 crores. With an advisory board nominated by the government it would be maintained by NABARD. The Fund would support activities for developing and promoting financial inclusion.

## Nachiket Mor Committee

In January 2014, the Nachiket Mor Committee (NMC) on Comprehensive Financial Services for Small Business and Low Income Households had pointed out, among others, that 60 per cent of the rural and urban population had no functional bank account and 90 per cent of the small business had no formal institutional support for their financial needs. As a result unregulated private lenders had tried to fill the consequential vacuum. The Committee had made a series of recommendations to fill this gap.

One suggestion of NMC was to establish payments banks for deposits and payments and wholesale banks for credit outreach with relaxed entry point norms of Rs 50 crores. It also recommended that by January 1, 2016 every Indian over 18 years of age should have a universal bank account.

## Regulation and supervision

In the background of the lessons learnt from the global financial crisis the cornerstone of RBI's approach on regulation and supervision was financial stability. The Financial Stability and Development Council (FSDC) was set up in December 2010 to give specific attention to financial stability. Measures were in place to assess systemic risks as well as those that could arise due to larger economic issues. These according to the regulator helped the banks to remain 'robust with high capital adequacy', although as it conceded 'the rising NPA levels emerged as a concern'[6]. The banking public continued to retain their confidence in the stability of the system.

It was also felt necessary to improve the quality of supervisory processes and techniques. A High Level Steering Committee (HLSC) under the Chairmanship of Deputy Governor, K. C. Chakrabarty was set up by RBI in 2012 to study this issue. It was the view of HLSC that the banks' supervisory processes should go beyond regulatory compliance; it was necessary for them to study the risks and evolve strategies to mitigate them if and when they materialise.

By 2014-15 the strategy of the regulator was to move away from the performance based CAMELS (capital adequacy, asset quality, management, earning, liquidity and system and control) framework to risk based supervision (RBS). Progressively more and more banks were brought under this framework; by 2016, according to RBI, 36 major banks had shifted to this more dynamic model of supervision based on risk assessment.

## Restructuring of standard advances

As mentioned in an earlier chapter, non-performing assets (NPAs) of the banks had started looking up by the turn of the first decade. RBI had repeatedly urged upon banks to contain the increase through proper appraisal of loans and timely monitoring of the borrowal accounts to keep watch on the symptoms of irregularity so that prompt corrective actions could be taken.

In the backdrop of the financial crisis of 2007-08, to help the borrowing units which were viable but due to economic downturn had become irregular, RBI introduced a new debt restructuring scheme in 2008. Under the scheme banks were allowed to restructure standard, sub-standard and doubtful debts subject to certain conditions. The borrowing company could be given extension of repayment period, the rate of interest could be reduced and the repayment holiday might be extended. The restructured standard accounts would be treated as standard assets thereby helping the banks also to limit the deterioration in the quality of advances. As per RBI's report, the PSBs were the largest beneficiaries of the debt restructuring exercise. It was reported by RBI that between March 2009 and 2011 the share of restructured advances as a percentage of total advances had gone up from 2.16 to 2.66 thereby mitigating the likely increase in the volume of NPAs. How long the restructured accounts would remain standard assets was, however, a matter of concern to the regulator.

In June 2015, the RBI introduced what was known as Strategic Debt Restructuring (SDR). Under this scheme the banks participating in Joint Lenders' Forum (JLF) and having the security for the overdue loans could convert the loans into equity shares of the borrowing company at a price fixed as per the formula prescribed by the RBI. This conversion of overdue loan into equity would be exempt from the SEBI's Issue of Capital and Disclosure Requirements Regulations 2009 subject to certain conditions. The JLF would ultimately gain the majority holding and could appoint professional management to run the company. The equity acquired should be divested at the earliest possible time.

But the scheme, though launched in June 2015, did not result in successful takeover till a year thereafter. One problem was that banks would convert only enough loan to equity so as to gain control over the enterprise but they would not sacrifice beyond. A takeover by a prospective buyer was thus unattractive. A second scheme called Scheme for Sustainable Structuring of Stressed Assets (S4A) was launched in June 2016. Its purpose was to give the assisted concerns a chance for sustained revival. Under the scheme the debt would be divided into two parts. One part of the debt would be treated as sustainable to be serviced from the project itself after a reasonable time for generation of revenue. The part which was in excess of this would be converted into equity or redeemable preference shares. The requirement was that the first part should be over 50 per cent so that promoters would still have control over the firm.[7]

## Better corporate governance

Corporate governance in PSBs was a major issue of concern for both the regulator and the owner for a long time after the reforms began. The following observation made by a Deputy Governor in 2012 was instructive [8]:

> While over the last one decade, the governance requirements have been considerably enhanced in India, good governance has to be a continuous and ongoing process.... As such the Board of Directors and the senior management have a great oversight responsibility in ensuring that the respective banks lay down robust compliance culture and corporate governance framework which is reviewed periodically for its efficacy and efficiency.

During the current round of reforms a renewed emphasis was laid on better corporate governance. In 2014, the Committee to Review Governance of Boards of Banks in India headed by P.J. Nayak appointed by RBI made a number of recommendations. These out-of-the-box suggestions invited mixed reactions.

## The contaminated loan portfolios

After the Global Financial Crisis, the banks in India had started experiencing a downslide in their earnings. The principal factor responsible for this was the decline in the quality of loan assets, which added to the volume of NPAs. From a low of 2 per cent of advances in 2009, the level of NPAs started surging to 2.2 in 2011 and far more steeply to exceed 11 per cent in March 2015. There was a perception that through CDR, banks were trying to evergreen overdue debts and classify them as standard assets. During August–November 2015, the RBI conducted a special inspection of the loan accounts of the banks; the process was termed Asset Quality Review (AQR). Loans which were restructured under CDR but had not in fact become standard assets were to be treated as NPAs from the date of restructure and appropriate provisioning as per the standard guidelines was required to be done by the affected banks. Governor Raghuram Rajan had observed that instead of providing band-aids, a deep surgery was needed to cure the illness.

In its *Financial Stability Report,* June 2016 while conceding that AQR had affected the banks' profitability the regulator was optimistic of its long-term impact:

> While AQR has resulted in unprecedented pressure on the profitability of some banks in the short-term, the push towards cleaning up of banks' balance sheets is expected to improve their market valuations through a greater trust in accounting numbers, augment their capacity to lend more and support the economic growth in the medium to long run.

As anticipated this change in the approach to classification added to the misery of the banks. When the economy had not yet started recovering, debt servicing as per the revised schedule was difficult. The consequential default in restructured loans would only swell the contaminated portfolios. The total stressed assets had scaled almost to 20 per cent of gross advances by 2016. Several banks with already depleted earnings could not make adequate provisions pushing up the net NPA as well. For the first time after the three weak banks had turned around in the beginning of this century, over a dozen banks posted losses during 2016.

While the intention of the RBI was laudable, the timing of the surgery advised by the Governor was inappropriate particularly in the backdrop of a serious slowdown in the critical real sectors of the economy.

## Institutional structure

As part of the continuing reform process certain institutional changes were also made in the financial sector. These were related to customers, to competition, to introducing specialised agencies and to enhance governance.

For the benefit of the customers, the Banking Codes and Standards Board of India was further expanded with membership increasing from 67 banks in 2006 to 121 banks in 2012. BCSBI, as an autonomous body, was intended to ensure fair treatment to customers. In 2014, a Charter of Customer Rights was also introduced for safeguarding their rights. To facilitate redress of customer grievances banks were directed to appoint Internal Ombudsman.

With a view to promoting further competition among banks the RBI gave licences to Bandhan Financial Services Private Ltd and IDFC Bank to start banking operations. Bandhan Bank and IDFC Bank started their operations in 2015.

For accelerating financial inclusion, guidelines for opening specialised 'Payments Banks' and 'Small Finance Banks' were issued by RBI in 2014. In 2015-16 budget the government announced the setting up of Micro Units Development Refinance Agency (MUDRA Bank) Ltd. MUDRA Bank would be responsible for regulation of micro finance institutions (MFIs) and provide them refinance. Registered in March 2015, under the Companies Act, 2013 it was a wholly owned subsidiary of the Small Industries Development Bank of India (SIDBI) to carry out activities relating to development and financing of small micro-enterprises.

## The questions that came up

Looking at the catalogue of measures taken by the RBI and the government, one is tempted to observe that the reforms process between 2010 and 2015 were not path breaking; the principal focus was to make the banks stable and sound and steadily to deepen financial inclusion. As the PSBs were government undertakings with majority ownership vested with the government the banking public had no anxiety about their stability. The major development was the migration of banks to the Basel III framework. The other development was the renewed emphasis on social banking with a different nomenclature now, namely, financial inclusion. This was perhaps calculated to answer the criticism that the reforms were instrumental in moving away from social banking which was the key objective of state control over the financial resources.

While the RBI's efforts to make the banks robust and competitive were praiseworthy, questions do arise on its failure to pick up the clear signals of an impending downfall during 2015-16. This could be better understood by a study of the rapid and steep build up of the stressed assets of PSBs eroding their earnings forcing them into huge losses and inviting widespread criticism of both the banks and the regulator. In the ensuing chapter an attempt is made to study the issue of NPAs during 2010 and 2016.

## References

1. RBI, 2011: Report on Trend and Progress of Banking in India (RTPBI).
2. BIS: October 2015: A brief history of the Basel Committee.
3. RBI, 2013: Annual Report (AR).
4. RBI 2011: RTPBI.
5. RBI 2014: AR.
6. RBI 2013: AR.
7. Montek Singh Ahluwalia 2016: Fixing public sector banks *Livemint*: June 24 2016.
8. Anand Sinha, 2012: Indian Banking – Journey into the Future-*RBI Monthly Bulletin*, February 2012.

# Chapter - 17

# A Precipitous Fall-2015-16

After nearly two decades of reforms in the banking industry and the commendable performance of PSBs, they started experiencing serious downward slide during the second decade of this century. The challenges foreseen by the top functionaries of the regulator as aired during different occasions literally materialised. In this chapter efforts are made first, to focus on the state of affairs as on 2015-16, followed by an analysis of the causes leading to the present crisis.

## Progress at a glance

In terms of statistical data the banking industry expanded during the period 2010 to 2015 as shown in the Table 1. While the number of branches registered steep growth from 85,393 in 2010 to 1,25,672 in 2015 the thrust was evidently on expanding the branch network in rural and semi-urban areas. Out of the 40,279 new branches opened as much as 15,874 were in rural areas and another 12,963 in semi-urban centres. The population per branch came down further from 13,800 to 10,300 during the period. The renewed emphasis on reaching out to unbanked and under-banked centres to deepen financial inclusion had necessitated this shift.

The aggregate deposits and advances of SCBs also grew steadily during the five year period. But they do not by themselves reveal the emerging crisis in the industry.

**Table 1: Progress of commercial banking at a glance 2010-2015**

| *Sl. No.* | *Parameter* | *As on March 2010* | *As on March 2015* |
|---|---|---|---|
| 1. | Number of commercial banks | 169 | 152 |
| 2. | Number of branches: out of which: | 85,393 | 1,25,672 |
| | *Rural* | 32624 | 48498 |
| | *Semi-urban* | 20740 | 33703 |
| | *Urban* | 17003 | 22997 |
| | *Metropolitan* | 15026 | 20474 |
| 3. | Population per office (in thousands) | 13.8 | 10.3 |
| 4. | Deposits of banks in India (`Rs. Crore) | 44,92,826 | 88,98,901 |
| 5. | Credit of banks in India (Rs. Crore) | 32,44,788 | 64,99,829 |
| 6. | Deposits Banks as percentage of National Income (at current prices) | 86.6 | 80 |
| 7. | Credit Deposit Ratio | 72.2 | 73.0 |

*Source:* RBI BSR.

## The slide began after the global crisis

The Indian banking sector was fairly immunised against the contagion of the financial crisis that shook the developed economies in 2007-08 thanks, as acknowledged widely, of the practical and down-to-earth approach of the RBI at the relevant time. Indian banks withstood the impact without any need for bailouts from the government and without affecting the confidence of the depositors as proved by the highly successful public issue of equity shares by a few PSBs around this time.

But the symptoms of a downward slide were becoming clearer from 2010 as evidenced by the performance parameters of the banks both in the state and private sectors. In critical areas like credit expansion, deposit growth, NPA containment, earnings, productivity and returns on equity and assets there was a progressive decline during this period.

## A painful business growth

The volume of deposits of the banking industry no doubt rose up during the early years of the second decade. During 2013-14, the deposits of PSBs went up by the 14.68 per cent. But next year the rate of increase declined to 9.20 and in 2015-16 it further fell down to 4.06. In fact, large PSBs like Bank of Baroda and Bank of India registered a negative growth in their deposits. The Chennai-based Indian Overseas Bank experienced a steep fall of 8.75 per cent in its deposits.

The advances showed a different trend, though. While in 2013-14 the advances of PSBs increased by over 14 per cent, next year the rate of increase was in single digit at 7.35 per cent. In 2015-16, the advances shot up by 10.47 per cent. Yet, Bank of Baroda, Bank of India and UCO Bank showed a decline ranging between 10 and 15 per cent. Five other PSBs too showed a decline in the range of less than one to seven per cent. In fact, UCO Bank and Indian Overseas Bank had recorded a negative growth for the second successive year.

A matter of grave concern, though, was the sharp bulge in non-performing assets (NPAs) of all banks. The PSBs were the worst hit by the scourge. The gross NPAs of PSBs shot up from Rs 74,614 crores in 2010-11 to Rs 2,78,468 crores in 2013-14 and further steeply to Rs 5,39,956 crores (out of total advances of Rs 55,93,577 crores) in 2015-16. The net NPAs skyrocketed from Rs 36,071 crores to Rs 1,59,951 crores and further to Rs 3,20,376 crores during the same period (Table 2). In 2016 (calendar year) it further jumped up and by the time 2017 *Economic Survey* was released the share of NPAs was estimated to be of the order of almost 20 per cent of total credit.

**Table: 2: NPAs of PSBs between 2011 and 2016**

*In Rs Crores*

| *Year ended March* | *2011* | *2015* | *2016* |
|---|---|---|---|
| Gross NPAs | 74,614 | 2,78,468 | 5,39,956 |
| Net NPAs | 36,071 | 1,59,951 | 3,20,376 |

The bulging volume of stressed assets required higher provisioning knocking out the surplus from the operating profits of most PSBs. The operating profits increased from Rs 1,27,652 crores in 2013-14 to Rs 1,38,441 crores the next year. But in 2015-16 the OP slid down to Rs 1,36,926 crores. As a result of huge provisioning for the NPAs, 13 PSBs incurred net loss ranging between Rs 506 crores incurred by Corporation Bank to Rs 6089 crores by Bank of India. All put together, the PSBs incurred a net loss of Rs 17,993 crores as against the aggregate net profit of Rs 37,540 crores in 2014-15.

This in turn affected the returns on assets and equity. The ROA which was at 0.97 per cent in 2010-11 declined to 0.46 per cent in 2014-15 and turned negative at (-)0.20 per cent in 2015-16. A similar trend was visible in RoE which declined from 16.90 per cent in 2010-11 to 7.76 per cent in 2014-15 and further fell down to (-)3.47 per cent in 2015-16. Table 3 provides information on the performance of PSBs between 2011 and 2016.

**Table 3: Business data of PSBs during 2011 and 2016**

| *Particulars* | *2011* | *2015* | *2016* |
|---|---|---|---|
| **Capital** *(Rs crores)* | 19,055 | 17.096* | 19,194 |
| **Reserves and surplus** *(Rs crores)* | 2,71,196 | 4.85,575 | 5,14,184 |
| **Deposits** *(Rs crores)* | 43,72,985 | 71,94,192 (9.18) | 74,86,178 (4.06) |
| **Loans & advances** *(Rs crores)* | 33,05,632 | 54,76,250 (7.35) | 55,93,577 (2.14) |
| **Credit-deposit ratio (%)** | 77 | 76.11 | 74.72 |
| **ROA (%)** | 0.97 | 0.46 | -0.20 |
| **ROE (%)** | 16.90 | 7.76 | -3.47 |
| **Spread (%)** | 3.52 | 2.25 | 2.19 |

*There was reduction and restructuring of the equity of some of the PSBs resulting in a net reduction in capital of PSBs by 14.03 per cent (excluding SBI, IDBI and Bharatiya Mahila Bank).

Figures in brackets represent increase in percentage over the previous financial year.

*Source:* IBA: Performance highlights of PSBs –different years

The state of affairs of selected banks is given in Tables 4 and 5. Among them were some of the largest banks like Bank of Baroda, Bank of India and Canara Bank which were known for their consistently good performance. Among the mid-sized PSBs were IOB and Corporation Bank which had a long record of sustained business growth. Even the UCO Bank which had weathered a serious crisis earlier suffered a huge loss.

**Table 4: Performance of selected banks during 2015-16**

| *Advances* | | *Deposits* | |
|---|---|---|---|
| ***Bank*** | ***Growth (-) %*** | ***Bank*** | ***Growth (-) %*** |
| Bank of Baroda | 10.35 | Bank of Baroda | 7.05 |
| Bank of India | 10.66 | Bank of India | 3.55 |
| Canara Bank | 1.61 | - | |
| Central Bank | 4.49 | - | |
| Corporation Bank | 3.27 | - | |
| Indian Overseas Bank* | 6.34 | Indian Overseas Bank | 8.75 |
| Syndicate Bank | 0.67 | - | |
| UCO Bank** | 14.55 | UCO Bank | 3.37 |
| Vijaya Bank | - | Vijaya | 0.71 |
| *2014-15: 2.35 | | | |
| **2014-15: 1.49 | | | |

**Table 5: List of PSBs which incurred losses and amount of loss incurred in 2016 (*in Rs Crores*)**

| | ***Bank*** | ***Amount*** |
|---|---|---|
| 1. | Allahabad Bank | 743 |
| 2. | Bank of Baroda | 5396 |
| 3. | Bank of India | 6089 |
| 4. | Canara Bank | 2813 |
| 5. | Central Bank of India* | 1418 |
| 6. | Corporation Bank | 506 |
| 7. | Dena Bank | 935 |
| 8. | Indian Overseas Bank** | 2897 |
| 9. | Punjab National Bank | 3974 |
| 10. | Syndicate Bank | 1643 |
| 11. | UCO Bank | 2799 |
| 12. | State Bank of Patiala | 972 |
| 13. | IDBI Bank Ltd | 3665 |

*In 2013-14: Rs 1263 crores; ** In 2014-15: Rs 454 crores
*Source:* IBA data.

This was not a sudden development revealed after the financial results of 2015-16 were announced by the banks. A few banks had already shown negative results during the earlier years. When the results of the quarter ended December 2015 were announced, alarm bells sounded. The provisioning required towards bad loans was so overwhelming that several PSBs had their earnings knocked off.

There was, according to the 2017 *Economic Survey,* no economic crisis as experienced during 1997 Asian Crisis or during the 2007-08 financial crisis of the West. The Indian crisis was initially attributed to what came to be termed as 'Twin Balance Sheet' problem involving contaminated loan assets of lenders and the overleveraged balance sheets of the debtor companies.

### What went wrong?

Despite the progress of reforms, the PSBs continued to remain fragile as observed in Chapter 11. That the lessons of earlier experience were not learnt was evident from the progressive deterioration in the functioning of PSBs during second decade of this century. The immediate trigger was the AQR conducted by the RBI and its direction to cleanse the balance sheets as a one-time exercise (a surgical treatment, prescribed by Raghuram Rajan!). The crisis was building up when, in the beginning of the second decade the banks went for massive lending to large industrial houses undertaking projects with long gestation period. These were factors outside the purview of the financial sector. There were factors within the sector which inevitably would expose the dark underbelly of PSBs over time. Both the regulator and the owner had also certain role in pushing the banks to an unprecedented crisis. These factors can thus be broadly grouped under four heads:

1. External factors
2. Internal factors

3. Government's failures
4. Regulator's failures.

## External factors

After a sustained growth for over many years from the beginning of reforms, the Indian economy had slowed down around the end of the first decade of this century. The growth rate which was at a level of nine per cent per year around 2007-08 declined to about six per cent in 2012-13. Although the industrial sector showed a remarkable growth between 2009 and 2012, the slowdown in the industry started from 2012-13. The existing capacity remained unutilised in some sectors; new projects got bogged down by bureaucratic red tape and environmental conflicts. There were reports that bad governance, cost overruns, stalled projects, and pricing constraints had affected the viability of many of the companies involved[1]. Successive droughts affected agricultural production which in turn affected the demand for consumer goods. In 2012-13, industrial production went up by one per cent and the next year it was just 0.4 per cent. The growth in coal, fertiliser, electricity, crude oil, natural gas, refinery products, steel and cement industry-which were considered core, was 6.5 per cent in 2012-13 and it declined sharply to 2.7 in 2013-14. While the borrowings increased, the earnings came down causing stress on their repayment capacity, documented the *Economic Survey 2014*. The position worsened during the next two years with the rate of growth declining to 2.4 per cent in 2015-16. The infrastructure industries declined from 4.5 per cent in 2014-15 to 3.7 per cent in 2015-16.

Many borrowers had heavily borrowed creating over-leveraged balance sheets (a position where borrowed funds were disproportionately larger than owned fund). When the debts were already stuck, fresh lending was scarce compounding the problem further. The balance sheets of the borrowers were severely affected. The inability to recover the overdue advances from such companies affected the banks' balance sheets. It was as the 2017 *Economic Survey* said, a *Twin Balance Sheet Problem* where both the banks and the corporates had impaired balance sheets.

There were also complaints that business houses were able to pressurise circumspect bankers to sanction and disburse loans ignoring commercial prudence exposing the banks further. 'Tycoons had the upper hand in negotiations with their lenders because they knew that red tape, patronage and antiquated legal systems would make it all but impossible to seize the assets of defaulting firms', commented *The Economist*[2], London.

There was a long history of large industrial houses borrowing heavily from PSBs and not repaying promptly. In fact, a report of the Confederation of Indian Industry's Task Force on Non-Performing Assets (CII Report) submitted in 1999-2000 to the then Finance Minister Yashwant Sinha had stirred the hornets' nest. The CII report had recommended liquidation of loss making banks (like Indian Bank, UCO Bank and United Bank of India). During a debate on the issue it was brought to the notice of the Parliament that some large business houses owed about Rs 45,000 crores to PSBs.[3] To enable them to borrow further and also to mitigate the incidence of NPAs the scheme of Corporate Debt Restructuring was introduced with periodic changes primarily to suit the big borrowers.

The situation progressively worsened. In November 2014, the RBI governor had said that the corporates were indulging in 'riskless capitalism' meaning that during boom period they would augment their earnings on their equity whereas during downward slide of business they would pass on the losses to the banks as unpaid debts.[4]

The FSR of December 2015 had revealed that the share of large borrowal accounts with outstanding dues of Rs 5 crore and above was as much as 87 per cent in September that year. These borrowers were medium and large sized corporate customers. The Ministry of Finance had also revealed that 30 top borrowal accounts contributed to as much as one-third of the bad advances of PSBs in December 2014. A report called *"House of Debt"* brought out in October 2015 by Credit-Suisse Securities Research and Analytics had placed before the public domain that the loans borrowed by ten large corporates namely, Lanco, Jaypee, GMR, Videocon, GVK, Essar, Adani, Reliance ADAG, JSW and Vedanta had continuously increased reaching a level of Rs 7.33 lakh crores amounting to 10 per cent of the banks' advances[5].

It is pertinent to recall that in the wake of financial sector reforms development financial institutions were discontinued and the consequential vacuum in infrastructure financing had to be filled up by PSBs. With their own stakes being low, when the projects got delayed and the promoters incurred losses they could escape their liability and shift the burden to the banks. Considering the clout these industrial houses had, the relationship lending degenerated into corruption or the banks succumbed to pressures from powerful connections.[6]

Thus, the setback in industrial growth and the pressure on the PSBs to bail the ailing industrial borrowers became the principal external factors affecting the asset portfolios of PSBs.

## Internal factors

PSBs were indeed under the dual control of the RBI as the regulator and the government, as majority stakeholder. Within this framework and the policy guidelines issued by them the banks were given substantial autonomy on internal management. One principal objective of reforms in the banking sector was to make the PSBs autonomous in matters of internal management with the government keeping an arm's length.

The autonomy given to the PSB managements covered wide range of human resources issues like recruitment, training, placement and promotion of staff, evolving appropriate internal systems and controls on bank's operations, business strategies and plans and upgradation of technology from time to time. In short, they were intended to be autonomous corporations.

Most PSB managements, however, did not live up to the new challenge of autonomy. This in turn contributed in a large measure to the inability of the PSBs to maintain their house in order causing serious institutional damage. (*Considering the importance of the internal factors a more detailed discussion is made in the next chapter.*)

## Regulator level failures

The RBI as regulator had tremendous power to oversee the banks. Did it discharge its role effectively? It is useful to focus on the means and medium through which RBI could exercise this power. They were broadly as follows:

(a) Mandatory access to all information about the banks.

(b) Mandatory annual financial review of banks.

(c) Board level participation with an RBI nominee on PSB's board.

(d) Regular meetings with the chiefs of banks.

(e) Power of giving direction to individual banks.

These were the avenues conventionally at the disposal of the RBI to monitor the working of banks. After 1991 with the onset of reforms, RBI had been given more powers to ensure the compliance of banks with the guidelines under different Basel norms. Not only at the macro-level but at the micro-level that is, at the level of an individual bank could the RBI monitor if the banks were on the right reformist track. Even in selection of the top management personnel like chairmen, managing directors and executive directors senior RBI officials would be involved.

With such an array of powers and access to information, it would be reasonable to expect that RBI should be able to gauge the functioning of individual banks. If so, how does one explain the inordinate delay on the part of the regulator in diagnosing the crisis and initiating corrective action during 2014 and 2016? The scams and scandals that hit the banking industry regularly, the serious problems of New Bank of India ultimately leading to its enforced merger with Punjab National Bank, the near bankruptcy of three PSBs in the 1990s, the circumstances leading to the failure of Global Trust Bank and its compulsory merger with Oriental Bank of Commerce and the downward drift of PSBs from 2012 leading to the crisis of 2014-16 could not have escaped the vigilant eyes of an independent regulator. Where and why did the RBI dither in intervening at the nick of time?

## Government's failures

The government as the majority stake holder in PSBs and also as the guardian of the nation's financial resources had wide ranging powers over the banks. The formal powers were related to:

(a) Appointment of chairmen and whole-time directors
(b) Appointment of other directors to the boards,
(c) Meeting CEOs and other top management personnel of banks,
(d) Issuing guidelines on matters of internal management of a bank,
(e) Calling for any information from the banks,
(f) Appointing its own nominees on the boards of every bank, and
(g) Fixing accountability

From time to time, the government had been giving more and more autonomy to PSBs. Where legislative reforms were needed it had the powers to change the law to suit the evolving situation.

With all this, how was it that the government also soft-pedalled the interventions warranted? The explanation could be found in the inability of the political class to concede autonomy in the real sense to government undertakings for various reasons. As already discussed in an earlier occasion[7] much of the criticism against the government banks springs from the continued failure of the owner to treat them as professional business corporations.

A continued major failure of the government as owner was in the process of selection and fixing the term of appointment of the CEOs and other whole-time directors. The shortcomings pointed out by Narasimham Committee-II and experts in the field further stymied the working of PSBs even during the current decade. The terms of CEOs were also not uniform; more often than not it would be between one year to two years with inherent disadvantages.

The appointments to boards of directors too continued to be guided by extraneous considerations. A casual scrutiny of the profile of directors published in the PSBs' annual reports would beg the questions about their professional competence and suitability as part of the top policy-making body of a commercial institution. Three illustrations extracted from such reports of two south based banks are provided here[8] :

> *AKP* is BE in Electronics and Communication, a successful entrepreneur. He is active in undertaking social welfare activities and tasted success at a very young age. He is an extensive traveller and a constant reader of diverse subjects. He has participated in conferences, seminars, workshops conducted by reputed institutions in India and abroad. He is the Chairman of *ABC* Group, which has business interests in Real Estate, Hospitality, Film Financing and Capital Market investments. Earlier he served as a government Nominee Director and shareholder director in a PSB.
>
> *CRN* is a social worker hailing from Davangere, Karnataka. He possesses poised attitude for upliftment of the underprivileged and is having keen insight into

the banking problems. He has got innate ability to take quick and reasonably precise decisions and a patient listener to each and every individual. He travelled extensively including remote rural areas and possesses the first hand knowledge of the economic situation prevailing in the country and the tasks ahead to make the economy vibrant and resilient.

*MBR,* aged 52 years, hails from ....village in ....... Mandal, ..... district, AP. He was appointed as part time Non-Official Director by GoI on September 22, 2011. He is an agriculturist and a well-known social activist. He works for the upliftment of the downtrodden and growth of agriculture in his area and nearby districts.

Another practice which hampered the autonomy of the boards was the continued treatment of government and RBI nominees as superior to the other members. Certain committees of the boards were exclusive preserves of the RBI and government directors; other directors had no place in those committees. For example, in the audit committee, employee directors could not be members. Although this undesirable practice went against the principle of equality of all directors, no effort was made to set it right. As a matter of practice, the CEO, the government director and the RBI director were more equal than the other directors and had the last word in the deliberations in the board.

A related shortcoming was the inability of the Finance Ministry to make the appointees answerable for non-performance and accountable for even established acts of omissions and commissions. There was a tendency to pass on the blame to junior level officials in cases of large advance related frauds. This was what a deputy governor of RBI said in July 2013[9]:

> .....there is a tendency to hold only the junior level officials involved in post-disbursement supervision accountable and ignore the lapses on the part of

higher officials who were involved in sanctioning of the advances, unless of course, the case becomes a high profile one or if some personal vengeance is involved. Our experience is that the accountability examinations do not comment on lapses of sanctioning officials even while the fraudulent intentions of the borrower might have been overlooked by the sanctioning officials ab initio....

There was also the practice of senior bureaucrats, supervisors and regulators on retirement, joining the companies over which they had links while in service. The same authority commented about this in November 2013[10]:

> We see many instances of close relatives of the officials working for the commercial entities which these officials also supervise.... Do we make an analysis of how many of these recruitments are based on merit and how many of these are accommodations? Sooner or later, such issues are also likely to come up for debate in our society. It is important, therefore, that we take cognizance of the problem before it snowballs into a major controversy. Further, there is also this issue of bureaucrats, regulators, supervisors taking up appointments with the entities they regulated/ supervised, soon after their retirement.

In 2016, the CVC had advised the government that in view of the rising instances of misconduct and frauds involving the CEOs and other whole-time directors it was necessary to initiate disciplinary action when they were in service and continue it after retirement so as to act as a deterrent[11].

All these factors cumulatively affected the PSBs over time causing a major setback during the period under review.

## References

1. *Economic and Political Weekly,* 2016 'Spectre of Debt', May 28.
2. Issue dated Mar 4, 2017.
3. V. Sridhar, 2000: A controversial report, *Frontline,* January 8.
4. Prasenjit Bose, 2016: No bailout with taxpayer money, *The Hindu,* February 16.
5. Prasenjit Bose, 2016: *ibid.*, and *Economic and Political Weekly,* 2016, *ibid.*
6. Ashima Goyal, 2016: *Banks need an autonomy stimulus, The Hindu,* March 1.
7. In Chapter 10 on fragility.
8. The names have been withheld; Annual Reports of two banks for FY2013.
9. K. C. Chakrabarty, 2013: *Frauds in the Banking Sector: Causes, Concerns and Cures,* Address delivered on July 26, 2013 during the National Conference on Financial Fraud organised by ASSOCHAM at New Delhi.
10. K.C. Chakrabarty, 2013: *'Vigilance Administration: Encouraging Probity in Public Life'* Keynote address delivered at a Seminar organised by the Centre For Integrity, Governance & Training on Vigilance Administration on November 11, 2013.
11. Report by: *PTI,* August 19, 2016.

# Chapter - 18

# The Crisis of 2014-16: Internal Factors

## Governance, the core issue of reforms

One goal of the reforms was to enhance the governance standards in the banks so that they would be efficiently managed. The irony of the reforms process was that within one year the banking industry was rocked by the securities scandal; that exposed the contradictions between intent and practice. Thereafter too at frequent intervals scams followed. If the earlier scams were due to a nexus between outsiders and those within, the NPA crisis of 2014-16 was the result of several cumulative factors. Many of these figured repeatedly in the past but long term measures were not forthcoming from the policy makers.

Although the government had the power to appoint and dismiss the CEOs of PSBs, those who were appointed had a great responsibility in living up to the role expected of them as leaders of dynamic institutions. Many of them failed in reaching these levels. This was evident from their own conduct- some of which had come into public domain- and the resultant leadership failures. The leadership failure affected the governance standards. Because of poor governance standards the internal checks and balances became fragile with lapses in enforcing accountability standards. Coupled with these was the lack of attention to efficient management of human resources. In what follows these issues are dwelt at length.

The failures were primarily visible in the following functions:

(a) Providing good leadership,
(b) Enhancing the standards of governance,
(c) Internal checks and controls,
(d) HR management,
(e) Accountability,
(f) Whistle-blowing.

These need to be deliberated at length.

## Leadership failures

Until 2015, the CEO of a PSB held the dual posts of chairman of the board and managing director; he was designated Chairman & Managing Director (CMD) of the bank. In State Bank of India these positions were separated long back. Till the middle of 1990's the government had the practice of elevating a senior official within a bank to the post of CMD of the same bank. A decade earlier to this, the government had started posting executive directors (EDs) in PSBs with a view to grooming them to become CMDs.

After the 1990's, the government started appointing outsiders for the posts of CMD and ED. A senior official of one PSB could be posted as ED of another PSB; after he put in some experience he could be elevated there or shifted to another bank as CMD with a fixed tenure that would be for a maximum of five years or his attainment of the age of 60. If, on completion of his term he was still less than 60, his term would be extended till 60 or he could be moved to another bank, generally a bigger one in size.

After the nationalisation, one major governance problem that remained unaddressed was the absence of a standard tenure for the CMD. The situation did not change after the reforms began. The Narasimham Committee-II had recommended a reasonable tenure of three to five years; the government in its March 2005 package of autonomy to PSBs had announced that the CEOs and EDs would be appointed for a minimum term of three years. Even thereafter many appointments were for periods less than three years. There were instances of tenures being just one year or 15 months even as late as 2010[1]. The situation obtaining in the pre-reforms era (as illustrated in Chapter 3) and after a dozen years of reforms (as shown in Chapter 11) remained substantially unchanged.

Where the period was short, it was difficult for a CEO to bring about desirable changes in the administration, policy and direction of growth. The incumbent's performance could not be reviewed by the owner; the CEO would be happy to spend his time playing safe. Or else, to make a grand show he would announce a new strategy and ambitious long term plan for the bank without assessing its strengths and weaknesses knowing full well that he would not be there to make even a mid-term appraisal of the implementation of the plan he had announced. On the other hand if his actions caused setback there would be no time to hold him accountable for failure to deliver[2].

Posting outsiders as CEOs of PSBs had certain implications. Most PSBs had a cultural legacy of the past which could not be wiped out over night. For a CEO coming from outside, to understand this legacy would take time. His unfamiliarity with the organisational culture could cramp his ability to take the people with him. He would be new to the top managerial personnel of the bank; to understand their strengths and weaknesses would require time. As he would have spent his professional career elsewhere developing an attachment to the new institution would not be easy.[3] While it would take time for him to integrate with the bank, the staff would continue to consider him an outsider. In an institution with huge manpower which would actually run the show on a day-to-day basis, the wave length between the head of the institution and the ground staff could be of critical importance.

It was often noticed that to make his arrival known he would unilaterally declare some rosy goals; he would announce a new organisational structure like circles, verticals and groups with new designations; there would be attempt to graft certain systems of his earlier institution; in some cases, the banks' logos and base line of the logo were changed by hiring external advisors. In the name of evolving new strategies or business process reengineering global management consultants would be hired[4]. There would also be temptation to declare very high business goals; when such goals would be unattainable, there would be pressure to bring bulk business in the form of large deposits and huge advances, sometimes circumventing the bank's own declared business policy. The short-term goals would get priority over their long-term sustainability.

If tenure was one problem the second problem arose out of the nexus between political leadership and the appointees. The leadership skills were subservient to their skills in acting at the behest of the political leadership. The 'behest culture' referred to by former RBI governor S.Venkitaramanan[5] in 1996 continued through till the current decade.

This behest culture enabled the more enterprising among the CMDs and EDs to deflect charges of corruption and malfeasance against them through the connections they had developed. Even when there was prima facie case against them the government would not act or act belatedly. The following few instances culled out of media reports and personal correspondence corroborate this:

1. In August 2007, a Karnataka based bank's CMD was booked by CBI at Trivandrum for taking a bribe for sanctioning a loan of Rs 1.40 crores.[6]

2. In 2007-08, a senior executive of Mumbai-based PSB had complained to the CVC about certain misdemeanours of its CEO. The CVC first dismissed his complaint but an investigation made later by CVC and the Ministry of Finance indeed found the CEO responsible for irregularities in the bank. By that time the CEO had already demitted the office.[7]
3. In 2011, the CMD of a Karnataka-based PSB was indicted by a direct enquiry conducted by CVC in response to a whistle-blower complaint. The CVC had said this in its letter of June 2011: 'the CMD has abused his authority, by transgressing his power with malafide intent and has shown undue accommodation and favours while awarding consultancy as well as retainership, outsourcing of ATM activities, while granting advances and in respect of alteration to the decision-making process of the bank to accommodate certain parties while sanctioning advances.' The CVC advised the DFS to take steps to restrain him from further abusing his authority.[8]
4. When a newly appointed CMD of a south-based bank landed in Mumbai airport, the general manager had come to receive him. While loading the luggage of the CMD in the bank's car, the car accidentally got locked with the car keys inside. It could not be opened. In the meantime the official profusely apologised and made alternate arrangements to carry the VIP to the bank's guest house and also arranged for urgent clothes for changing over. The general manager was, however, suspended stating the reasons as follows '...Our CMD could not enter the vehicle to proceed to guest house. CMD was made to wait for more than an hour (sic) at the airport and could leave in alternative taxi arranged without baggage.'[9]

5. In 2013, Central Vigilance Commission (CVC) had sought action against the CMD and ED of one PSB for their 'high-handedness, arbitrariness and manipulation' of appraisal reports of a general manager in the bank, with a view to deny him promotion. In fact at the relevant time he was not working with them. An official in the Finance Ministry was hand in glove with these officials and did not take any action; the CVC sought action against the said official in the ministry.[10]

For long the Chairman & Managing Director (CEO) was the key person in every PSB. Over the years, with the business volume growing, the powers of loan sanction were progressively decentralised. Smaller and retail loans which were as per the bank's norms would be sanctioned by the branch heads subject to certain conditions. Larger loans would be processed and sanctioned by committees comprising senior officials in the controlling offices. Very large advances would go through a grid generally consisting of the CEO, the ED and senior general managers. But the EDs and the general managers would rarely raise their little fingers against the wishes of the CEO; if they did their career prospects might be affected. When it came to accountability, however, no one was responsible when a committee took a decision.

The personal conduct and behaviour of CEOs should inspire respect down the hierarchy of an institution. This was not the case in a couple of PSBs as illustrated in the following incidents[11]. Information about such behaviour moves very fast in the institution causing an adverse image of the CEO.

When a new CMD joined a south-based public sector bank he placed orders for four new high end luxury cars, one each at Mumbai, Delhi, Bangalore and his bank's headquarters. The cars in the other metros were to ferry him from the airport to the local office during his official visits there. In the headquarters he took one more car to be parked with a driver at his residence to enable his better half to go shopping. Another CMD found that the official bungalow where he was to stay had furniture not appealing to the taste of his wife. They were changed. The flooring also needed overhaul to suit his taste. After his tenure of one year a new CMD joined. The entire furniture had to be replaced. The floor tiles had to be dug up and in their place wooden flooring with carpets were ordered to be fixed.

A new CMD of a PSB found that the wash room of his tastefully furnished and designed chamber was 'sub-standard'. It was fine for seven CMDs who had preceded him. For the new official it had to be redone.

The CMD of one bank directed the manager of a branch located close to a sea to make all arrangements for stay, food and conveyance for a group of his relatives in a resort on the sea shore. All the expenses of his personal guests for three days were paid by the branch which in turn claimed the reimbursement of the same from the corporate office.

The Chairman of another bank would always instruct his secretariat to book his air ticket in the business class: the airline would give him an extra ticket without any additional charge to enable his spouse to travel with him. Another CMD, on his joining his post, instructed the security department to post security staff exclusively to his secretariat. The staff, including the senior executives had to pass through the security net to enter his office. Another worthy chief executive mandated that out of the two elevators in the corporate office, one should always be kept exclusively for his use. For the rest of the staff, the other one was deemed sufficient.

The CMD of one bank immediately after his joining wanted all the name boards to be replaced; he advised the department concerned to supply expensive cash counting machines to every branch irrespective of the volume of cash they had handled. Both the assignments were given to someone close to the CMD.

A CMD while returning from a temple on a Sunday saw that the name board of a rural branch on his way was dangling. As it was a holiday the branch was closed. He got out of the car, talked to the local *paan* shop owner who informed him that in a gale which had hit the area a few days before, the board slid down from its perch. The chief instructed the accompanying zonal head to place the manager under suspension for not protecting the bank's interest! The official reasoned out that the failure did not warrant suspension. The CMD instructed him to transfer the branch manager- who had only three months to superannuate- to a controlling office in a north Indian centre.

Bank officers know that changing logos and name boards, replacing the printing, advertising and travel agencies, bringing in new consultants and creating more posts in the name of restructuring the organisational set up are common strategies of new CMDs to give a message down the line –'I know what is good for this bank'. The CMD coming from a different organisational culture declares that what was followed by his predecessors and the bank itself for decades is not suitable in the present circumstances. In the last decade, banks like Bank of Baroda, Canara Bank and Union Bank of India had changed their logos. Did the change enhance their respective images? Did the new logos bring a steady growth to them? Or did the consultants and the advertising agencies make money?

As discussed in an earlier chapter (Chapter 10) the leadership in PSBs- as in any other enterprise- would be a decisive factor affecting their performance. The weaknesses pointed out earlier continued to remain unaddressed. As a result, during the 25 years of reforms where the banks failed to perform or were driven to suffer losses a major blame should be on the failure of their CEOs to provide effective leadership. CEOs involved in scandals, tainted by allegations of malfeasance and under scrutiny by investigating agencies like CVC or CBI and those who were unable to reach out to the employees could hardly inspire the work force however loyal they were to their institutions.

## Governance standards

The second major internal factor for the recurring problems of PSBs is poor governance standards. While it was almost totally absent till 1991, efforts were made to bring in some norms in accordance with the Basel Committee standards (as listed in chapter 11).

The banks were, however, slow in adopting these standards. A major failure which came to public domain was the absence of accountability. M.S.Verma Advisory Group on Banking Supervision had found that accountability for non-performance at any level including that of the board was nearly absent and it would end up with efforts to fix accountability at the management level for loans and advances that go bad. The group had called for greater accountability of directors. The situation has not changed much.

The audit function on which Basel Committee had laid stress did not inspire confidence. The quality of both internal and external audits was a subject of debate. The certificates from external auditors attached to the annual reports had helped conceal the shortcomings in the accounts rather than reveal the true state of affairs. If they were professional, the financial irregularities that hit the financial sector periodically should have been noticed in time. The internal auditors also suffered from serious complex of superior-subordinate relationship which cramped their independence. As a result internal audit was generally unable to point out serious irregularities involving senior executives of the banks[12].

On the standards of governance regarding loans, the workshop of officers' directors held in 2000 (quoted earlier in Chapter 10) had identified three factors affecting the loan portfolio of banks: external pressures, attitude of senior bank officials and inadequacy of credit management skills of officials handling the portfolio. The workshop illustrated the problem as under[13] :

> Influential politicians and bureaucrats and powerful businessmen and industrialists constitute the power brokers who bring pressure at corporate level - to book loan proposal, to expedite processing, to sanction the limits at break-neck speed and to disburse the credit without waiting to comply with the terms of sanction.
>
> To appease the persons with clout one category of senior officials pressurise the officers down the line - in the branch, in the Zonal Office, and in the Credit Division to put up the proposals quickly. If the junior officers note the negative features of the proposals they will be treated harshly. Branch Managers are threatened with dire consequences if they do not oblige the executive concerned. There is also a small section of branch managers who use and abuse their delegated powers of lending and often go beyond their powers without attracting even mildest rebuke from the controlling offices - because of their ingenuity to conceal the irregularities or because they have godfathers in the controlling offices.

The information shared on the process of sanction, its later rationalisation when the loan becomes bad and the approach to accountability throws enormous light on the standards of governance:

> While recommending the sanction it is declared that the market is very good, that the promoters are well experienced and qualified, that adequate security is offered by the party and so on to give a rosy picture. But later when a loan so sanctioned becomes bad

standard reasons are advanced - market has collapsed, cost has escalated, borrowers are unhelpful and security has eroded.

If there is a loss compelling provisioning and write off, accountability is fixed on the junior officials; when the needle of suspicion points towards the sanctioning authority, a standard clause is added in the relevant note: "a committee of executives has resolved that the staff lapses have not contributed to the loan becoming bad"!

As recently as 2007 a deputy governor of RBI attributed many risk management failures to breakdown in corporate governance. This was in turn due to poor management of conflict of interest, inadequate understanding of key banking risks, and poor Board oversight of the mechanisms for risk management and internal audit.[14] Six years later a similar view was expressed by another deputy governor. The crisis underscored flaws in bank's risk management practices and insufficient understanding by supervisors of the risks posed by increasing complexity of products and services.[15] These authorities strengthen the perception that governance in PSBs even after repeated exhortations was weak making them vulnerable to crisis.

## Ineffective internal checks and controls

In principle, every bank has its own internal checks and controls. At the highest level is the board which is expected to formulate policies and call for periodic reports from critical departments of the bank. There are directors representing different interests most of them appointed by the government. There are nominees of RBI and the Ministry of Finance. There are chartered accountants too. There are two representatives of employees also. The CMD and ED are part of the board and are the link between the board and the institution. That ideally would make the board very competent and capable of exercising adequate checks and controls on the bank's management.

The top management of a typical bank consists of the general managers who have their own responsibility areas. They are not only required to monitor and guide the field level functionaries, they are obligated to report matters to the CEO.

In the post-reforms era as recommended by the Basel Committee, internal machineries for oversight functions have been continuously streamlined. New departments with very senior officials in charge of them have been created to address emerging needs.

What are the internal checks and controls and how do they operate? The following account from a paper[16] is instructive:

> There are internal checks and controls intended to ensure the health of a loan account in every bank. The first set of such checks is at the sanctioning stage itself. People working in the field level are generally in the know of things regarding every loan account, for the simple reason that the disbursements of sanctioned loans take place at the branches. The loan applications have to be sent through a branch, formal recommendations are required to be given by the branch concerned; the processing cell at the controlling office has to scrutinise the application thoroughly and point out shortcomings or adverse features if any. After such adverse features are rectified the loans can be sanctioned. The disbursement of sanctioned loans has to take place according to the terms of sanction. All these are intended to ensure the quality of the loan asset.
>
> The second set of checks is in the form of periodic internal audit. The internal audit department has the responsibility of auditing large loan accounts to ensure that the terms of sanction are followed and post-sanction monitoring is done as per a standard system. If there are failures the auditors need to report them

and the bank's controllers should take steps to regularise the account. When a loan is above a threshold limit, there will also be a legal audit by the law department and a concurrent audit by an external firm of chartered accountants.

The third set of checks is in the form of periodic statements of working of the loan accounts sent by the branch to the controlling office. Independently of this the controlling office has also access to every account through the core banking network of the bank. Through this mechanism the early warning signals could be seen and corrective steps initiated at the right time.

With all such internal mechanisms in place how do loans go bad? Economic slowdown and market conditions could be the external factors. But they are the risks every business has and a lending bank does have a system to analyse the risks and build safety valves to safeguard the bank's interests in the form of charge on the immovable and movable assets of the borrower.

The risk of bad sanctions is primarily an internal threat generated by the actions or failures of officials within. The interference by the sanctioning authority who may advise the processing official to rewrite his recommendations or to modify certain common precautionary conditions generally prescribed before disbursement of the sanctioned loan to accommodate a favoured borrower can expose the lender to a definite risk. If the official refuses to toe the line he will incur the wrath of the sanctioning authority. An upright official may stand by his conviction. There are, however innumerable instances where the sanctioning authority overlooked the comments of the processing official and also directed the branches to dilute the terms of sanction to the detriment of the bank. When the sanctioning authority itself causes the risk what is the option available to the institution?

With all these changes and complex systems, what one noticed was that several banks faced crisis on different occasions. The question that defies satisfactory response is if the internal checks and controls were in place how was it that the top managements or the boards had no knowledge of a deterioration in the quality of loans or when the sanction itself was in violation of the banks' norms. When the leadership fails and the standards of governance are diluted, the 'behest culture' of CMDs and EDs would percolate down weakening the internal checks and controls.

## Poor HR management

Another major failure of the PSBs has been in the area of their human resources management. These failures have been recurring from the pre-reform through reform years. The 'golden handshake' in 2000 and the lack of a concerted effort to build a trained manpower to fill the vacuum due to retirements had worsened the manpower issue in PSBs. During the mid-2010 decade a majority of the bank employees who were all recruited in the post-nationalisation decade were also retiring on superannuation creating a vacuum.

The PSBs did not have a long-term plan to build a cadre of trained personnel to ensure succession. With the autonomy given to the banks in recruitment and stress on cutting establishment costs PSBs were discreet in recruitment of new staff. As there was already shortage in many branches sparing the employees for training was not practicable. Rotation to build multi-skills among the officers was almost given up. Manpower training became low priority issue in PSBs.

With rapid strides in the volume of business, the PSBs needed officers who could shoulder higher responsibilities. They had to promote internal people who did not have adequate skill and knowledge. People recruited from outside would need more time to know the nuances of operations.

As a consequence of these developments the branch managers and field level executives were greatly handicapped in handling jobs that needed credit appraisal skills, professional integrity and independence to stand up to unscrupulous leaders at the top and the crafty borrowers. The decision-making in respect of loans, the monitoring of loan accounts and recovery efforts in overdue loan accounts suffered. This in turn affected the capacity of the PSBs to build leaders for the future.

The ICBP had identified four major problems related to HRM in banks: low motivation, fear of accountability, threat of brain drain and risk of non-availability of skilled manpower in future. It had recommended a new approach to the HRM policies of PSBs.[17] That approach remained a far cry till 2016.

## Lack of accountability

Another serious failure that had a long term impact on the functioning of PSBs was the absence of standard norms in fixing accountability for failures. Post-nationalisation, the banks had elaborate conduct rules and discipline and appeal regulations grafted from the government. In reality the approach of the government and the banks' boards did not inspire confidence on the impartiality in fixing accountability. In Chapter 3 the weaknesses of the system were highlighted. Even with the government's commitment to reforms the situation on accountability did not change substantially.

The RBI and the government had no doubt, laid great stress on enforcing accountability for failures of employees. There were guidelines issued by the Central Vigilance Commission (CVC) which focused on both preventive and corrective actions. In consultation with CVC full-time chief vigilance officers (CVO) were appointed in PSBs reporting directly to the CMD. Periodic internal inspection and special inspections when complaints were received could be undertaken to examine the lapses and fix accountability for both procedural lapses and mala fide actions. The CVO would give a status report to the board of the bank regularly on complaints received, investigations done on them and the actions taken. The CVO could undertake investigations on the basis of information received through whistle blower complaints about irregularities. The human resources department (HRD) of the bank would also submit reports to CMD from time to time. All these were desirable measures to instil a sense of accountability.

The shortcoming was, however, in making top decision-makers of the PSBs accountable for their failures, lapses and deliberate acts detrimental to institutional interest as mentioned earlier in this section and observed by the M.S.Verma Advisory Group. This shortcoming continued to frequently figure in meetings of CVC, CBI, RBI and Ministry of Finance as illustrated below.

In a conference of chief vigilance officers of PSUs including banks held in August 2013, the Deputy Governor of RBI, K.C. Chakrabarty had said: 'Majority of the frauds are *wrong sanctions at the highest level of the banks*' (emphasis added). The Director of CBI Ranjit Sinha participating in the discussion had found fault with two issues namely, fixing of accountability and denial of sanction to prosecute the delinquent officials. He found no justification for denial of sanction for prosecution when the officials had caused huge losses to the banks. Former Governor of RBI, C. Rangarajan had underlined that both preventive vigilance and punitive vigilance were very important factors in maintaining discipline in the banking and financial sector and those who violated procedures and rules should be appropriately punished.[18]

The practice of soft-pedalling the actions against the upper echelons of the hierarchy has been a common strategy. In the post-nationalisation history of nearly 45 years of Indian banking there have been only two cases of CMDs being prosecuted and found guilty of malpractice. (UCO Bank's K. Margabanthu in August 2009 for his involvement in the 1992 Securities Scam was one and the other was, Indian Bank's M. Gopalakrishnan). The departmental actions in the form of disciplinary proceedings against erring top executives have been at the proverbial snail's pace. In November 2003, in the backdrop of CVC investigation, the then Punjab & Sind Bank's CMD, N S Gujral was asked to go on leave before his term ended. In August 2007, Central Bureau of Investigation filed a charge sheet against Vijaya Bank's CMD M.S. Kapoor for taking bribe. Nothing was, however heard about the cases against them. Corporation Bank's Ramnath Pradeep was left scot-free despite a recommendation by the CVC for action.[19]

According to a government statement in the Parliament given in August, 2012 complaints were received against over 65 chief executives and functional directors of Public Sector Enterprises and financial institutions; to investigate these complaints a group of officers was constituted in terms of a Department of Public Enterprises memorandum dated March 11, 2010 and May 11, 2011. As many as a dozen bank chiefs (including former CEOs) figured in that list.

At almost all lower levels in the banks if targets are not reached, NPAs go up or certain prescribed parameters are not reached the branch managers or the zonal heads are targeted by transfers to inconsequential positions and sometimes disciplinary action for loan losses. In contrast, there is no instance of a bank CEO in India having been hauled up for his/her failure or when the bank suffers losses during his/her tenure. On the other hand they build up the clout required to get a clean chit followed by cushy assignment in the private sector or very often in the central government agencies. [20]

Had there been timely and deterrent actions against erring top officials, the PSBs would have been far healthier today. In a public institution operating on people's trust standards of accountability should be high and fair.

## Whistle-blowing

One area often ignored is the empowerment of the bank staff who naturally know more about the internal state of affairs of their bank. If they are encouraged to speak or communicate freely about the shortcomings, the questionable decisions of CEOs would have been exposed well in time.[21]

For long, the system of whistle blowing was not formalised in the banking industry. There was no protection to the whistle blowers. The employees and officers of the PSBs were (and are even now) bound by their conduct rules. In the first instance, they could not complain to the owner or the regulator about questionable loan sanctions or deliberate failure to act on the early warning signals. If ever they did, the owner or the regulator would forward the complaint to the bank's Chairman for comments. There was no protection of the identity of the complainant. Acts of reprisals could take place against the complainant; there would rarely be an independent investigation by an outside agency. If employees as a collective group through their union raised the issue there would be victimisation of the office bearers and the industrial relations climate would be strained.[22] The media also could not be trusted entirely as the bank managements would extend patronage to the newspaper to find out the identity of the informant.

To overcome the shortcoming, in May, 2004, the CVC, introduced a scheme called Public Interest Disclosures & Protection of Informer (PIDP Scheme) covering all public sector undertakings and government departments. The CVC would accept complaints about acts of corruption allegedly committed by the officials within the bank. Such complaint should contain verifiable facts; the complainant should provide his/her name and full address and it should be sent in a closed cover with a superscription reading, 'Complaint under the Public Interest Disclosure'. Nowhere in the text should the identity of the author be indicated.

The complaint would be investigated by the CVC without disclosing the identity of the complainant and if the allegations are substantially true departmental action and if need be criminal proceedings would be recommended by CVC.

The PIDP Scheme expressly provides safeguards against possible victimisation of the complainant by the accused. The complainant can petition the CVC and seek protection. Where the circumstances warrant, the CVC would direct the concerned government authorities to take appropriate actions.

The scheme's intentions were good. The implementation, however, did not conform to its spirit. There were several cases of senior executives indicted by CVC but the government sleeping on the recommendations of CVC to take follow up action. There were instances of complainants being victimised by the powerful CEOs.[23]

Had the scheme been implemented in its letter and spirit some cans would have been opened acting as a check on the unscrupulous among the senior bankers. Demonstrative actions taken within a reasonable time would have deterred them from indulging in their questionable practices; this in turn would have reduced the incidence of NPAs in PSBs.

## Lessons from UK

In the wake of the global financial crisis of 2007-08, a Parliamentary Commission on Banking Standards in UK (PCBS) was mandated to go into, among others, professional standards and culture of their banking sector, corporate governance, transparency and conflicts of interest, and their implications for regulation and for Government policy. It submitted its report in 2013 along with far reaching recommendations[24]. The findings of PCBS provide important lessons to Indian regulators and the policy-makers. The shortcomings noticed by the PCBS in the areas of professional standards, corporate governance and transparency are found in the Indian banking system as well.

The proposals of PCBS were intended to enable trust to be restored in banking. It outlined five themes for consideration:

(1) making individual responsibility in banking a reality, especially at the most senior levels;

(2) reforming governance within banks to reinforce each bank's responsibility for its own safety and soundness and for the maintenance of standards;

(3) creating better functioning and more diverse banking markets in order to empower consumers and provide greater discipline on banks to raise standards;

(4) reinforcing the responsibilities of regulators in the exercise of judgement in deploying their current and proposed new powers; and

(5) specifying the responsibilities of the Government and of future Governments and Parliaments.

In restoring the trust in our banking system and making it healthy and strong, our policy-makers will be better advised to bear these themes in mind.

## Conclusion

The PSBs did have appropriate internal machinery intended to regulate their working in conformity with the standards required for large financial institutions. That such machinery was not empowered adequately to meet its purpose is a reflection on how the PSBs were run. The consequence was that the sector witnessed periodic crises with huge loss of public money as well as loss of institutional credibility. Future process of reforms will have to address this issue.

## References

1. Corporation Bank had between 2005 and 2013 five CMDs two of whom had tenures of less than 15 months each; Canara Bank had three CMDs between July 2008 and September 2014, one of them had 15 months' term; these are examples.
2. Report of the Independent Commission on Banking & Financial Policy (ICBP) 2006, p. 86.
3. This writer while interacting with new CMDs had observed that while addressing the staff for quite some time he would say, 'in your bank..' and 'in my bank...'.
4. In fact between 2000 and 2015 almost every bank went on hiring consultants without of course an audit of the impact of the proposals of such consultants. More information on this is available in Bhat, T R 2016: *Hiring of global consultants by PSBs: without transparency and accountability* (unpublished).
5. S.Venkitaramanan, 1996: *Bankers and their dilemma* in *Times of India,* August 25, 1996, already quoted in Chapter 3.
6. *The Hindu,* August 17, 2007.
7. Rommel Rodrigues, *The Indian Express,* December 1, 2010.
8. This author's letter dated August 23, 2011 to PMO; there were reports in *The Statesman* and *The Hindu* around the same time on the CVC investigation.
9. 'Locked out of car, Indian Bank CMD slams door on regional head' *Indian Express*- New Delhi, May 25, 2011.
10. 'CVC seeks action against Indian bank CMD, ex-ED', *TNN* Aug 31, 2013.
11. Reproduced from different issues of *Officers' Voice,* Corporation Bank Officers' Organisation, 2013 and 2014.
12. T.R. Bhat, 2002.
13. The Loan Portfolio of Banks, Editorial, *Officers' Voice,* August 2000.
14. Vittaldas Leeladhar, 2007: ' Indian Financial Sector Reforms'- lecture at Annual Washington Conference 2007.
15. K. C. Chakrabarty Post-Crisis: The New Normal, *RBI Bulletin* December 2013.
16. T.R. Bhat, 2013: Whistle blowing in the banks *(unpublished)*
17. ICBP 2006, Chap XI.
18. *The Hindu*: New Delhi, August 21, 2013.
19. T.R. Bhat, 2013.
20. *Officers' Voice,* June 2012.

21. S.Venkitaramanan, 1996: Bankers and their dilemma in *Times of India,* August 25, 1996.
22. In the mid 1980's, when Canara Bank Officers' Association came out with a circular highlighting the misdemeanours of a senior executive related to the CEO and the protection given to him, the top office bearers were subjected to a series of disciplinary actions. A senior office bearer was dismissed alleging that he, by issuing a circular to his members had tarnished the image of the bank. He had to seek judiciary's interference.
23. A few examples of failure to take action are already given earlier. A more detailed information is available in T. R. Bhat, 2013.
24. The Stationery Office Limited, London, June 2013: Changing banking for good: Report of the Parliamentary Commission on Banking Standards.

# Chapter - 19

# The Fresh Round of Reforms- 2015-17

The problems experienced by public sector banks from 2014 to 2016 warranted two-pronged strategy. In the short run they needed capital and in the long run, measures to sustain their health were to be evolved. What measures did the RBI as regulator and the government as owner take to put the banks back on the rails?

The RBI under the governorship of Raghuram Rajan had, in 2015-16 launched a serious measure to cleanse the contaminated loan portfolios of the PSBs through AQRs Rajan famously said 'the time of band-aids was over; a surgery was needed' to free the banks from the legacy of stressed loan assets. Surprisingly, when the initial three year term of Raghuram Rajan ended in September 2016, the government did not renew it; instead deputy governor Urjit Patel was appointed the new Governor of RBI effective September 2016.

## Government acts

Sensing the urgency in helping the public sector banks, the government initiated a series of measures to stem the rot that had set in. In a conclave called *'Gyan Sangam'*, of top bankers, the RBI and finance ministry officials held in January, 2015, the government conducted an exercise to examine the various options for reforming the ailing PSBs. As a sequel to this conclave, in August the same year the government announced a seven-point action plan to revitalise the ailing banks. These measures labelled as *Indradhanush* were as follows:

1. Appointment of heads of public sector banks,
2. Setting up of Bank Boards Bureau,
3. Capitalisation of public sector banks,
4. De-stressing assets of banks,
5. Empowerment of bank managements,
6. Framework of accountability, and
7. Governance reforms.

## Setting up of Bank Boards Bureau

A key decision taken by the government was to set up a Bank Boards Bureau (BBB). According to the Finance Minister this was to be the 'first step towards a banking investment company which will hold all the share-holding assets of the government with the banks'. The BBB was constituted in April 2016 with Vinod Rai, former Comptroller & Auditor General of India as the Chairman. The selection of candidates for appointment as CEOs and executive directors would be undertaken by the BBB. Over a period, it would act as banking investment company (BIC) as recommended in 2014 by the PJ Nayak Committee on Governance of Boards.

Simultaneously as recommended by the PJ Nayak Committee the post of Chairman and Managing Director of PSB was, in 2015, bifurcated into two: there would be a non-executive chairman of the board and a managing director to be the chief executive officer (CEO) of the bank. The government appointed CEOs to a few banks; a few of them were from the private sector which caused discontent among the senior officials of the PSBs as they felt that they had as good a competence as those selected from the private sector. The largest national trade union of officers in banking industry, All India Bank Officers' Confederation (AIBOC) went to the court challenging the decision of the government. The government said that the new appointment made would be subject to the outcome of the case.

## Recapitalisation

Another major measure was to recapitalise the PSBs to shore up their financial strength. Starting from the financial year 2015-16 the government committed to inject Rs 70,000 crores during the period ending 2018-19. The first dose of Rs 25,000 was released in 2015-16. In the 2017 budget the government allocated another Rs 10,000 crores for recapitalisation. It should however be noted that compliance with Basel III standards by March 2019 would need a total additional capital of Rs 2.40 lakh crores. The method of raising the balance Rs 1.70 lakh crores was not spelt out either in the 2016 budget or the 2017 budget.

## Accountability

There was evidence of an attempt to fix accountability on top level executives of the PSBs. In August 2014, the then Chairman & Managing Director of Syndicate Bank, S.K. Jain was arrested on allegations of demanding bribe from a borrower. He was later on dismissed from the bank. In March 2016, Central Bureau of Investigation registered criminal cases against senior and top officials of the same bank based in Delhi and Rajasthan branches for defrauding the bank to the extent of Rs 1000 crores.[1] In 2015, there was a foreign exchange scam involving Bank of Baroda and HDFC Bank which came under CBI scanner. Government and RBI directed the banks to publish a list of wilful defaulters and initiate criminal action against such defaulters. Liquor baron Vijay Mallya was one among the industrialists to be hauled up for such prosecution.

## Turnaround plans for 10 banks

In March, 2017, the government announced a turnaround plan for 10 PSBs as a precondition for capital infusion of Rs 8586 crores. It required a commitment from the board, the management and the staff and their unions to achieve quarterly milestones. The milestones related among others, to management of bad debts, disposal of non-core assets, closure of loss-making branches and arrangement of capital from the market. The names of PSBs and the assured capital support are given in Table 1:

**Table 1: Amount of capital infusion proposed by the government in March 2017**

| | *Name of Bank* | *Capital in Rs crores* |
|---|---|---|
| 1. | Allahabad Bank | 418 |
| 2. | Andhra Bank | 1100 |
| 3. | Bank of India | 1500 |
| 4. | Bank of Maharashtra | 300 |
| 5. | Central Bank of India | 100 |
| 6. | Dena Bank | 600 |
| 7. | IDBI Bank | 1900 |
| 8. | Indian Overseas Bank | 1100 |
| 9. | UCO Bank | 1150 |
| 10. | United Bank of India | 418 |

These were substantive measures intended to refurbish as well as turnaround the ailing PSBs. Although there was no concrete action to address the problem of governance, the Finance Minister was in February 2016 on record about the government's commitment to run the banks professionally and continue with them under the public ownership as during the last three-four decades PSBs had reached out to areas where there was no banking.[2]

## Mergers of SBI associates

With a view to building up size the government in 2016 initiated the process of merger of the five associate banks of State Bank of India (SBI) with SBI itself. The process was completed by March 2017. Earlier two associate banks namely, State Bank of Saurashtra and State Bank of Indore were merged respectively in 2008 and 2010 with the SBI. Along with the SBI associates, the new generation government owned Bharatiya Mahila Bank, set up in 2013 as an exclusive bank for women was also merged with SBI. With these mergers, SBI was expected to have a market share of nearly 25 per cent of the deposits and advances; and would be one among the top 50 banks of the world.

## Bankruptcy Code, 2016

In 2016, the government enacted a new bankruptcy law called *The Insolvency and Bankruptcy Code, 2016 (IBC, 2016)*. It was a comprehensive legislation consolidating the existing laws related to reorganisation and insolvency. It was intended to create a framework for quicker winding up or strategy for turnaround of sick companies.

## Demonetisation

In November 2016, the government took a major decision to demonetise the large value currencies. The rupee notes of the face value of 500 and 1000 constituting 86 per cent of the currency in circulation became worthless effective from the midnight of November 8. The earlier instance of demonetisation of large value currency was in 1978; that however had affected less than one per cent of the currency in circulation without causing any disruption to the ordinary citizens. Although the 2016 November decision did not have anything to do with the reforms, the banks were under tremendous pressure to exchange demonetised notes before end December 2016. The supply of new notes was slow and the cash dispensing machines had to be recalibrated to dispense new notes of Rs 500 and Rs 2000. Recalibration involved time. In paying cash across the bank counters there were limits which further strained the banks. Long queues in front of bank branches for exchange of currencies and depositing the notes into the accounts were the order of the day till end December. PSBs had a harrowing time in tackling the irate customers and reconciling the cash received and passed over to the RBI. It took almost five months to return to normalcy.

The PSBs were affected in two ways. For nearly two months from November they had to keep aside all their normal work including sanction and disbursement of loans and efforts to recover overdue loans. A positive outcome of the government decision was that the banks received huge inflow of deposits of demonetized currency. This enhanced the liquidity levels of all banks.

## Proposal for PARA

The government in its 2017 Economic Survey mooted the proposal to set up a government owned asset reconstruction company. Called PARA (Public Sector Asset Rehabilitation Agency) the company would assist in take-over of large bad loans facilitating resolution of the twin balance sheet problem of banks and over-leveraged borrowing companies.

## Move towards consolidation of PSBs

A recurring theme of the approach of both RBI and government was the need for consolidation of PSBs into five or six large banks. In fact, during the second conclave of Gyan Sangam organised by the government in 2016 consolidation through mergers of PSBs was a major issue of discussion. It should be remembered that Narasimham Committee-II did suggest merger of banks to create large sized banks to enable them to compete globally. The recommendation was in cold storage. Given the problems of erosion of the financial position of most PSBs during 20014-17 the priority was for turning them around. The consolidation exercise was restricted to SBI group till the year ended March 2017.

## Issues left open

In the string of measures put in place and announced by the government the issue of dilution of government stake in PSBs was left untouched. Right from the start of reforms, debate has been going on, on the need to reduce the government ownership in PSBs below 51 per cent.

The P J Nayak Committee (2014) was the latest panel to suggest repeal of Bank Nationalisation Acts to pave the way for privatisation of the PSBs. In 2017, a deputy governor of RBI once again argued in favour of reducing government stake in the PSBs on the ground that tax payers' money should not be lost.[3] Considering what the Finance Minister had declared in 2016, it would be safer to say that reduction of government holding below 51 per cent would not be in the agenda of the government for some more time to come.

## The questions that remain

The problems faced by the banks in general and the PSBs in particular during 2014-17 were grave enough to cast a doubt on the efficacy of reforms. It was obvious that despite the sustained process of reforms spread over two decades the PSBs went for almost a precipitous fall. During the global financial crisis of 2007-08 it was the foresight of the RBI that prevented the contagion from spreading to the Indian financial sector. While that foresight was nowhere to be seen until the banks were deep down in the red, the government was always dictated by the short term compulsions preventing the PSBs from working with high professional standards required for financial institutions. These inevitable inferences lead us to the questions of the future policy requirements for the public sector banking in India.

## References

1. Report by Sandeep Bamzai *'The ugly truth about our banks' The Pioneer:* 03 June 2016.
2. Report in *The Hindu,* 2016: *Owning without interfering,* February 16.
3. Viral V Acharya, 2017, *'Some Ways to Decisively Resolve Bank Stressed Assets'*, speech delivered at the Indian Banks' Association's Banking Technology Conference, Mumbai, on February 21.

# SECTION - V

# The way forward

# Chapter - 20

# Merger of PSBs, How Feasible is the Option?

## Earlier approach towards merger of PSBs

In the background of the 2014-17 problems faced by the Indian banks, the demand for merger of public sector banks is once again a subject of serious debatc. The debate, in fact, is as old as the date of nationalisation. Immediately after nationalisation, there was a view that instead of retaining the nationalised banks' individual identity all of them could be merged into a single entity with a name like National Banking Corporation of India. The logic was perhaps the merger of insurance companies after they were nationalised. In 1956, after the life insurance business of about 245 private (Indian and foreign) insurance companies was taken over by the government, a single all India institution in the name of Life Insurance Corporation of India (LIC) was established. When general insurance business was nationalised in 1972, the business of 107 insurance companies was taken over and the General Insurance Corporation of India (GIC) was established as a holding corporation with four subsidiaries carrying the original names with headquarters in different cities- National Insurance Company, New India Assurance Company, Oriental Fire & General Insurance Company and United India Insurance Company. Over the years, both the national level insurance corporations were able to integrate the taken-over companies and their staff into the new set up. In 2000, the subsidiaries of GIC were delinked from the parent corporation and made independent public sector insurance companies.

When the Imperial Bank of India was nationalised in 1955 and State Bank of India was set up the government continued its organisational structure. A little later the banks in the then princely states were nationalised and they were constituted into seven subsidiaries of SBI with headquarters in their original places. The SBI continued to control and monitor the working of the subsidiaries, later on known as associate banks. Their names-State Bank of Bikaner & Jaipur, State Bank of Hyderabad, State Bank of Indore, State Bank of Mysore, State Bank of Patiala, State Bank of Saurashtra and State Bank of Travancore -were similar indicating their parentage, organisational set up and the service conditions governing the employees were more or less similar to those of the parent bank. This arrangement continued till about 2008 when the process of mergers of the associate banks began.

For reasons of their own, the political decision-makers did not take any decision on the merger and consolidation of the nationalised banks. The Bank Nationalisation Acts of 1970/1980 provided for the continuation of the taken-over banks with their workforce, head office, administrative set up and even the CEOs (who were designated as custodians till regular chairmen were appointed by the government as the new owner). The Acts had given powers to the government to appoint the boards and the chairmen. Every bank was allowed to operate as an autonomous corporation with overall direction and control by the government as the owner.

## The logic of individual identity

The retention of the individual identities had helped the banks to a large extent. Each one was a part of a local regional culture. Many of them were founded during the pre-independence days; some had great lineage of nationalist leaders committed to promote self-reliance and habit of savings among the ordinary people. The employees were also grounded on the local environment; they could speak to the vastly illiterate or poorly educated clientele in their own language which would naturally strengthen the comfort zone for both. Such a common wave length with the customers helped the banks to make deep inroad into the unbanked areas during the immediate post-nationalisation years when the emphasis was on taking the banking to the country side. The bank managers were for long VIPs in small villages and semi-urban areas. In smaller cities too the business and trading classes developed affinity to certain local banks; this helped the banks to build enduring relationship without much of the high-flying publicity of the current environment.

In both rural and urban areas there used to be a continued personal relationship stretching beyond the mundane customer-banker relationship. Banking institutions although owned by a distant government in Delhi were part of the social milieu in most places.

For these reasons, the political leadership of the day perhaps allowed the individual identities to continue and compete with each other. With a vigilant regulator like the RBI around, branch licensing would ensure that there would be no overlapping of branches or poaching on each other's clients in smaller townships. A kind of healthy competition evolved itself to make the PSBs expand and grow both vertically and geographically. When performance efficiency and profitability gained currency PSBs looked beyond their original areas of operation to expand branches and business while retaining their individual characteristics including the logos!

## The renewed debate and action

With the reforms coming up in the 1990's and beyond, the question of merging the PSBs into four or five entities gained currency again. The I Narasimham committee emphasised the need to build size to face global competition; one way was to merge government owned banks into four or five large banks. Leading bankers, IBA, RBI and even government started playing the same tune. One chairman contended that mergers would reduce cost and increase productivity; another said that Indian banking was highly fragmented with hundred odd commercial banks, numerous co-operative banks and regional rural banks, and he batted for consolidation; one more who later moved to RBI felt that consolidation would help leverage synergies where factors such as size, spread, technology, human resources and capital could be reconciled. The RBI also advocated mergers through amendments to relevant legislation.[1] The principal arguments were that

(a) Size would bring in economies of scale,
(b) Mergers would cut costs and enhance efficiency,
(c) Size would enable the banks to face global competition, and
(d) Indian banks could become global players.

These arguments are continued to be advanced even 25 years after the reforms began. For instance, in its discussion paper[2] put on the public domain in August 2013 the RBI contends that consolidation of Indian banks would enable them 'to cater to the global needs of the economy by becoming global players'. It further argues that consolidation would help the banks 'to become stronger with capacity to meet corporate and infrastructure funding needs.' The paper, however, underlines four factors to be taken care of:

(a) consensus at the management and employee levels,
(b) integration of heterogeneous work culture,
(c) alignment of different technology platforms, and
(d) absence of correlation between size and efficiency.

In 2016, the government fired the first salvo by directing the merger of SBI's five remaining associates and the Bharatiya Mahila Bank with SBI. And in early 2017, both the government and the RBI indicated that the time was opportune for merger of PSBs into four or five larger entities.

## Experience the world over

World over, the experience of building size is not uniformly positive. A look at the findings of different studies and experience in specific cases will corroborate this premise.

A report brought out by Federal Reserve Bank of New York in 1997 based on a study of several mergers suggests that there is no evidence of improvement in efficiency after the mergers. Another study conducted in 2002 by A.T. Kearney, a consulting firm says that only 29 per cent of mergers and amalgamations (M&As) delivered the expected benefits. The reasons were primarily the lack of communication within the organisation and unrealised synergy and financial expectations.[3]

A study made by Bank of International Settlements in 1999 concludes: 'Studies continue to indicate that the experience of the majority of mergers is disappointing as organisational problems are systematically underestimated and acquirers tend to overpay for targets.' Analysing this report *The Economist* lists out three dangers of mergers[4]:

(a) mergers may reduce competition and hurt consumers,

(b) bigger banks are not necessarily any safer than smaller ones,

(c) the alleged benefits of merging for banks' profitability often prove illusory.

A report published in *The Economist,* points out that that both merging companies and the merged entities lost their values after the mergers.[5] The report was based on a study of 4136 companies of USA conducted by three American economists between 1998 and 2001. The study revealed that the merging firms lost their market value by $158 billion and the shareholders of the buying firms saw their wealth eroded by an aggregate of $240 billion.

In an authoritative book[6] documenting the impact of mergers in banking it is established that 'bank managements remain preoccupied with a merger consolidation process and the executives are as prone as those in other industries to the delusion that they can enrich shareholders through M & As. One problem is the trade-off between speed of execution which maximises savings and the need to build a common culture'.

The Japanese experience further corroborates this trend. Through mergers and consolidation four large groups emerged in Japan by April 2001. There was little cause for celebration, though. Poor lending decisions continued to plague the merged mega banks. In 1999, three banks, Industrial Bank of Japan, Fuji Bank and Dai Icho Kangyo Bank merged to form a mega holding company called Mizuho Holdings Incorporated (MHI). MHI was projected to earn by 2005-06 about 800 billion yen equivalent to a return on assets of the order of 12 per cent as against its loss of 1.048 trillion yen in 1999. The group posted the biggest corporate loss in May 2003 amounting to 2.38 trillion yen ($20.35 billion). It had become the world's biggest bank in terms of assets[7].

The Japanese story is further interesting and gives useful lessons. In the year March 2003, seven largest banks of Japan posted a loss of 4.6 trillion yen ($839.3 billion) which was equivalent to the size of Nigerian economy. The banks promised to return to profits the next year. But a study by Barclays showed that these banks even in their pre-merger days had promised profits every year since 1993 but were never able to match their promised numbers. The surging NPAs had knocked off their profits. At that time itself their NPA was as high as

8.50 per cent. It was the tradition in Japan that the government would bail out the ailing banks by taking them over, turning them around and thereafter handing them over back to the private owners. Between 1996 and 2003 the government had pumped in 37 trillion yen for such bailouts.

If size were to ensure performance and enhance competitive strength why did the largest banks of the world that were in Japan suffer repeated losses warranting state support for bailout?

*The Economist* was of the firm view that the trend was being too much influenced by misguided governments[8].

## The social cost

The mergers are intended to help reduce financial cost. There are, however, huge social costs in the form of job losses. For example, the merger of Bank One of America with J.P.Morgan Chase announced in January 2004 was expected to shave off 10,000 jobs to save $2.2 billion over three years. The merger of Deutsche Bank and Dresdner Bank in Germany announced in March 2000 was to result in a loss of 16,500 jobs to save $2.77 billion. In India, after the merger of Bank of Madura Ltd (BoM) with ICICI Bank Ltd, in 2000, the employees of BoM were offered voluntary retirement scheme to reduce the manpower. Those who did not opt for voluntary retirement were transferred out of their places forcing many to opt out of the merged bank. After the merger of New Bank of India with Punjab National Bank in 1993, the employees of NBI carried a feeling that they were treated as second class citizens by PNB. A similar feeling prevailed when Global Trust Bank was compulsorily merged with Oriental Bank of Commerce in 2004. When State Bank of Saurashtra and State Bank of Indore were merged with SBI there was considerable discontent among the employees of the associate banks.

The customers also feel alienated when after the merger a bank's identity is lost. In Canada, where mergers resulted in the country being dominated by six big banks the consumer groups and representatives of small business started complaining that the banks were unresponsive to their needs and that decrease in competition would fuel the bankers' arrogance. The Canadians were piqued by the increased transaction costs, higher service charges and reduced interest rates.[9]

Mergers would result in relocation of branches to reduce cost and ensure synergy. In reality such relocation would primarily be dictated by the urge to reduce cost. This could result in denial of easy access to banking in far flung locations.

When building size becomes the driving force preference will be given to large borrowers. The cost of appraisal, monitoring and supervision of such advances is relatively smaller than those of smaller loans. The returns in large advances are apparently higher. This approach could result in ignoring the smaller clients –both depositors and borrowers.

With the greater autonomy proposed to be given to the banks in the matter of opening and closing branches, axe could fall on the seemingly non-profitable branches in rural and semi-urban areas. This will add to the huge social cost of mergers.

## Big is not necessarily efficient

That size does not ensure or guarantee efficiency is established by several reports and studies. Size breeds greater risks and when the risks materialise the controllers come to their protection at the cost of tax payers' money as it happened during the global financial crisis of 2007-08. In India, when there was a near run on ICICI Bank in 2008, the RBI had directed the PSBs to supply unlimited amount of cash to the troubled bank. The operation of market discipline is circumvented by regulatory intervention translating the perception of 'too big to fail' into a reality. As the exchequer would come to the rescue in contingencies created by the banks themselves, they tend to be reckless exposing the system to greater risks.

For long, the biggest among nationalised banks like Punjab National Bank, Bank of Baroda, Bank of India and Canara Bank were considered to be strong and healthy. Yet each one of them was involved in one or other scandals starting from the Harshad Mehta affair. SBI was found negligent in entertaining the business of Harshad Mehta, Bank of Baroda had unduly favoured CR Bhansali in CRB Capital Markets case and Bank of India was implicated in the Pay Order scam. In 2015, Bank of Baroda was involved in 6100 crore foreign exchange remittance fraud. These banks suffered heavily during the crisis of 2014-17. In the year 2015-16, Bank of Baroda suffered a loss of Rs 5396 crores, Bank of India, Rs 6089 crores, Canara Bank, Rs 2873 crores and PNB, Rs 3974 crores. If size were guarantee of efficiency how did these banks come to grief? The regulator and the owner with all the powers and authority of control and supervision have not been able to read the signals in time when the current size of the affected banks is not comparable to that of the global giants. By merger and consolidation how effective will be the control over them?

A financial analyst wrote this in 2013 in *Al Jazeera*[10]:

> In 2011, 29 banks in the world were so large that, if even one of them failed, it would take a huge chunk of the global economy down with it. Because this fear hangs over the head of our governments, they are afraid to charge big banks with criminal activities. In addition, mega-banks are able to intimidate regulators when new banking laws are being negotiated.

In 2013, JP Morgan Chase, one of the largest global banks, had to enter into a settlement with US Federal authorities for its questionable role in selling mortgage based securities during the 2007-08 crisis[11].

In April 2016, Wells Fargo the largest mortgage bank in US and third largest in assets entered into a settlement of $1.2 billion fine with US Department of Justice. Its failure was in deceiving the government into issuing thousands of risky mortgages[12].

The global financial crisis of 2007-08 is a further testimony to the premise that big is not necessarily efficient; rather the bigger the institution, the greater is the risk that it takes. When the risk becomes real, to prevent a collapse of the faith in the system, bailout efforts are made as demonstrated at great financial and social cost in the western world.[13] The enactment in USA of Dodd–Frank Wall Street Reform and Consumer Protection Act (Dodd-Frank Act) in 2010 by the Obama Administration was the fallout of that crisis. The stated objectives of that act are important lessons for our policy-makers:

> To promote the financial stability of the United States by improving accountability and transparency in the financial system, to end "too big to fail", to protect the American taxpayer by ending bailouts, to protect consumers from abusive financial services practices, and for other purposes.

In 2014, the Federal Reserve Board had issued further directions under section 622 of the Dodd-Frank Act imposing restrictions on the size of the post-merger financial entities so that the risk of too big to fail would not become real.

## The inconsistency in policies

A major plank of reforms in the financial sector has been enhancing efficiency through competition. It necessitates opening up the sector for more players. In the reforms era new banks have been licensed to be opened. Foreign banks also have been allowed to expand their network. From the early years of this century a new concept of local area banks has been introduced. From the middle of this decade new specialised financial institutions like payments banks and small finance banks have also been permitted. For instance in September 2015 the RBI granted licence to 10 small finance banks[14] . These small banks will accept deposits and lend to unserved sections of people subject to certain conditions stipulated by the regulator. All these measures are intended to increase competition and offer specialised financial services.

While advocating more players and licensing them to increase competition, simultaneously the argument for merger and consolidation is advanced. After the merger of associate banks with SBI, the case for merger of PSBs has gained further prominence. A deputy governor[15] of the RBI made the case for consolidation in the following words:

> As many have pointed out, it is not clear we need so many public sector banks. The system will be better off if they are consolidated into fewer but healthier banks... some banks can be merged, as a quid pro quo for timely government capital injection into the combined entity. It would offer the opportunity to rejig management responsibility away from those who have under-performed or dragged their feet the most. Synergies in lending activity and branch locations could be identified to economise on intermediation costs, allowing sales of real estate where branches are redundant. Voluntary retirement schemes can be offered to manage headcount and usher in a younger, digitally-savvy talent pool into these banks.

In April 2017, Governor Urjit Patel said that merger of PSBs would help address the issue of stressed assets and improve their health. Around the same time, the Finance Ministry itself made a statement of its plan to examine the strategy of mergers of PSBs.[16]

Our policy-makers give a lot of credence to views of the global consultants and analysts. In 2016, Moody's Investors Service had cautioned against mergers in India in the context of the nature and magnitude of the NPAs of PSBs.

Mergers could offset the potential long-term benefits, according to the said agency.[17]

## Competition Commission and size

In 2002, Indian government enacted the Competition Act which was further amended in 2007. In October 2003 the Competition Commission of India (CCI) was set up. The CCI consists of a Chairperson and six members appointed by the Central Government. While passing the Act the then Finance Minister Jaswant Singh had stated that it 'is to prevent MNCs from abusing the market and indulging in unfair trade by using their *size and muscle power.'* (emphasis added). The following are the responsibilities of CCI as stated in its website:

> It is the duty of the Commission to eliminate practices having adverse effect on competition, promote and sustain competition, protect the interests of consumers and ensure freedom of trade in the markets of India.
>
> The Commission is also required to give opinion on competition issues on a reference received from a statutory authority established under any law and to undertake competition advocacy, create public awareness and impart training on competition issues.

The CCI further states in the same place:

> Competition is the best means of ensuring that the 'Common Man' or 'Aam Aadmi' has access to the broadest range of goods and services at the most competitive prices. With increased competition, producers will have maximum incentive to innovate and specialise. This would result in reduced costs and wider choice to consumers. A fair competition in market is essential to achieve this objective. Our goal is to create and sustain fair competition in the economy that will provide a 'level playing field' to the producers and make the markets work for the welfare of the consumers.

If size and muscle power could be abused by the MNCs, how far are the Indian corporates including PSBs free from such a tendency? The latest example of the use of such clout was of the SBI after its associate banks were merged with itself effective from April 2017. Within a few days after the merger, the SBI announced, much to the dismay of the customers that the service charges on various facilities would stand revised.[18]

> Effective April 1, State Bank of India, the behemoth that has grown bigger following the merger of its five associates with itself, will levy fresh charges on account holders, including on their minimum balance, ATM use and cash-handling. For example, if the monthly average minimum balance falls below Rs 5000 in savings accounts in metros a levy of Rs 100 plus service charges will be applicable. ATM charges beyond the mandatory limit will be doubled from Rs 5 to Rs 10 plus service charges. For debit cards there will be a charge of Rs 30 per quarter if the average balance is less than Rs 15,000.

For cash withdrawals also the bank would levy charge of Rs 50 plus service tax per every transaction in excess of three in a month.

These restrictions affect the customers of small means who find it difficult to keep large balances or who need to withdraw cash more frequently. Said a customer of State Bank of Hyderabad as reported in a newspaper[19]:

> "I am a contract worker with the Greater Hyderabad Municipal Corporation with an earning of Rs 7,000. How do I keep Rs 1,000 in my account," asked Ratnamma, a customer of State Bank of Hyderabad.

During the merger of Global Trust Bank with Oriental Bank of Commerce the government had given tax concessions to the OBC to enable it to absorb the pressure on its earnings in the transitional period. For the failure of the management of a lending bank or the failure of a borrower company which results in loss to the lending bank providing tax relief to the bank which takes over the losing lender is an unjust burden on the tax payer.

## Need for caution

The home-grown wisdom of one of our distinguished central bankers, Y V Reddy is extremely illuminating[20]:

> There is a global consensus that banks that are 'too big to fail' are sources of serious risk to financial stability. It is also recognised that it is not simply the size but a bank's systemic importance that makes them 'too big to fail'. Thus, if links are permitted between large corporate houses and banks, they become too important systemically to be allowed to fail. Globally, there is also a discomfort even with current proposals to allow such big banks with safeguards for two reasons: first, the formal recognition that they are 'too big to fail' encourages them to take excessive risks; and second, in any case regulatory capture is far more likely by such large entities. There is a preference to avoid such banks from emerging, and the feasibility of breaking up banks that are 'too big to fail' is being considered. In fact, there is a movement that insists that banks that are 'too big to fail' are 'too big to exist'. These considerations are reinforcing the global mood to deny a bank licence to real sector entities like, say, General Electric in the US.

They hold good even today.

## Need for an India-centric model

The primary priority in the policy and the strategy should be strengthening the systems and controls; for mergers by themselves are not the goals.

Most of the recommendations for mergers and consolidation have come from western consultants, Indian economists or bankers influenced by western models of banking and Indian industry chambers who are far removed from the ground realities of Indian banking. The peculiarities of Indian economy cannot be addressed by transplanting western models of financial architecture into our economy. Those models have not proved successful in their own countries; how far can they be appropriate for emulation by India?

For over four decades and a half Indian PSBs have complemented the development efforts of the government. Those efforts need further support; they need priority, not mergers and consolidation of PSBs. Banks in India need to have a primarily India-centric model integrated with the economic policies of the state and aspirations of a largely illiterate banking clientele who need hand –holding and not a highly tech-savvy service.

## References

1. See the reports related to (a) S.S. Kohli, PNB, in an interview to *Hindu Business Line*, November 17, 2000; (b) A.K. Purwar, SBI Chairman, *HBL*, September 30, 2003; (c) V.Leeladhar, IBA, *Financial Express,* August 31, 2004; and (d) a Report by *Economic Times*, dated November 8, 2002.
2. RBI DBOD and DEPR (Department of Economic Policy and Research) Aug 2013: *Banking Structure in India - The Way Forward -Discussion Paper.*
3. Reported in *Business Standard*, November 27, 2002.
4. August 28, 1999.
5. February 21, 2004.
6. Steven I. Davis*: 'Bank mergers: Lessons for the future'*, 2000, Palgrave Macmillan, UK.
7. *Business Standard*, May 28, 2003.
8. August 28, 1999.
9. Cherian Thomas, *Business Standard*, March 18, 1998.
10. Nick Fillmore, *Al Jazeera,*14 Sep 2013.
11. *The Hindu*, Editorial-October 29, 2013 '*Wide-ranging implications.'*
12. *Reuters* report dated April 10, 2016.
13. Refer to the Chapter on Global Financial Crisis.
14. *FE Online* , September 17, 2015.

15. Acharya, V.V., 2017: 'Some Ways to Decisively Resolve Bank Stressed Assets', Speech delivered at the Indian Banks' Association Banking Technology Conference, Mumbai, on February 21, 2017.
16. *'Centre for more PSB mergers',* Reported in *The Hindu,* April 30, 2017.
17. *'Not an opportune time for consolidation of public sector banks, says Moody's': Hindu Business Line,* June 29, 2016.
18. *Hindu Business Line 'SBI customers will have to pay higher service charges from today'* April 1, 2017.
19. *Hindu Business Line,* April 1, 2017.
20. *Global Crisis, Recession and Uneven Recovery* 2011, Orient BlackSwan.

## Chapter - 21

# Is Privatisation an Option?

### Background of the demand

It is to be recalled that when 14 banks were nationalised in 1969, the takeover was successfully challenged in the Supreme Court compelling the government to reintroduce the Bank Nationalisation Act in 1970 plugging the loopholes found by the court in the impugned act. Two decades later with the onset of economic liberalisation the demand to privatise the public sector banks (PSBs) regained currency. Broadly the reasons advanced for privatisation of PSBs could be listed as follows:

(a) PSBs need huge capital to meet the capital adequacy standards set by Basel Committee; the government does not have so much of money to spare; through privatisation the required capital could be found.

(b) The performance of the banks will improve if their control vests with private owners.

(c) It is not the business of the government to be in business.

The II Narasimham Committee was in favour of reducing the government shareholding to 33 per cent. In 2000, the then RBI Governor Bimal Jalan speaking at a seminar in National Institute of Bank Management had said that it might be difficult to raise the capital needed to meet the capital adequacy norms due to high government holdings in PSBs[1]. In 2014, the PJ Nayak Committee on Governance of PSB Boards advocated denationalisation of PSBS and SBI by repeal of the Bank Nationalisation Acts and SBI Acts and incorporation of all banks under the Companies Act. It had also recommended setting up of a Bank Investment Company (BIC) to which the Government should transfer its share holdings in banks. Innumerable analysts and consultants have repeatedly played the same tune after the reforms set in.

It is appropriate that these reasons in support of privatisation are examined in detail.

## Need for more capital

Until 1991 the level of capital a bank possessed was not an issue of debate. The fact that the PSBs were wholly owned by the Government of India was a critical factor to strengthen the trust the people had in them. That they were under the supervision of the Reserve Bank of India further enhanced the trust in the banks.

The importance of capital as a buffer to the losses a bank may suffer was underscored by the Basel Committee and the standards set by it. It is pertinent to recall that the failure in 1974 of Bankhaus Herstatt, a German Bank with assets worth $800 million and its impact on Japanese and Italian banks dealing with it had triggered a debate on the need for adequate cushioning to safeguard the banks against such failures. The capital adequacy norms which came to be formulated were thus primarily for the banks with international business. And most of the Indian banks did not have global presence which could affect the banks dealing with them. The share of Indian banks' foreign business in their total business was negligible. Further, as they were owned by the government the risk of depositors losing their money was virtually non-existent.

Yet with a need to fall in line with global trend of reforms in the financial sector, the government decided to follow the Basel norms for capital adequacy. Under Basel I the banks were mandated to have a capital adequacy ratio of nine per cent by 1999; the II Narasimham Committee revised it to reach 11 per cent over time. According to RBI's Report on Trend and Progress of Banking in India 2011 all banks were much above the required level of nine per cent by 2010-11. Basel III norms required still higher capital level to cover different forms of short-term and long-term risks.[2]

Under the latest norms, the PSBs require huge capital estimated to be Rs 2.40 lakh crores by 2019. Under the *Indradhanush* package of measures the government has committed to provide a recapitalisation amount of Rs 70,000 crores leaving a gap of Rs 1.70 lakh crores. As the government has not spelt out alternative plans to bridge this gap, one option for the PSBs is to go for public issues. With several PSBs there is still some headroom to raise capital from the public through follow-on offers. The amended provisions of Bank Nationalisation Acts permit dilution of the government holding up to 51 per cent. Infusion of capital by the government is a policy decision to be taken by the government.

There has been a view that as the government is investing tax-payers' money unless there is reasonable return the government should not pump in money. The perception is that the return on equity has been very low. As recently as February 2017, a deputy governor of RBI contended that injecting more capital without adequate return is a drag on the tax-payers' money[3].

How far is this argument reasonable? A study conducted by State Bank of India's economic research cell gives a different picture. The study says that in the decade ended 2014 the government injected about Rs 60,000 crores of additional capital to the PSBs. The government received during this period a dividend of about Rs 64,000 crores amounting to about 20 per cent and roughly Rs 130,000 crores as income tax from these banks. 'Thus, on a combined basis, dividend and tax paid to the government was more than 300 per cent during the past decade.'[4]

The capital required by the PSBs to meet the Basel III norms by 2019 is Rs 2.40 lakh crores. The gross NPAs of the PSBs were about Rs 5.40 lakh crores as on March 2016 and in March 2017 they were estimated to breach the limit of Rs 7 lakh crores. Compared to this, the gap of Rs 1.70 lakh crores is not a difficult task to achieve.

## Performance and ownership

One frequently advanced argument for privatising the PSBs is that private sector companies are more efficient than their counter-parts in the public sector. There is overwhelming evidence that performance and efficiency are ownership neutral. Notwithstanding periodic crises in the banking industry the Indian PSBs have acquitted themselves well in relation to overall performance.

In a paper published in 2004, a deputy governor complimented the performance of PSBs in these words[5]:

> ...since the initiation of reforms, financial health as well as efficiency of the public sector banks closely matched and some times surpassed those of the private sector including foreign banks. Therefore, there is no definite observed link between efficiency and ownership in the contemporary Indian banking system.

Almost a decade later RBI confirmed this again[6]:

> In fact, many studies in the Indian context have not found any significant difference between the performance indicators of PSBs *vis-à-vis* private sector banks in the post-reform period. This suggests that, with operational flexibility, public sector banks are competing relatively effectively with private sector and foreign banks.

There is also a huge weight of evidence that the banks in the private sector are not necessarily paragons of efficiency. Three former RBI governors during different occasions had cautioned about the risks to which private banks are exposed. Commenting on the experience of private banks before 1969, S.Venkitaramanan had observed[7]:

> Many private banks before 1969 were virtually feudal fiefs of their owners. To privatise the banks in distress does not ensure that there will be no more problems, although temporarily, the fisc may earn a respite.

I.G. Patel, during whose time the banks were nationalised found infirmities in private ownership[8] :

> Private ownership too has its infirmities. There is no such thing as perfectly competitive market divorced from political realities. The choice is of the lesser evil-which may not be the same at all times and in all places.

With the natural tendency to grow in size and volume of business banks have potential to become too big. When they are owned by the government there is greater accountability for the government itself. When they are controlled by the private shareholders, the regulator's efficacy can get hamstrung by the size. Privatisation of PSBs can lead to this risk. For these reasons Y.V. Reddy, another governor quoting the approach of controllers globally, had said that banking licences to too big entities like General Electronic were not encouraged. He had underscored the need for reinforcements rather than dilution of guidelines on appropriate ownership and governance[9].

Driven by the urge to enhance the return on equity the private players would tend to circumvent the regulatory mechanism as it happened in case of mandatory priority sector lending and find newer avenues to augment the income. This approach could alter the nature of banking itself from the conventional business of lending and acceptance of deposits with its adverse impact on production credit[10].

## The conduct of private banks

The functioning of Indian private banks has frequently been subject of debate at different levels right from the pre-nationalisation days till the present era. In every one of the major scams that hit the financial sector, post-reforms, the main players were the institutions in the private sector. There have been recurring instances of the RBI penalising the private banks for violating the regulatory instructions[11].

After nationalisation many banks in the private sector failed and the RBI and the government had to bail them out by declaring moratorium and later merger with PSBs. Even after the reforms began the process continued. Between 1996 and 2007 as many as 10 private banks including the Global Trust Bank had to be merged with the state owned banks as given in the Table 1. A few private sector banks merged with the new generation banks. But where bailout was required the banks in the government sector had to come to the rescue.

**Table 1: List of private banks merged with PSBs between 1993 and 2007**

| | *Name of Bank* | *Merged with* | *Year of merger* |
|---|---|---|---|
| 1. | Kashi Nath Seth Bank Ltd | State Bank of India | 1996 |
| 2. | Bari Doab Bank Ltd | Oriental Bank of Commerce | 1997 |
| 3. | Bareilly Corporation Bank Ltd | Bank of Baroda | 1999 |
| 4. | Sikkim Bank Ltd | Union Bank of India | 1999 |
| 5. | Benares State Bank Ltd | Bank of Baroda | 2002 |
| 6. | Nedungadi Bank Ltd | Punjab National Bank | 2003 |
| 7. | South Gujarat Local Area Bank Ltd | Bank of Baroda | 2004 |
| 8. | Global Trust Bank Ltd | Oriental Bank of Commerce | 2004 |
| 9. | United Western Bank Ltd | IDBI Ltd | 2006 |
| 10. | Bharat Overseas Bank Ltd | Indian Overseas Bank | 2007 |

The banks in the private sector have also been as vulnerable to frauds as PSBs. In fact, according to one source, as on March 2013, foreign and private banks accounted for as much as 82.5 per cent of the reported frauds in the banking industry. In terms of amount PSBs accounted for 83 per cent, though.[12]

The conduct of the top banks of the world has always been a matter of intense scrutiny by the western media itself. In a report published after the 2007-08 global financial crisis *Al Jazeera,* points out that Bank of America, HSBC, JP Morgan Chase, Barclays, Goldman Sachs and Credit Suisse were either guilty of or admitted to doing fraudulent dealings or money laundering. They were heavily penalised by the regulators.[13] The analyst also said that none of the top echelons of the banks were prosecuted or jailed.

There have also been complaints against several private banks about the charges they levy, the rules regarding the minimum balance to be maintained and the penalties they impose on different occasions, many of which are not spelt out while opening new accounts. On the steps for recovery of advances given to small borrowers, private banks in India have been frequently hauled up by judiciary for employing strong-arm tactics.

In 2005, on complaints against banks for manipulating certain IPO issues RBI conducted investigations. Ten banks were found guilty and varying amounts of fines were levied on them by RBI. Out of the ten, seven were private banks and foreign banks.[14]

It is nowhere established that private ownership of banks has enhanced performance and efficiency.

## Doing business is not government's business?

A common theme of the argument for privatisation is that it is not the business of the government to be in business.

Many eminent economists, central bankers and experts had in the 1960's underlined the need to nationalise banks. The grounds were economic. A change in the ownership would remove the stranglehold of the few industrial houses on credit and reduce their control over the community's resources, ensure balanced regional development, channelise credit to selected activities and give stability to financial institutions and inspire depositors' confidence.

These grounds found resonance in the objectives of the Bank Nationalisation Bill 1969:

> The banking system touches the lives of millions and has to be inspired by larger social purposes and has to subserve national priorities and objectives such as rapid growth in agriculture, small industries and exports, raising of employment levels, encouragement of new entrepreneurs and the development of the backward areas. For this purpose, it is necessary for government to take direct responsibility for the extension and diversification of banking services and for the working of the substantial part of the banking system.

The first 25 years of nationalisation saw that the banking sector moved in the direction set forth at the time of take-over in 1969. Several official and non-official studies confirmed this trend.

When the government itself was the owner of the business enterprise it could reorient its business policy to meet the needs of a larger purpose. Therefore, the idea of government ownership and control over resources had its grounding in the economic compulsions of the country.

Current evidence indicates that there is still a wide gap to be filled in terms of geographical reach, the need to free the farmers from the grip of moneylenders and availability of resources for socially and economically marginalised segments to integrate into the development model. Obviously, profit orientation will run into rough weather in such activities. Herein comes the relevance of government playing a direct role in running the business of banking.

## Emphasis to be on performance, not ownership

There is no economic rationale or social sanction for further privatising the PSBs. The mind-set developed during the quarter century of liberalisation has to be revised with out-of-the-box thinking. Considering the need to accelerate financial inclusion and the process of reaching out to more people and places as of now, there is no viable alternative to continuing the PSBs as undertakings of the government. In evolving an appropriate development strategy the concept 'one size fits all' has no place.

## References

1. Business Standard, January 7, 2000.
2. See Chapter 17.
3. V.V. Acharya: Address to IBA, February 21, 2017 *Some Ways to Decisively Resolve Bank Stressed Assets.*
4. Soumya Kanti Ghosh, 2015: *Chastising public sector banks for every failure is a Comedy of Errors, The Economic Times,* January 21.
5. Rakesh Mohan, 2004: *Financial Sector Reforms in India: Policies and Performance Analysis,* RBI Bulletin, October.
6. 2013: *Banking Structure in India - The Way Forward-A discussion Paper.*
7. *Bankers and their dilemma* in *Times of India,* August 25, 1996.
8. I.G Patel, 2002: *Glimpses of Indian Economic Policy An Insider's View,* Oxford University Press.
9. Y.V.Reddy, 2011: *Global Crisis, Recession and Uneven Recovery,* Orient BlackSwan.
10. C P Chandrasekhar, Parthapratim Pal: *Financial Liberalisation in India: An Assessment of Its Nature and Outcomes, Economic and Political Weekly,* March 18, 2006.
11. Bhat, T R. 2002: *Privatisation of Public Sector Banks: without social sanction or economic justification,* paper published in *Privatisation of Banks in India-Present Position and future options, edits Joshi., G.V and others, Mangalore University.*
12. *Frauds in the Banking Sector: Causes, Concerns and Cures,* Inaugural address by K. C. Chakrabarty Deputy Governor, Reserve Bank of India on July 26, 2013 during the National Conference on Financial Fraud organised by ASSOCHAM at New Delhi.

13. September 14, Nick Fillmore: *Giant banks still play roulette with our future.*
14. RBI-Report on Trend and Progress of Banking in India 2006 Box II.17: IPO Irregularities and the Involvement of Banks.

# Chapter - 22

# Facing the Future Challenges-the Way Forward

## The positive gains made by PSBs

Both during the post-nationalisation and the reform periods, public sector banks have demonstrated their internal strengths and their capacity to face new challenges. There is abundant data on the continuously expanding reach of PSBs to the unbanked locations; promoting banking habits in formerly unbanked areas and meeting the exacting needs of a developing economy. The performance of the PSBs as measured by the standard parameters has been creditworthy over the years.

The institution of public ownership has ensured stability of the financial system. Notwithstanding the serious scams of the early reforms era or the heavily contaminated loan assets resulting in huge write-offs of loans and consequent loss suffered in the recent years, the PSBs have continued to enjoy the faith of the people. Unlike in the well developed financial systems abroad, Indian banking has not witnessed runs on the PSBs or liquidation of stressed banks. Despite the severe stress of 2014-16 which stretched into 2017, there are signs of recovery after the cleansing of the balance sheets subsequent to the RBI's asset quality reviews of 2015-16.

The PSBs have time and again demonstrated their ability to stand up to pressures from the policy-makers. The most recent examples are the way the pressures to exchange demonetised currencies were handled in November and December 2016 and the sustained efforts to popularise what was earlier known as no-frills accounts and in 2015 rechristened as Jan Dhan Accounts.

For the banking public, PSBs have remained easily accessible; their dealings have been transparent; their charges have remained reasonable. Lakhs of small borrowers have found PSBs a source of support for their self-employment. For these people, branches of PSBs are not made of just bricks and mortar but of animate, living and interactive human beings.

These have been the unique achievements of the PSBs during the nearly half century of government ownership. These achievements need to be contrasted with the sustained campaign to deride the whole concept of public sector banking and the repeated advocacy of privatisation of PSBs. It is an irony that such suggestions are made by official committees comprising experts from diverse disciplines except from the stakeholders like the customers who benefit from, and patronise the PSBs and, the bank managements and the staff who contribute to their strengths. A section of financial media has also played the same tune.

## Continued relevance of PSBs

Will the PSBs be relevant in the years ahead? Despite the phenomenal progress made by and the striking achievements to the credit of the PSBs, the circumstances which compelled state takeover of banks years ago continue to subsist today. The state of affairs of the economy and compelling needs of development that is sustainable provide an enduring rationale for an India specific banking policy distinct from the western models. PSBs have a specific role to play in providing cost-effective banking service the foundation of which is the faith of the vast sections of people who need to learn the advantages of financial literacy. There is enough evidence to establish that the non-state players for whom revenue generation is the end of all activities are not suited to this job.

## Way forward

If the PSBs should continue to be under the control of the state, what should be the focus of the future strategy for making them efficient and robust? The focus areas are broadly the following:

(a) Recapitalisation,
(b) Appointments and accountability,
(c) Managerial autonomy,
(d) Standards of corporate governance,
(e) Human resources management strategies.

## (a) Recapitalisation

Considering the uniqueness of PSBs and the need for them to be under the state control, it is necessary that from time to time the government should support efforts at capital infusion. Evidence available shows that the government has received adequate return on the investments it has made over years in the form of capital injection into PSBs. Apart from the return the government receives on its share of capital, the long-term return to the economy in the form of catalysing employment generation through finance to small enterprises, promoting agriculture and small industries is confirmed over the years.

Where will the government bring in the money from? Raghuram Rajan had said early in 2016[1]:

> We believe enough capital is available. While the profitability of some banks may be impaired in the short run, the system, once cleaned, will be able to support economic growth in a sustainable and profitable way.

Recapitalisation, therefore, should not be a problem. With a series of measures calculated to enhance the efficiency of PSBs, the quality of assets should improve and consequently the earnings. Where head room is available the PSBs could raise the capital from the market through public issues. That the banks on the verge of being closed were able to come out of the woods and raise capital from the public is a point in its favour.

The capital that will be required in the immediate future is a small fraction of the huge amount of NPAs due from the corporate houses. If efforts are made to recover some of the stressed assets the financial position of the PSBs should further improve.

We need also to remember that with all the stress on capital adequacy and Basel norms the global financial crisis did occur causing huge suffering to the society and necessitating large state sponsored bailout packages to put the financial system back on the rails. In contrast with this experience, Indian banks particularly those in the state sector have done well after the reforms and recorded continued reduction in NPAs and increase in profits and profitability. After the global financial crisis also they performed well. This is periodically confirmed by several authorities.

### (b) Appointments and accountability

A key issue deserving continued focus is related to the appointments of the chief executives for PSBs. There have been recurring instances of leadership failures in PSBs, a major blame for which should be laid before the government itself. It is, therefore, necessary that the top level appointments in the banks should be through an independent process solely guided by the candidates' proven track record, integrity, leadership qualities and suitability to face the challenges. The newly constituted Bank Boards Bureau should have the necessary autonomy to select the personnel without interference from the political leadership.

As earlier recommended by the Narasimham Committee-II and as confirmed by the government, the tenure of appointments of the CEOs should be for a minimum period of three years. The fresh round of appointments made by the current government after the *Indradhanush* package has not adhered to this commitment, though. PSBs cannot function without reasonable stability of top management and the government as owner has a critical role in ensuring this. It also follows that the current practice of shifting the CEO from one bank to another midway in the tenure is not in the interest of either bank.

The organisational culture of every PSB is unique by itself. When an outsider is brought in as the CEO, there is always an attempt to bring in a new culture alien to the legacy of the host institution. It takes years to graft a new culture and the progress gets stunted during the interregnum. It is therefore desirable to appoint some one from within the institution who meets the requirements set by the guidelines for appointments.

Currently two or more executive directors are appointed for every PSB. The intention of the government is to groom them to become CEOs in due course. This also needs changes. If they have to succeed as CEOs and the CEO should have a minimum term of three years the EDs should be in the age group of 50 to 55. Appointing some one with just one or two years to superannuate from the service (at the age of 60) does not serve the purpose of grooming him to shoulder higher role. Therefore, in appointing a senior official as ED s/he should have a fairly long left over service. Further, in appointing two or more EDs the government does not stipulate their functional role. It is necessary that each ED is assigned with a specific function like administration, operations, credit management and so on.

At present the age of retirement for the CEO of a PSB is 60 years. In the private sector the CEOs can continue beyond 60. Because of poor succession planning of the past years, the top executives of PSBs, when they become eligible for appointment as ED or MD, would be left with a short tenure. Further, those who retire at 60 and have a good track record are able to get attractive assignments in the private sector. Their capabilities could be utilised by the government for the PSBs if the age of superannuation is raised to say 65. That will help retention of talent and experience. That will also pre-empt the tendency of innovative CEOs from building bridges with the companies or organisations dealing with the PSBs for post-retirement assignments.

There were also instances in the past where about-to-retire CEOs of PSBs were appointed to Central Vigilance Commission which created doubts about their impartiality in taking decision on complaints against their former colleagues. It is therefore desirable that greater scrutiny of the candidate's suitability to the job has to be undertaken. If CEOs retire at 65, the prospect of their being appointed for such assignments gets reduced.

There is also a need to make the top management functionaries accountable for non-performance and for acts of omission and commission. The current system of suddenly transferring a CEO from a big PSB to a smaller one tantamounts to condoning non-performance. On the lines suggested by the UK Parliamentary Commission in 2013[2], an independent team of directors of the board could undertake a periodic assessment of the performance of the CEO and submit reports to the government. When there is evidence of failure or deliberate acts inimical to the well-being of the bank the government should wield the stick against the delinquents both as a penalty and as demonstration of its commitment to probity in public institutions.

There is a felt need to professionalise the board of PSBs. It is for the policy-makers to decide on the continuation of the nominees of the regulator and the government on the boards of the PSBs. The appointment of the other directors as provided for under the Banking Companies Acquisition & Transfer of Undertakings Acts and the State Bank of India Act should be through a transparent selection process governed by minimum standards of professional exposure, knowledge related to banking and specialised fields relevant to banking. Even in appointment of shareholder directors in PSBs with private shareholdings it is observed that they move from one board to another by using their clout with the government and the institutional investors who have a decisive say on the outcome of elections in the annual general body meetings of the PSBs. This practice needs to be reviewed.

### (c) Managerial autonomy

A recurring problem of PSBs commented upon by different committees and authorities is the absence of managerial autonomy. The present Finance Minister had declared in February 2016 that the government 'is committed to zero interference and letting the institutions run professionally'[3]. A time has come to ensure that the government and its wings keep an arm's distance from the management of the PSBs. Once the broad policy guidelines are laid by the government as the owner it should be the responsibility of the board of individual bank to run the bank. If there are failures or lapses the government has the power to question the CEO; that does not justify its interference in day-to-day decision-making in the matter of loans, administration, branch opening or fixing of premises for office.

### (d) Standards of corporate governance

Another recurring issue that figured in the discussions on the agenda for reforms is the standard of corporate governance in PSBs. The Raghuram Rajan Committee (2008) laid stress on better governance within the framework of state ownership. The PJ Nayak Committee went to the other extreme of recommending privatisation of PSBs for better governance. There has been progressive improvement in the governance standards compared to the levels prevailing before the reforms, but a lot still needs to be done in the area as elaborated in earlier chapters.[4]

Both the owner and the regulator have to take further measures to strengthen the standards of governance beyond the current approach of reporting in the annual reports.

### (e) Human resources management strategies

Human resources management (HRM) is the most neglected discipline in the management of PSBs. Although the government has repeatedly proclaimed its intentions to give full autonomy to the bank managements in the matter of management of staff from recruitment till retirement the reality is different.[5] Four areas deserve specific mention here:

(i) Need for greater autonomy to the boards in recruitment of staff.

(ii) Clear policies of training focusing on skill building, knowledge widening and tending the attitude of the employees to meet the changing dynamics of business.

(iii) Evolving long ranging internal succession plans.

(iv) Evolving policies of rewards and punishments linked to measurable performance and lapses.

A renewed emphasis on evolving a truly participative and collaborative culture between employees as collective entity and the management teams is necessary. The revival in the early 1990's of Corporation Bank and of Indian Bank, UCO Bank and United Bank of India, the three banks labelled as weak during the beginning of this century and the SBI's programme of *Parivartan* launched during 2006-11 were possible through collaboration between recognised workmen and officers' associations. This evidence of positive impact on the working of institutions underlines the need for a trust based collaborative approach.

Much of the potential available in the system of bilateral discussions between the unions and the management remains untapped as they are limited to basically wage issues which cause periodic industrial relations issues in the banking industry. Even in wage settlement there is hardly any pro-action from the PSB managements thanks to the absence of autonomy in HRM. Apart from the wage settlements it is necessary, through appropriate forums, to carry the unions along, both at the national level and the bank level to promote a collaborative culture. Such efforts will create a sense of belonging to the institution and institutional loyalty among the staff.

## The pace of reforms

Admittedly the pace of reforms in the Indian financial sector has been gradual, very often inviting critical reactions against the initiatives of the RBI and the measures announced by the government. But the steady pace has helped the financial system in India. Slothful public institutions could gradually but surely move into the age of global change. That the PSBs were able to weather new challenges on their transition to a new age is a testimony to the suitability of the pace of reforms. There have been failures and continuing weaknesses; they have not, however, affected the stability of the financial system or the faith of the common people in the PSBs. With appropriate checks and balances it is possible to meet the needs of change through a gradual process of reform.

## Need for consensus

In a country as diverse as India changes cannot be

steamrolled without conscious effort at building up a consensus among the stakeholders. There have been divergent views on privatisation as well as mergers of PSBs; policy-makers have also been faulted for diluting the concept of social banking signified by opening branches in unbanked centres, rural lending and lending to small borrowers. The entry of commercial banks into development banking has also been an issue of debate. The current government has to strive to achieve a consensus among the stakeholders so as to mitigate the problems that could arise during the transition. The magnitude of the challenge in making the PSBs facilitators of an inclusive economic growth makes such consensus imperative; for the required transformation has to be carried out by the people within the banks.

## Policy issues

Modernisation of Indian economy needs a vibrant and healthy financial sector. PSBs are the mainstay of Indian financial sector. It is not that the new financial institutions like small banks and micro-finance institutions have no role in deepening financial inclusion. The public as customers and owners of PSBs continue to have trust in the state owned banks. The policy relating to them needs to focus on the twin issues of making them healthier and responsive to the society's needs in conformity with the national priorities and policy directions so that the lessons of the experience of 25 years of reforms are internalised.

## Built-in safeguards

In spite of continuous efforts by the RBI and actions by the banks, many large borrowers have been able to get away with their wilful defaults. The share of 'large borrowers' defined as those with total exposure of Rs 5 crore and above- was as much as 87 per cent in September 2015. These have serious destabilising effect on the financial system. Certain systems to act as built-in safeguards against the unscrupulous power-players from within acting in nexus with outsiders need to be strengthened. For example, as repeatedly demanded by unions and recommended by parliamentary committees, the names of top 100 borrowers of every bank should be made transparent. As public money is involved in lending and losses arising out of NPAs would affect the health of a public institution, the people have a right to know the names of the largest borrowers. The defence of protecting customer confidentiality is not tenable.

The second measure would be in bringing the loan write-offs above a threshold limit under the audit of Comptroller & Auditor General. Write-off involves a huge drain on a bank's revenue. It brings some relief to the borrower who for reasons beyond his control suffers loss and is unable to repay the bank loan. But when the beneficiary does not deserve such munificence and if the decision-makers in a bank decide to write-off the debt such action is suspect. Write-offs of such nature are not in the interest of the society. It is therefore desirable to subject write-offs of large loans to audit by CAG. The likelihood of an audit by a statutory agency would act as deterrent against malpractices in write-offs.

The third measure would be strengthening the system of whistle-blowing within the PSBs. This could be done in two ways: prompt time bound action on complaints and complete protection to the complainants. A transparent and efficacious scheme of whistle-blowing will act as a deterrent against malpractices at the top echelons of the banks.

A fourth measure is that within the board of directors everyone should be treated as equal both in letter and spirit of the Bank Nationalisation Acts. Such equal treatment has the potential to make the boards more professional in their conduct in safeguarding the institution's interest over personal loyalties.

## References

1. Raghuram, G. Rajan: reported in *The Hindu*: New Delhi, February 8, 2016.
2. The Stationery Office Limited, London, June 2013: Report of the Parliamentary Commission on Banking Standards London: Changing banking for good.
3. Editorial February 16, 2016 *The Hindu.*
4. Chaps.12 and 18.
5. See chapters 6 and 18.

# The Epilogue

As a staunch advocate of people's control over the commanding heights of the economy, this author has a soft corner for the public sector banks. Although at a number of places critical observations have been made about the failure of the financial system controlled to a large extent by the government, those failures are not of the institutions; on the other hand they have to be attributed to the policies or poor implementation of some of them. The PSBs by themselves have displayed their strengths as well as potential for growth over the years. These strengths have to be sustained and the potential exploited in the days ahead.

Post-2016-17 NPA crisis of Indian banks, efforts have been made both by the regulator and the government to help the PSBs to tide over the problems. There are signs of recovery as revealed by a better performance of some of the PSBs during the year ended March 2017.

In the backdrop of the experience of the 25 years of reforms and the lessons learnt the measures needed to face the challenges could be classified into short-term and long-term measures.

In the short run, the focus has to be towards making the PSBs come out of woods by addressing the issues of NPAs, business growth and earning profits once again. In the long run, focus should be on strengthening the systems related to inclusive growth, autonomy, governance and harnessing the human resources. Restructuring of

PSBs through mergers and diluting the government share holding are not critical for making the banks stronger and healthier.

Although deregulation is a key theme of globalisation and in turn of financial sector reforms, the recurring bank crises in the free world and problems in the Indian context have raised the importance of re-regulation. PSBs, owned as they are by the government, fit into this newer framework of regulation.

# Postscript

*(After the book went to the press, a scheme of capital infusion into the PSBs was announced by the government in October 2017. The modalities of translating the scheme announced by the government are yet to be fully unveiled. This short note is added to give a bird's eye view of the scheme and its implications.)*

## Recapitalization plan unveiled in October 2017

The Reserve Bank of India (RBI) had observed in its *Financial Stability Report*, June 2017 (p. 2) that the banking stability indicator had worsened between September 2016 and March 2017 due to deterioration in asset quality and profitability. The report forewarned that a severe credit shock was likely to impact capital adequacy and profitability of a significant number of banks. The results of the first quarter of 2017-18 further confirmed this deterioration. The credit growth continued to be in single digit hovering around 5 per cent, a sixty-year low in the history of Indian banks. The country's gross domestic product (GDP) during the year ended March 2017 had witnessed sharp fall caused by several factors. The economic activity continued to cause alarm during the next six months.

The volume of non-performing assets (NPAs) of banks continued to grow, crossing according some sources Rs.10 lakh crores; bank unions put it at Rs.15 lakh crores. The RBI advised the banks to invoke the provisions of the newly enacted Insolvency & Bankruptcy Code (IBC, 2016) to resolve 12 selected large corporate NPAs which accounted for over 50 per cent of the total of the bad loans. The progress in resolution was, however, tardy compelling the RBI to advise the banks to go in for 'larger haircuts' meaning greater losses. This would erode their capital further. A proactive measure on the part of the government to bailout the ailing PSBs was imperative.

In this backdrop the government, in late October 2017, announced a massive plan of recapitalization of PSBs. It had two objectives: bailing them out from the entrenched NPA crisis and stimulating them to lend more.

According to the announcement of the government, the plan included a package of Rs 2.11 lakh crores of financial support to the PSBs. Out of this, Rs 76,000 crores would be in the form of equity capital to be provided by the government and/or raised from the capital market. About Rs 1.35 lakh crores would be in the form of recapitalization bonds. These bonds would be issued by the government and subscribed by the PSBs using the excess deposits they had accumulated after the demonetization of higher denomination rupee notes in November 2016. With the help of the cash so generated the government would shore up the capital support by infusing additional equity to selected PSBs over a period of two years. This in turn was expected to spur economic growth which had sunk to around 5 per cent per annum - the lowest in several years.

### The wisdom of the measure

Considering the gravity of the crisis faced by the PSBs which had adversely affected economic growth, the government's package was generally welcomed. There were also criticisms against infusing more capital into the already struggling PSBs, contending that such bailout of PSBs for their inefficiency was a recurring burden on the tax-payer. The former RBI governor, Y. V. Reddy suggested that the package should be designed with extreme care to ensure that there was no disproportionate burden on taxpayers. A former Finance Secretary, D K Mittal cautioned that periodic pumping of capital to PSBs by itself would not be sufficient unless capital infusion was backed by improvement in governance standards.

As mentioned in several chapters of this book, PSBs will continue to be relevant given the reality of Indian economy. The government had very limited choice to make: either privatise the government owned banks or strengthen them with a series of measures. When privatization of PSBs has far reaching implications the government's decision in infusing more capital is a pragmatic choice. To that extent the measure is laudable.

The flip side of the plan is the missing emphasis on the measures to enhance governance standards. Along with the package of capital infusion the government should initiate measures to enhance governance, to professionalise the top management and reorient the human resources policies to enable the PSBs to effectively face the emerging challenges. Unless these complementary measures are taken there could be pressure to pump in more capital to PSBs regularly.

# Select Bibliography of Books and Articles Referred to in the Text

**Author, year of publication, Title of the Book/Article, Publisher/name of Journal**


1. Bank of International Settlements: 2015: A Brief History of Basel Committee.
2. Bhat, T R 1998: Voice of CBOO- Collection of Editorials in Officers' Voice 1982-1998, Pub: CBOO, Mangalore.
3. Bhat, T R. 1999: In search of an identity, CBOO through 25 years; Pub: CBOO, Mangalore; Pub: CBOO.
4. Bhat, T R. 2002: Privatisation of Public Sector Banks: without social sanction or economic justification, paper published in Privatisation of Banks in India-Present Position and future options, edits Joshi, G.V and others, Mangalore University.
5. Da Costa, E P W, 1985: Reserve Bank of India –Fifty Years, 1985, RBI.
6. Davis, Stephen, 2000: Bank mergers: Lessons for the future, Palgrave Macmillan UK.
7. Government of India, 1991: Report of the Committee on Financial Systems headed by M. Narasimham
8. Patel, I.G., 2002: Glimpses of Indian Economic Policy An Insider's View, Oxford University Press.
9. Rangarajan, C and Jadhav, Narendra, 1992: Issues in financial sector reform published in Bimal Jalan (Edit) 1992: The Indian Economy-Problems and Prospects Viking/Penguin India.

10. Reddy, Y.V., 2011: Global Crisis, Recession and Uneven Recovery Orient BlackSwan.
11. Reserve Bank of India, Annual Reports, Reports on Trend and Progress of Banking in India for different years.
12. Shukla, S.P. 2006: Report of the Independent Commission on Banking and Financial Policy , AIBOC.
13. Tandon, Prakash 1989: Banking Century-A Short History of Banking in India and the Pioneer: Punjab National Bank, Penguin.
14. The Stationery Office Limited, London, June 2013: Changing banking for good: Report of the Parliamentary Commission on Banking Standards.

**Articles/reports referred to in the Book:**

1. Arun Kumar, 1992: Financial Scam: Wages of Deregulation, paper published by Public Interest Research Group (PIRG), Delhi.
2. All India Bank Officers' Confederation, 1999: AIBOC's Study of PSBs sought to be termed as 'Weak' with specific reference to UCO, UBI and Indian Bank.
3. Acharya, Viral V., 2017: 'Some Ways to Decisively Resolve Bank Stressed Assets Speech', speech delivered at the Indian Banks' Association's Banking Technology Conference, Mumbai, on February 21.
4. Ahluwalia, Montek Singh, 2016: Fixing public sector banks *Livemint*: Jun 24.
5. Bamzai, Sandeep, 2016: 'The ugly truth about our banks' *The Pioneer:* 03 June.
6. Bhat, T.R., 2002: Corporate governance in banks-Paper presented in Bank Economists' Conference, December.
7. Bhat, T.R., 2004: GTB Fiasco-The Lessons, *Officers' Voice*, November.
8. Bhat, T. R. 2013:Whistle blowing in the banks *(unpublished)*.

9. Bhide, M.G., and others 2001: Emerging Challenges in Indian Banking Stanford University Working Paper No. 103.
10. Bhide, M.G; Prasad, A; Ghosh, Saibal, 2002: Banking Sector Reforms- A Critical Overview, *Economic and Political Weekly,* February 2.
11. Bose, Prasenjit, 2016: No bailout with taxpayer money, *The Hindu,* February 16.
12. Brahmananda, P.R., 2000: Bank nationalisation-Story of ad hocism and arbitrariness; *The Hindu,* July 26.
13. *Business Standard*: August 18, 1992: Syndicate Bank Chief Asked to go on leave.
14. Chandrasekhar, C.P. and Pal Parthapratim, 2006: Financial Liberalisation in India- An Assessment of Its Nature and Outcomes: *Economic and Political Weekly,* March 18.
15. Chakrabarty, K.C. 2013: Frauds in the Banking Sector: Causes, Concerns and Cures, Address delivered on July 26, 2013 during the National Conference on Financial Fraud organised by ASSOCHAM at New Delhi.
16. Chakrabarty, K.C., 2013: 'Vigilance Administration: Encouraging Probity in Public Life' Keynote address delivered at a Seminar organised by the Centre For Integrity, Governance and Training on Vigilance Administration on November 11, 2013.
17. Chakrabarty, K.C., 2013: Post-Crisis: The New Normal *RBI Bulletin,* December.
18. Dalal, Sucheta 2001: Nedungadi Bank and the saga of RBI inaction, Article in *Rediff.com* May 10, 2001 (downloaded on January 15, 2017).
19. *Economic and Political Weekly,* 1992: Securities Scam: The Systemic Origins -A Special Correspondent, September 5.
20. *Economic and Political Weekly, 2002*: Special Statistics-31: Money, Banking and Finance, February 2.

21. *Economic and Political Weekly,* 2002: April 20, 2002: Governance In Banks- Cleaning the Augean Stables, April 20.
22. *Economic and Political Weekly,* 2016: 'Spectre of Debt', May 28.
23. *ENS* Economic Bureau, Delhi, 2008, September 30.
24. *The Economist.*, 2017: Issue dated Mar 4.
25. Fillimore, Nick: Giant banks still play roulette with our future, *Al Jazeera,*14 Sep 2013.
26. Ghosh, Soumya Kanti, 2015 : Chastising public sector banks for every failure is a Comedy of Errors, *The Economic Times*, January 21.
27. Goyal, Ashima, 2016: Banks need an autonomy stimulus, *The Hindu*: March 1.
28. Government of India, 1994: Action taken report on the Recommendations of the Joint Parliamentary Committee which enquired into the Irregularities in Securities and Banking Transactions, July 1994.
29. Government of India, Ministry of Finance, 2011: Press statement dated February 20.
30. Ghosh, D.N: 2000, Weak Banks: A Strategy for Self-Renewal, *EPW,* Jan 29.
31. Ghosh. D.N. 2003: Market Scandals and Regulatory Governance, *Economic and Political Weekly,* May 17.
32. *The Hindu,* 2004: The crisis of Confidence, Edit: Jul 27.
33. *The Hindu,* August 17, 2007.
34. *The Hindu*: New Delhi, August 21, 2013.
35. *The Hindu*: February 8, 2016.
36. *The Hindu,* 2016: Owning without interfering, February 16.
37. *Hindu Businessline:* various issues.
38. Indian Banks' Association, various issues of *IBA Bulletin.*

39. *Indian Express*- New Delhi, May 25, 2011: 'Locked out of car, Indian Bank CMD slams door on regional head.'
40. Kurup, N.P., 1994: Muddle of Partial Privatisation of Banks, *Economic and Political Weekly*, September 10.
41. Leeladhar, Vittaldas, 2007: Indian Financial Sector Reforms, Address to Annual Washington Conference 2007, *RBI Bulletin*, April.
42. Leeladhar,V., 2007: India's Preparedness for Basel II Implementation- Special Address delivered at the Panel Discussion during "FICCI-IBA Conference on Global Banking : Paradigm Shift", held on September 13, 2007, Mumbai.
43. Mukherjee, Arindam and Ghosh, Shekhar 1997: The Anatomy of a Fraud, *Outlook* Magazine, June 11.
44. Mohan, Rakesh, 2004 : Financial Sector Reforms in India: Policies and Performance Analysis, *RBI Bulletin* October.
45. Mohan, Rakesh, 2005: Address to the 21st Annual General Meeting and Conference of the Pakistan Society of Development Economists, Islamabad, 21 December.
46. Mohan, Rakesh, 2006: Reforms, productivity and efficiency in banking: the Indian experience, *BIS Review* 15/2006.
47. *Newsweek*, 2008, October 27.
48. *Officers' Voice,* monthly journal of Corporation Bank Officers' Organisation, various issues.
49. Palande, Pravin, 2014: Economic Milestone: Stock Market Scam (1992) *Forbes India* 22 August.
50. *PTI report,* August 19, 2016.
51. Ram Mohan, T. T. 2007: *Banking Reforms in India- Charting a Unique Course- Economic and Political Weekly*, March 31.

52. *Rediff.com* report dated February 03, 2003: Clearance for merger with PNB lifts Nedungadi Bank (downloaded on January 15, 2017).
53. Rommel Rodrigues, 2010: *The Indian Express* December 1.
54. Reddy, Y.V., 2008: Global Financial Turbulence and Financial Sector in India: A Practitioner's Perspective Address at the Meeting of the Task Force on Financial Markets Regulation organised by the Initiative for Policy Dialogue at Manchester, United Kingdom, on July 1.
55. Reserve Bank of India, DBOD and DEPR (Department of Economic Policy and Research) August 2013: Banking Structure in India - The Way Forward - Discussion Paper.
56. Shah, Mihir, 2007: The crowning of the moneylender, *The Hindu,* September 1.
57. Sridhar, V. 2000: Banking-A controversial report *Frontline* Magazine: January 8.
58. Sridhar, V. 2004: The collapse of a bank, *Frontline*, Aug. 14 – 27.
59. Subbarao, Duvvuri, 2010: Financial Inclusion: Challenges and Opportunities, *RBI Bulletin,* January.
60. Subba Rao, Duvvuri, 2011: Five Frontier Issues in Indian Banking: *RBI Monthly Bulletin,* January.
61. Sinha, Anand, 2012: Indian Banking – Journey into the Future - *RBI Monthly Bulletin,* February.
62. *TNN,* August 31, 2013, report titled 'CVC seeks action against Indian bank CMD, ex-ED.'
63. Thakurta, Paranjoy Guha, 1985: Fraud at Bank of Baroda : Cover Page article in *Update*, August 23-September 5.
64. Thingalaya, N K. 1997: Banking Development in Independent India, *Pigmy Economic Review*, July-August 1997, monthly economic journal of Syndicate Bank.

65. Thorat, Usha, 2008: Inclusive Growth - The Role of Banks in Emerging Economies, *RBI Bulletin*, March.
66. *Times of India*, June 29 and 30, 1992.
67. Venkitaramanan, S, 1996: Bankers and their dilemma in *Times of India*, August 25.
68. Venkitaramanan, S.,1999: Cure For The Sick, *The Telegraph*, Kolkata May 31.

# Index

**C**

**E**



**F**



**G**